Pluralism in the World Religions

A SHORT INTRODUCTION

OTHER BOOKS IN THIS SERIES

RELATED TITLES PUBLISHED BY ONEWORLD

Pluralism in the World Religions

A SHORT INTRODUCTION

Harold Coward

ONEWORLD
OXFORD

PLURALISM IN THE WORLD RELIGIONS: A SHORT INTRODUCTION

Oneworld Publications
(Sales and Editorial)
185 Banbury Road
Oxford OX2 7AR
England
http://www.oneworld-publications.com

Oneworld Publications
(US Marketing Office)
160 N Washington St.
4th Floor, Boston
MA 02114
USA

ISBN 1-85168-243-0

Cover design by Design Deluxe
Typeset by LaserScript Limited, Mitcham, UK
Printed and bound by Clays Ltd, St Ives plc

CONTENTS

PREFACE

Religious experience has been defined as the quest for ultimate reality. In pursuing this quest, religions often seem to have an inherent drive to claims of uniqueness and universality. Many religions exhibit an inner tendency to claim to be *the* true religion, to offer *the* true revelation as *the* true way of salvation or release. It appears to be self-contradictory for such a religion to accept any expression of ultimate reality other than its own. Yet one of the things that characterizes today's world is religious pluralism. The world has always had religious plurality. But in the past two decades the breaking of cultural, racial, linguistic and geographical boundaries has been on a scale that the world has not previously seen. For the first time in recorded history we seem to be rapidly becoming a true global community. Today the West is no longer closed within itself. It can no longer regard itself as being the historical and cultural centre of the world and as having a religion that is the sole valid way of worship. The same is true for the East. Today everyone is the next-door neighbour and spiritual neighbour of everyone else.

In Canada almost all our cities set aside a special day for a cultural fair. Music, dance, handicrafts and food from many different cultures are offered by the members of the respective ethnic communities, now Canadian citizens. In addition to these domestic experiences, we are travelling more and having the existential experience of other cultures. The same thing is happening with exposure to other religions. I don't have to go to India to encounter Hinduism. In Calgary there are a large Hindu community, two Jodo Shinsu Buddhist congregations, Zen and

Tibetan Buddhist groups, three Islamic mosques and five Jewish synagogues – to say nothing of the many so-called new religions, such as transcendental meditation and Hare Krishna. Today every religion, like every culture, is an existential possibility offered to every person. Alien religions have become part of everyday life, and we experience them as a challenge to the truth claims of our own faith.

The aim of this book is to examine the way a number of religions have reacted and are reacting to the challenge of pluralism. My hope is that such a study will help people from various traditions better understand each other's religion and learn the true dimensions of spiritual life in a pluralistic world.

In revising the original 1985 edition of this book, I have consulted leading scholars of each religion and used their advice to update each chapter. Significant new material has been added. I have also included a Baha'i chapter to reflect the Baha'i Faith's status as a new world religion that has a unique approach to religious pluralism. A change in my own viewpoints is reflected in the final section of chapter 7 on 'The future of religions in dialogue'.

I wish to thank Novin Doostdar of Oneworld for encouraging me to undertake this revision. It has been a pleasure to work with Novin and the staff at Oneworld Publications.

I wish to thank Professor Balasubramanian and the members of the Dr S. Radhakrishnan Institute for Advanced Study in Philosophy, Madras, India, for extending to me the invitation to deliver a special lecture series which provided the original opportunity for this book. I am also grateful to many colleagues who have read and criticized drafts of various portions of the manuscript: Peter Craigie, Thomas Dean, Eva Dargyay, Yvonne Haddad, T. R. V. Murti, Hugo Meynell, Andy Rippin, Moshe Amon, Leslie Kawamura, Martin Jaffee, Paul Knitter, Fred Denny, Seena Fazel, Anantanand Rambachan and David Loy. Thanks are also due to Vicki Simmons for her careful typing and preparation of the revised manuscript, and to June Thomson for her assistance in library research.

Harold Coward

1 RELIGIOUS PLURALISM AND JUDAISM

Judaism is an appropriate tradition in which to begin the study of religious pluralism and the world religions.[1] From the destruction of the Second Temple in Jerusalem (*c.* 70 CE) and especially since the failure of the Bar-Kokhbah revolt (*c.* 135 CE), Jews have lived as a diaspora – as widely scattered communities of believers living as minority groups within other societies. The dispersion and scattering of the Jewish people began as early as 586 BCE with the fall of Jerusalem and the Babylonian exile. Thus for twenty-five hundred years the Jews, often struggling to maintain Jewish identity and existence, have constituted subcultures in the midst of other and larger cultures. The experience of being a minority group in other cultures, which is now becoming more commonplace for all the world religions as religious pluralism spreads, has been the norm for Judaism for countless generations. From the biblical period to the present, Judaism has had to formulate its beliefs and practices in the face of challenges from other cultures and religions. The events of the twentieth century, and the Holocaust in particular, have given fresh intensity and sharpness to the old question: 'How does one sing the Lord's song in an alien land?'

Another reason for beginning this study with Judaism is that of the three Western monotheistic religions of biblical origin (Judaism, Christianity and Islam), Judaism was the first to achieve its distinctive forms and beliefs. These forms and beliefs provided the context out of which Christianity and Islam arose. This integral relationship (somewhat like that of Hinduism and Buddhism in the East) has caused Jewish philosophers and theologians to examine their stance in relation to the viewpoints of the other traditions with which they are so closely connected.

THE BIBLICAL RESPONSE TO RELIGIOUS PLURALISM

The Jewish Bible or Torah recounts how Israel became separated from the vast array of different religions that characterized the ancient Near East. The Jews trace their origin to Abraham, who left Mesopotamia and migrated to Canaan. The religious significance of Abraham's journey is that in leaving Mesopotamia he also left the worldly gods, idols and nature deities in order to serve the Lord who is creator of heaven and earth. According to Jewish thinking this event marked the appearance not only of a new people but also of a new religious idea – one God, the creator, separate from and transcendent over all creation.[2]

The early experience of the Jewish people with the God of Abraham took the form of a covenant relationship. Scholars suggest that this covenant relationship may have been set in the form of the vassal treaties that were common at that time. For example, in reporting the liberation of the Jews from bondage in Egypt, the book of Deuteronomy understands the Jews next to be in bondage to God through the covenant entered into by Moses. Instead of being held in worldly vassaldom as they were in Egypt, the Jews are committed to a relationship of service and obedience to God. As Peter Craigie writes, 'Like the other small nations that surrounded her, Israel was to be a vassal state, but not to Egypt or to the Hittites; she owed her allegiance to God alone.'[3] It is this notion of being committed to God that is fundamental to Jewish theology and to Jewish understanding of the relationship of other peoples to God. Since God has entered into a special covenant relationship with the Jews, there is no reason why God could not enter into other relationships with other peoples. Although the religions practised by other peoples are routinely referred to in the Torah as 'abominations', in Deuteronomy and the later prophets (e.g. Ezekiel) the idea is presented that God could enter into relationships with other nations. Thus, from the Jewish biblical perspective, the various religions may be seen as the expressions of the relationships obtained between other peoples and God. Whereas for the Jews it is the Mosaic covenant – and later the Davidic covenant – that is true and authoritative, for other peoples (e.g. the Christians or Muslims) it will be their particular relationship with God that will be true and authoritative. Indeed in the most ancient covenant relationship, described in Genesis, chapter 9, verses 8–17, God enters into a covenant with Noah, his family and every living person and animal. In the Noahic covenant we see a simple but powerful statement of God's love for all people. A later resonance of this theme is recorded in the Song of Moses:[4]

> When the Most High gave the nations an inheritance, When he separated the sons of mankind, He fixed the boundaries of the peoples According to the number of the sons of God. (Deut. 32:8–9)

Israel is one among the many nations that received their inheritance from and had their boundaries fixed by God. Craigie notes that the exact sense of the phrase 'according to the number of the sons of God' is difficult to determine but seems to refer to a divine council of angels or sons of God with one for each nation or people.[5]

The personal nature of the covenant relationship between God and God's people is emphasized in Judaism. The Israelites experienced the divine as a very personal God who presided over their destiny. R. J. Zwi Werblowsky writes, 'God was not just there and acting; he was turned towards man, asking for him and calling for his co-operative response.'[6] God's calling to humanity was experienced as God's word spoken through Moses and the prophets. In the Jewish understanding God calls human beings, and all they have to do is listen and obey. This conception of the one Lord to whom the Israelites owed loyalty and obedience was the unifying power within Judaism. Instead of seeing a variety of gods performing particular functions (e.g. special gods for the different natural powers) or controlling specific geographical locations or representing the metaphysical forces of good and evil, the Jews experienced the one God as the transcendent source and unity of all being.[7] Thus the theological interpretation of the Babylonian defeat of the Israelites was not that Yahweh, the God of the Jews, had failed, but rather that Yahweh, the Lord of all, was using the Babylonians as an instrument to punish the Jews for their failure to keep their covenant agreement with God. When the defeated Israelites were carried off into Babylonian exile (587–538 BCE), this was understood as God's punishment of Israel for its conscious neglect of the covenant.[8] This mode of reasoning is still held by many orthodox Jews.

In the Babylonian exile the Jews switched completely to monotheistic practices and developed the tradition of not mingling with other nations. Living in Babylon produced an agonizing reappraisal aimed at ridding the Jews of any practice that might have evoked the divine punishment of the exile (Lev. 17–26; Ezek. 40–48). Also during the exile a change in the Hebrew alphabet took place: the Canaanite alphabet was replaced with the Aramaic. About one thousand years later the oral tradition was consolidated in the form of the Babylonian Talmud.

The end of the Babylonian exile and the return to Palestine marked the beginning of a more exclusivist approach to other peoples and religions. To a large extent this was the result of these Jews having lived among gentiles in a way that the pre-exilic Jews had not experienced. Under the leadership of Ezra and Nehemiah, both of whom were intense, rigid individuals, a strong feeling of religious separation was nurtured.[9] This emphasis was probably needed at the time to help the demoralized struggling community of those who had returned to Palestine to re-establish their identity and rebuild Jerusalem. But the proscription against mixed marriages (Neh. 10) and the condemnation of other peoples laid the foundations for the more exclusivist attitude that tended to dominate in the post-exilic period. There are other places in the Hebrew scriptures where there are condemnations of other religions and insistence that Yahweh is the only true God or that all other gods must bow before Yahweh (Deut. 5; Exod. 20). But even in the midst of the renewed exclusivism following the post-exilic period the books of Ruth and Jonah claim that Yahweh's concern extends far beyond Israel's borders; in the life of a Moabite woman named Ruth and in the repentance of the foreign city Nineveh, Yahweh's compassion for all human beings triumphs over narrow provincialism. Thus Israel was not to assume an exclusive claim on God but to fulfil its covenant responsibility of being a light to the nations.

During the third century BCE Jewish communities in Egypt began the revolutionary development of worshipping outside the Temple in Jerusalem. This practice of prayer outside the Temple gradually evolved during the first century CE and onwards into the synagogue.[10] The synagogue later served as a prototype for the Christian church and the Islamic mosque.

CLASSICAL AND MEDIEVAL RESPONSES

With the Persian victory over Babylonia in 539 BCE and the end of the Babylonian exile, some Jews returned home to Judaea. Others, however, remained in Babylonia forming a Jewish community within Babylonian society. Two centuries later the process of dispersion was more extensive as a result of conquests by Alexander: there was a large and important Jewish community in Alexandria, and there were similar communities in Antioch, Rome and most of the larger cities of the Graeco-Roman world.

The first great thinker of the Jewish dispersion was the philosopher-statesman Philo Judaeus (20 BCE–50 CE) of Alexandria.[11] Philo was a loyal Jew who believed that in the Torah and through the prophets God had spoken decisively to Israel. Philo was also a lover of Plato. He argued that the same God spoke through Greek philosophy and Jewish religion. Philo asserted that God, as absolute spirit, completely transcends all human limitations. God relates to matter through a series of inter-mediaries (like Plato's ideas) that derive from the Logos or divine reason. The Logos, for Philo, was God's instrument for creative activity as well as the rational structure of the universe. The different religions (and Greek philosophy also) could be understood as various manifestations of the one divine Logos. Because of his blending of Greek and Hebrew thought, Philo had little influence on the conservative rabbis of his day. However, he had a strong and immediate influence upon Christianity as is evidenced by the appropriation of his conception of Logos into the Gospel of John. The idea of a single divine Logos manifesting itself in the various religious traditions has continued to be a favourite notion of theologians and philosophers of religion.[12] Philo influenced the teachings of the early Christian fathers such as Clement of Alexandria, Origen, and Gregory of Nyssa, but his works remained unknown to Jewish philosophers of the Middle Ages. It was not until the sixteenth century that, through Azariah dei Rossi, his works became known again among Jews.[13]

The first Jewish philosopher of the Middle Ages was Saadiah Gaon (882–942), head of the rabbinical academy near Baghdad.[14] He was strongly influenced by both Islamic Mu'tazilite Kalim and Platonic thought. Gaon formulated a Jewish Kalim which affirms that God is one but possesses many attributes. This promoted an understanding of the various religions as different attributes or manifestations of the one God.

The most important thinker of medieval Judaism was Maimonides (1135–1204). Besides the traditional Jewish studies, Maimonides, a physician by profession, was educated in Greek thought and the Islamic Kalim. He was at once a devout Jew and a thoroughly rational thinker. As a result of the persecution of Jews in Spain, he and his family wandered through Israel and North Africa, finally settling in Egypt, where he served as private physician of the Muslim ruler Saladin. He was fully experienced in the challenge of the dispersion – the challenge of living and thinking in a Jewish way in the midst of a foreign religion and culture. Maimonides believed that of all religions Judaism was the only faith revealed by God and that it alone was in every respect true. He states,

> The difference between our religion and the other religions, to which it is sought to liken them, is none other than like the difference between the living, sentient man and the image carved by the workman from wood.[15]

The basis of the discrimination against other religions is clearly the Mosaic prescription against idolatry. Contrary to Philo, for Maimonides there is to be no intermediary between God and humanity. To interpose any such object is to open the way to it becoming an object of worship and accordingly to sow the seeds of idolatry. Other religions are seen by Maimonides as human attempts to emulate the Jewish religion by constructing belief structures that, like the carved image, are false and idolatrous.

In spite of this rather narrow perspective, Maimonides shows himself to be surprisingly tolerant. Although in his view both Jesus and Muhammad were false prophets, their activities were a part of God's wisdom and paved the way for the spread of Judaism and the coming of the Messiah and the kingdom. The favourable point about Christians is that they regard the Torah as scripture. The favourable point about Islam is that like Judaism it takes a strong stance against idol worship. Maimonides even finds praiseworthy features among the gentiles and admits that the pious among them have a place in the 'world to come' if they have attained knowledge of the creator and have corrected their soul with practice of the virtues. For Maimonides the criterion for spiritual acceptability is clear:

> Anyone who corrects his soul with purity of morals and purity of knowledge in the faith of the creator assuredly will be of the children of the world to come.[16]

Not all of the medieval Jewish community agreed with Maimonides' rationalistic and somewhat exclusivist view of God and religion. About the same time, the mystical tradition of the Kabbala was gaining strength in Jewish circles. The most famous book of the Kabbala, the *Zohar*, which may have been written in Spain (*c.* 1285) by Moses de Leon, has many Gnostic and Neoplatonic ideas. God is seen to be the Absolute beyond all human predications. Between God and the world are a series of emanations, with human beings as the worldly receivers. The logic of the Kabbala resembles that of Philo's Logos – one Absolute of which there are many manifestations, or one God phenomenalizing through the forms of the various religions.

MODERN RESPONSES

Even though Judaism existed in dispersion throughout the medieval period, within its scattered communities it was, in effect, a closed society. Jews lived as one class within a rigid society. The impact of modernity has meant that now, more than ever before, Jews are freely associating with non-Jews. This fact has given a higher profile to the relation between Judaism and other religions. This is particularly true in the modern West, where more and more Jews are looking for a common denominator with the prevailing Christian culture. This is especially evident in one of the first significant Jewish works of the modern period, Moses Mendelssohn's *Jerusalem.*[17] Mendelssohn (1729–86) set out to bridge the gap between the medieval Jewish ghetto and modern Europe. He attempted to bring together the high recognition given to reason by Enlightenment philosophers such as Immanuel Kant with an unquestioning loyalty to the God of Sinai. In line with Kant, Mendelssohn argued that the truth of religion is not dependent upon supernatural revelation but is immanent in human reason and thus available to all. It was inconceivable to him that God could have revealed the truth to only part of humanity, leaving the rest without revelation and therefore without access to happiness. No one religion can be the sole instrument through which God has revealed truth.

> According to the tenets of Judaism, all inhabitants of the earth have a claim to salvation, and the means to attain it are as widespread as mankind itself.
> Providence made wise men arise in every nation and bestowed upon them the gift to look with a clear eye into themselves as well as around themselves, to contemplate God's works, and to communicate their insights to others.[18]

Thus for Mendelssohn, Judaism does not claim to possess the exclusive revelation of truth necessary for salvation. That is available to all people through reason. The unique revelation given to the Jews in the Mosaic law is a code of conduct that binds them to God and unites them as a people. The Mosaic law is unique and valid for the Jewish people alone. Its purpose is to guide the Jews in their moral and spiritual conduct and to make them ponder the nature and destiny of life. For Mendelssohn the God of reason and the God of Sinai are one and the same. All religions share the same truth given by God through reason, but each religion has its own unique code to give meaning and guidance to practical life. To those who would argue that the practice of religion, as well as its truth, must be one and the same for all, Mendelssohn responds as follows: 'It is not necessary for the entire flock to graze on one pasture or to enter and leave the master's house through just one door. It would be neither in accord with the shepherd's wishes nor conducive to the growth of his flocks.'[19] To require a union of religions is not tolerance but the very opposite. The exercise of reason and freedom of conscience requires pluralism in religious experience.[20]

Modernity also has brought a changed consciousness with regard to the dangers of idolatry. As Emil L. Fackenheim, a modern Jewish philosopher, writes, 'Surely in this modern, technological, demythologized world ancient idol-worship is dead and buried.'[21] Although Rabbinic law regards the worship of graven images as so dangerous that ownership is prohibited even when no worship is intended, the modern Jew, far from being tempted by idols, cannot understand how there ever could have been such an attraction. 'In fact,' says Fackenheim, 'this apparently once desperately serious business has become a mere joke, as in the story of the parishioner who informs his minister that whereas he has broken 9 of the 10 commandments, he has, he is proud to say, never worshipped graven images.'[22] For the modern Jew, idol worship no longer seems to be a real threat. In many instances images have been brought into the modern house of worship itself. But, says Fackenheim, it occurs to nobody that a stained-glass window depicting Abraham or Moses might become an idol. The very idea seems preposterous to a modern mind.[23]

As noted above, it was the ancient notion of idolatry that formed the basis of Maimonides' rejection of other religions. It seems the Jewish attitude toward other religions was rooted not in exclusivism but rather in the fear of idolatry. Because this fear of idolatry has no place in modern Jewish consciousness, the basis for the rejection of other religions also has been removed. Evidence for this is the modern Jewish willingness to participate in interreligious dialogue and the widespread interest in interfaith cooperation. Fackenheim concludes that no modern Jew would regard another religion as idolatrous simply because images or statues are a part of it – so long as the one, imageless God is the intended object of worship.[24] If the modern Jew thinks of idolatry at all, it is in terms of the worship of sex, money or nationalism (especially Nazi idolatry[25]) instead of the God of the Bible.

The viewpoint of the modern Jew opens the way for relations with Christianity, Islam and perhaps Hinduism; however, Buddhism – especially Mahāyāna Buddhism – may prove to be in a separate category. The Buddhist consciousness in which no transcendent God is recognized and the Mahāyāna awareness of the divine in the secular may be judged by the Jewish philosopher as a modern idolatry. In Fackenheim's view, idolatry is still possible if the notion of the one transcendent God is desecrated.[26] Jewish thinkers do not seem to have reconciled this understanding with Buddhism.

Other significant and worthwhile responses to the challenges created by Jews freely associating with non-Jews are represented by Franz Rosenzweig in Europe and thinkers such as Abraham Heschel, Robert Gordis and Jacob Agus in America. Let us first look at the thought of Franz Rosenzweig as it relates to other religions.[27] Rosenzweig develops his position in reaction to Hegelian idealism. In opposition to Hegel's focus on universal ideals, Rosenzweig concentrates on the individual's experience of the wholeness of the relationship between God, humanity and the world. None of the parts of this experience, none of the parts of this wholeness, can be understood in separation from the others. Any such separation brings with it a state of heathen imagery: 'There we find the tragic hero, dumb, alien to men and to God; the plastic cosmos – without a beginning and without an end, unrelated to man and God; the gods of myth in their hiddenness, far removed from the doings of men.'[28] This heathen view of the world is transcended by a revelation of the real relations that obtain among the human being, the world and God. Judaism is one such revelation. Christianity is another.

> Both are representations of the real world (and as such equal before God) and spell the end of the heathen view of the world. Judaism, which stays with God, stands in contrast with Christianity, which is sent out to conquer the unredeemed world and is forever marching toward God.[29]

Glatzer concludes that Rosenzweig's work is the first attempt in Jewish thought to understand Judaism and Christianity as equally true and valid religions. However, this does not lead to any suggestion of compromise or harmonization. It is Rosenzweig's view that the two religions will exist in parallel to the end of history: the Christian being eternally on the way, the Jew having the privilege of realizing eternity within time. Accordingly, Christians worship on the first day of the week whereas the Jewish holy day is the last of the week. As to whether Judaism is the truth or whether Judaism and Christianity together constitute the truth, Rosenzweig gives this response: truth is beyond humanity. He argues that 'Only God is Truth, Man (Jew, Christian) is given a part in truth (*Wahrheit*) insofar as he realizes in active life his share in truth (*bewahren*).'[30] Rosenzweig concludes his book *The Star of Redemption* by saying that the distant vision of truth does not lead into the beyond but 'into life'.[31]

Although there seems no philosophical reason why Rosenzweig's analysis should not apply to other religions as well as Christianity (at least to Islam and Hinduism), Rosenzweig clearly restricts true religion to Judaism and Christianity. He calls Islam a parody of Christianity and Judaism.[32] In one of his letters he comments on the inadequacy of Islam in relation to Judaism and Christianity:

> [The Muslim] has more in common with Goethe than with either Jew or Christian ... He doesn't know, and cannot know, the quite other-worldly attitude of the soul that yet breathes the world with every breath ... *How* that breathing of the world happens is the great contrast between Jew and Christian, but *that* it happens is their common ground. In Islam you will always find that God and the world remain perfectly apart, and so either the divine disappears in the world or the world disappears in God.[33]

Although he does not spell it out, he implies that Hinduism and Buddhism suffer the same failing when he concludes the letter by saying that the bringing together of God and the world is something 'only Jew and Christian can do, and no one else.'[34]

In regard to American thinkers such as Abraham Heschel, Daniel Breslauer has produced a helpful analysis in which he finds 'the ecumenical perspective' to be their distinctive mark.[35] The characteristic feature of this ecumenical perspective in modern America is that of 'the Jew embracing the non-Jewish religions as partisans in a spiritual battle.'[36] The Jew and religious non-Jew are seen as standing together against a demonic secularity. For example, the Jewish philosopher Abraham Heschel argues that it seems to be the will of God that there should be more than one religion. However, analysis indicates that this view is founded not so much on traditional texts or teachings as on Heschel's sense of the desperate state of the human spiritual condition. In Heschel's view, 'The Jew's task was to be deeply religious Jewishly and thus deepen the spiritual content of America communally.'[37] The role of modern American Judaism is to reawaken the religious life of all America. This new ecumenical role for American Judaism has a certain resonance with God's call to Abraham in Genesis, chapter 12, verse 3: 'By you all the families of the earth shall bless themselves.'

In this new ecumenical perspective, says Breslauer, the modern Jew sees diversity as a positive element. Diversity is creative when it yields a pluralism that is 'a situation in which various religious traditions interact with mutual self-respect and a sense of spiritual unity despite diversity'.[38] But the modern Jewish ecumenical perspective does not look to any 'common denominator' religiousness; rather it stresses a need for individual religions to retain their unique identity.

Another modern American Jewish thinker, Jacob Agus, describes pluralism as 'the apprehension of unity and polarity, it is the awareness of a bond in unity in some sense along with the realization of categorical separateness and disunity'.[39] The uniqueness of each religious tradition witnesses to the variety of possible responses to the divine. The richness of the variety is seen to strengthen the whole pluralistic spiritual community. As Abraham Heschel puts it,

> God's voice speaks in many languages, communicating itself in a diversity of intuitions. The word of God never comes to an end. No word is God's last word.[40]

Thus God is speaking uniquely to each religious tradition, and it is through the ecumenical efforts of each tradition that the others will come to hear the unique word that God has spoken to it. Only if one listens to all the languages of all the religions will one hear all of God's word that has been spoken. Hearing God's word in other religions stimulates one to creative development within one's own religion. In this way religious differences provide the challenge to keep religions alive and fresh. But such a stimulating variety is possible only when religions share a common universe of discourse and thus the necessity of the ecumenical perspective.[41] Religious pluralism, seen in this light, is judged to be inherently good for all religions.

In addition to stressing the importance of diversity, the Jewish ecumenical perspective also emphasizes unity. Several modern American writers identify the basis of this unity in diversity as 'the depth-dimension of faith'.[42] The depth-dimension refers to the internal, personal experience of religion that puts one in touch with the essence of religiousness. This essence or depth of religion is identified as a personal meeting with God – a meeting that occurs in eternity and transcends the historically and culturally conditioned external religious forms. However, it is through these forms of ritual and creed that one may step out of historical time and into moments shared with God. It is their inner sharing of God's eternity that is the common ground on which the diversity of the various religions inhere. In Heschel's view, whereas outer rituals and dogmas separate people, it is this deep inner spiritual intuition that unites them into one pluralistic community of spiritual persons.[43] At the level of outward experience, this depth-dimension is identified as a protest against any historical or conditioned form that is judged to be absolute. This essence of religiousness within each of the religions impels them to self-transcendence and renewal. Religious pluralism is helpful in this regard because it forcefully points to the insufficiency of any one answer.

This last point sounds amazingly akin to Paul Tillich's formulation of 'the Protestant Principle' – the rejection of any absolutizing tendency as a manifestation of institutional demonism.[44] That modern Jewish thinkers and Tillich should be so similar is not really surprising when it is remembered that the sources for both are the biblical prophets.[45] Tillich also shares the idea that the inner religious essence (for Tillich the Holy Spirit) is the dynamic and creative breaking out through secularism and demonism to new forms of religious self-transcendence.[46]

Although the idea of a purifying and uniting depth-dimension resonates strongly with Christianity (especially Protestantism) and also with Islam and Hinduism, it encounters serious problems in Buddhism. A depth-dimension defined as a personal meeting with God would not likely find any common ground with a Buddhist. Although the notion of creative renewal would be very acceptable, the Buddhist would most likely not agree that the inner sharing of God's eternity is a ground on which the Buddhist experience can inhere and be united with the other religions. While modern American Jewish thinkers do not seem to be aware of this particular problem, they have clearly gone much further than European thinkers like Rosenzweig in attempting to embrace, in the ecumenical perspective, all other religions as spiritual family.

However, it is also important to realize that the great modern Jewish thinkers (Mendelssohn, Fackenheim, Rosenzweig, etc.) reviewed above were and are barely read by any Jews who have not taken 'modern Jewish thought' courses in college. They are representative of a small intellectual minority of modern Jews. Most American Jews, for example, are pluralists simply as pragmatists and have little intellectual 'principle' behind their convictions. European Jews too have identified with the liberalization of religion and the creation of a pluralistic society as 'good for the Jews'. But there have also been very vocal holdouts: not only Hasidism and various forms of Eastern European Orthodoxy, but also significant streams of 'modern Orthodox' Judaism are pluralistic only to the degree that it is prudent. They are not less modern than those who opt for an intellectual pluralism – they simply argue that the culture of pluralism is bad for the Jewish people in so far as it diverts them from observance of the Torah covenant in preference for participation in gentile projects.[47]

Since the middle of the twentieth century Judaism has been caught up in two major historical events. On the one hand there is the Holocaust, Hitler's cold-blooded extermination of about six million Jews under the eyes of a passive Christianity. On the other hand there is the emergence of the state of Israel. As Zwi Werblowsky puts it, 'No Jew could fail to be touched to the quick by the existential significance which the age-old symbols of his faith had suddenly assumed – sanctification of the Name in martyrdom and the promise of a return to Zion.'[48] In terms of interaction with other religions the dangers of these two events were that 'suffering may lead to self-righteousness and injustice, faith in providence to arrogance, and Messianism to Chauvinism. Even religious Zionism is tempted to mistake for fulfilment what is really a trial and for accomplishment what is essentially another stage on the long road of Israel's Messianic destiny.'[49]

In its beginnings Zionism offered a response to the challenge of other religions. The response involved freeing Judaism from the Mosaic law. Then Jews would be able fully to join the secular modern world. In Israel today, however, the Zionist achievement has been taken for granted by a new messianic movement, Gush-Emunim, and by other religious groups to its right. They wish to 'hijack' Zionism and use it to create a 'Torah state' in which Jews would be separated from other nations. Money is now being collected in Israel and North America for the building of the Third Temple, and in recent years one of the *yeshivot* or seminaries in Jerusalem has been specializing in preparing priests for all aspects of Temple duties – including animal sacrifice. This movement is 'nationalist-fundamentalist' rather than pluralist in nature.[50]

In recent times the situation has become very complex. A narrow political Zionism has been opposed by some of the earliest Zionist leaders. Arguing against the German philosopher Hermann Cohen, Martin Buber advocates a spiritual Zionism in which Jews would serve God faithfully in their acts as well as their words. This would require the establishment of a human community according to God's will.[51] How to do this is not at all easy or clear. There is a Jewish state that must include Muslims, Christians and others as Israeli citizens – an empirical test of Israel as God's community on earth.[52] And at the same time Judaism must exist as a minority religion of Israelites who are loyal citizens of France, Germany, Great Britain, Canada, the United States and a host of other countries. The challenge of religious pluralism for modern Judaism continues to exist.

CONCLUSION

Judaism arose out of the pluralist context of the ancient Near East. The Jewish response to the challenge of religious pluralism has a long history dating back to the Babylonian exile in 586 BCE. During the classical and medieval periods important Jewish thinkers directly addressed the question of the relationship between Judaism and other religions. Philo viewed the various religions (as well as Greek philosophy) as different manifestations of the one divine Logos. Maimonides taught that of all religions Judaism was the only faith revealed by God and therefore true in every respect. His rejection of other religions was based on an interpretation of them as idolatrous forms and thus subject to the Mosaic prescription against idolatry. In the late medieval period the Kabbala became influential. The logic of the Kabbala was similar to that of Philo's Logos – namely, that there is one Absolute or God, of which there are many manifestations in the forms of various religions.

In the modern period Jews have begun to associate with non-Jews. The modern technological and demythologized world seems to have largely removed the threat and temptation of idolatry from Jewish consciousness. Three modern Jewish responses are the eighteenth-century emancipation movement of Moses Mendelssohn, the European thinking of Franz Rosenzweig, and the American ecumenical perspective of thinkers such as Abraham Heschel. Rosenzweig emphasizes the wholeness of the relationship between human beings, the world and God. This wholeness is revealed within Judaism and Christianity but not within the other religions. The modern American Jewish thinkers, by contrast, seem open to considering all religions as various manifestations of God's word. Diversity among religions is seen as a positive element creatively strengthening the total religious community in its opposition to surrounding forces of secular society. Unity between the religions is grounded in the individual believer's experience of the depth-dimension, the direct meeting with God. This is open to the experience of the believer in each of the traditions and thus provides the common ground for all of the religions.

However, not all modern European or American Jews adopt the intellectual response of their great modern thinkers. Most are pluralists for pragmatic or prudent reasons. With the American Jewish response we seem to have come full circle to a logic not unlike that of Philo's Logos model. There are also apparent affinities between the American Jewish response and Tillich's Protestant Principle. But perhaps the most serious challenge for Judaism comes in its response to Buddhism. As long as a religion is founded on the experience of a transcendent God, Judaism seems to be able to enter into spiritual partnership with it. But if that experience does not hold true for the Buddhist – if it is not a transcendent God that is being experienced – can the Jew still embrace the Buddhist as a spiritual partner? This question has yet to be faced by Judaism.

Some aspects of Zionism and the emergence of Israel have provided the opportunity for a resurgence of a narrow Judaism. This may be the familiar experience of a narrowing taking place once a religion is pressed into the service of political or national ends. In any case it has refocused the challenge of religious pluralism for Judaism in new and complex ways.

2 RELIGIOUS PLURALISM AND CHRISTIANITY

The relationship between Christianity and the other religions is one of the key issues in Christian self-understanding. Perhaps pluralism is so pressing a challenge because of the exclusivist missionary approaches adopted by Christianity over the past several hundred years. Many Christians have maintained that the presence of a sufficient number of missionaries scattered over the world would result in the conversion of all men and women to Jesus Christ. Today Christians recognize that, far from disappearing, the religions of Judaism, Islam, Hinduism and Buddhism are alive and well – in spite of all the Christian missionary efforts. This fact is causing Christians to reassess seriously their understanding of God's will, the scriptural teachings regarding Jesus, and the theological doctrines of Christology and evangelism. In the rapidly expanding body of literature resulting from the encounter with other religions, many Christian theologians are concluding that Christian theology cannot continue to be formulated in isolation from the other religions, and that, in fact, future developments in Christian theology will be the direct result of serious dialogue with the other religions.[1] One factor that has promoted this dialogue is the availability to theologians of excellent data about the other religions, this due largely to the efforts of scholars working in the areas of comparative religions and the history of religions. With this knowledge of other religions and with persons of other religions increasingly becoming part of the existential situation of Christian theologians, both theoretical and concrete realities are forcing these theologians to question the exclusivist claims of their Christian faith.

Certain theologians have described the task of theology in terms of an encounter with the other world religions. R. Whitson suggests that the task of theology is to open one's religion to another religious tradition.[2] John Dunne proposes experiencing the other religion and then reflecting with enrichment upon one's own religion.[3] Cross-fertilization can take place, the spiritual wisdom of the other religion enriching the experience of one's own religion. But such open approaches to the tasks of theology meet serious objection from Christianity's claim to uniqueness and normativeness. This claim is based most fundamentally upon Christology, or the Christian understanding of Jesus, and also upon the Christian doctrines of salvation and revelation. Lucien Richard states the problem:

> Can Christianity accept other religious traditions as valid ways to salvation without giving up its fundamental conviction about the absoluteness and uniqueness of Jesus Christ? Is it possible to believe simultaneously that God has acted decisively and for the salvation of all in the person of Jesus Christ and that Jews, Hindus, Muslims and Buddhists are warranted in remaining who they are and in following their own different ways to salvation?[4]

The theological problem is rooted in the Christological doctrines formulated at Nicaea and Chalcedon that made Christianity an exclusivist world religion. Over the centuries the Christian claim of the uniqueness and universality of Jesus has been grounded in the doctrine of 'hypostatic unity' defined at Chalcedon as follows: 'Jesus of Nazareth is unique in the precise sense that while being fully man, it is true of him and him alone, that he is also fully God, the second person of the co-equal Trinity.'[5] It is this fundamental doctrine that has seriously questioned and challenged the fact and experience of today's religious pluralism.

The Chalcedon formulation of the unique incarnation of God in Jesus has also resulted in the Christian church conceiving of itself as the one 'perfect society', frequently identified with the kingdom of God.[6] Being in full possession of all truth, the church has not felt any need to listen to voices and other religions from the wider world. Instead, the medieval Christian church retreated 'into a splendid isolation, concentrating on her inner life through a strong centralization and reacting defensively to the outside currents of thought and life'.[7] It is this attitude that has obstructed any meaningful contact between Christianity and other religions, except, of course, for missionary endeavours designed to convert non-Christians and so bring them into the church. However, following the Second Vatican Council, there has been a shift in the approach of the Roman Catholic church. In an attempt to remedy broken contacts with the surrounding world, the church has accepted dialogue with the world community of peoples and religions as a fundamental attitude. In part this shift in attitude has been caused by the growing pluralistic nature of the world. Christians everywhere live next-door to people of other faiths. Christians have found that their foreign neighbours are religious people living from within their own traditions, convinced that they too have a truth or a message for the world.[8] In a sense, in the desire to share their own truth with others, all religions have become missionary minded. It is this new situation that is forcing the Christian church to change from its all-knowing 'let us teach you' attitude to one of listening to the wisdom and questions that come from other religions. This new dialogical attitude is causing significant changes in the traditional Christian doctrine of the church: the narrow interpretation of the adage 'outside the church there is no salvation' is abandoned; the spiritual nature of other religions is recognized as is the presence of God's saving will within their teachings and practices.[9]

Although the churches are altering their ecclesiology so as to open the way for serious dialogue with other religions, the fundamental Christology that underlies traditional ecclesiology is only just beginning to change. Until the doctrine of the uniqueness of Jesus is examined and reinterpreted in relation to the claims to truth by other religions, the changed ecclesiology will lack a firm foundation – and thus will have little meaning. Consequently, the following discussion will focus on Christology in relation to other religions. The Christology of the New Testament will be examined; the views of the early church fathers will be considered; and the views of modern theologians will be studied.

THE NEW TESTAMENT AND OTHER RELIGIONS

Christianity took shape within the context of Judaism. Jesus was born into a Jewish family and raised by devout Jewish parents.[10] His scriptures were Jewish scriptures and his teaching method was not unlike that of the rabbis of his day. Yet at the same time Jesus saw himself as inaugurating something new. Although in the line of the prophets, he seems to have experienced himself as 'something more'. Whereas the prophets regarded themselves as but the mouthpieces of God, announcing their proclamations by 'thus saith the God', Jesus repeatedly used the words 'I say unto you' with the quiet assumption that he had the inherent authority to speak in such a fashion. This was one reason for the anger he aroused in the Jewish religious leaders, for to them such statements indicated Jesus was engaging in blasphemy by making himself equal with God.[11] Statements about his relationship to God certainly would seem to assert a unique status. In John's Gospel, Jesus is described as the Logos, the Word become flesh, and he is reported to have said, 'The Father is in me and I in him' (John 10:38) and 'I and the Father are one' (John 17:22). In Matthew's Gospel, Jesus is said to claim that all things have been delivered to him by the Father and that no one knows the Father except the Son and those to whom the Son chooses to reveal the Father. Such statements (even if they turn out to be faith statements of the early church rather than Jesus' own words) certainly laid the foundation for later claims regarding the uniqueness of Jesus. They also helped produce the split between Judaism and Christianity.

One aspect of Jewish self-consciousness, namely its sense of being the specially chosen covenant 'People of God' (Deut. 7:6), provided fertile soil for the development of Christian exclusiveness and missionary activity. The Jews were a people with a mission: 'Every knee shall bend before Yahweh, every tongue shall swear by him' (Isa. 45:23); and Jesus' time was one of unparalleled missionary activity by Judaism.[12] In Romans, chapter 2, verses 17–23, Paul describes the Jewish people as having absolute certainty that they possess the truth of God and have the duty to make this revelation known to all others. Although Jesus apparently forbade his disciples to preach to non-Jews, telling them, 'Go not to the Gentiles and enter no town of the Samaritans, but rather go to the lost sheep of Israel' (Matt. 10:5), we find the disciples involved in missionary works very soon after the resurrection. In the light of the resurrection, the early Christian community saw Jesus as the fulfilment of all the promises of the Hebrew scriptures and as the embodiment of God's saving action for all people (Luke 1:55, 73). The covenant established with God by Abraham and Moses became focused on the one person of Jesus Christ: 'And there is salvation in no one else, for there is no other name under heaven given among men by which we must be saved' (Acts 4:12). The Christian appropriation of the Jewish missionary motivation seems complete.

It is also important to recognize that in the Gospels as written by the early Christians, Jesus did not just present himself as a new prophet, but as God come among humanity. For example Jesus endorses the messianic declaration of Peter, 'You are the Christ, the Son of the living God' (Matt. 16:16). Jesus requires faith in his person equal to that which up until that time had only been placed in God: 'He who believes in me, rivers of living water will flow from his breast' (John 7:38). He speaks to people as only God could be imagined to speak: 'Go, your sins are pardoned' (Matt. 9:2). He changes the rules relating to divine worship and claims to be 'Lord of the Sabbath' (Mark 2:28). Jesus even goes so far as to attribute to himself the formula used on Mount Horeb to designate God, 'Before Abraham was, I am' (John 8:58). Jesus succinctly states the matter, 'He who sees me, sees the Father' (John 14:9). This direct identification of Jesus with God was proclaimed by the first generations of Christians.[13]

It is in the writings of Paul and John that the foundations are laid for later doctrines about the incarnation. In Romans, chapters 5–8, Paul describes Jesus as the second Adam, God coming as a new creation embodying the eschatological destiny of all people. Jesus Christ is Lord of all and the father of the new humanity. 'He is the image of the unseen God and the first-born of all creation, for in him were created all things' (Col. 1:15). According to Paul, Jesus Christ is a universal, active presence throughout the world and in the whole of human history; in short, he is the Logos. However, God's sending of the Son into the world is a decisive act of salvation and the unique manifestation of that divine Logos. Jesus Christ is a new incarnation but in continuity with God's past relationship with Israel. He embodies its fulfilment. God and Christ become the double object of Paul's faith.[14] Paul's is a mystical rather than a historical experience of Jesus – Paul had never seen Jesus, but Christ had come to him in a vision and had had an impact upon him like that of the God of Abraham of his Jewish experience. For Paul one comes to God with and in Christ. John, by contrast, focuses more on Christ. Although John shares the Jewish belief in the God of Abraham, his thought is concentrated on the person of Jesus, the Word that was made flesh and dwelt among humanity (John 1:14). For John, in his Gospel and letters, everything comes from Jesus. The whole of John's writing is dominated by his encounter with Jesus. It is thus even more Christocentric than the writing of Paul.

Lucien Richard summarizes the New Testament teachings as follows:

> What emerges out of the New Testament are two different strands of thought that serve as groundings for claims about uniqueness and finality. The universalism of the New Testament has its source and foundation in

the one person of Jesus Christ as God's very special agent and ultimate fulfilment of God's promises. The doctrine of the incarnation is an attempt to express Jesus Christ's special agency ... The other affirmation of the New Testament about Jesus Christ is that in him sacred history has already come to its end. Realized eschatology is one of the roots for the Church's claims about Christ's uniqueness and finality.[15]

Thus Christian claims of the uniqueness and finality of Christ are grounded in the two New Testament concepts of incarnation and realized eschatology. Both of these concepts are seen by contemporary Christian theologians as obstacles to Christian openness to other religions. Both lead to 'the absolutization and the freezing of attention on one human being and one moment of history'.[16]

But the New Testament also contains elements that can encourage a more open approach. The Jewish emphasis upon the God of Abraham as the sovereign God of all peoples carries over into the New Testament: Matthew sees Jesus more as a mediator than a full incarnation.[17] Peter's perspective focuses greatly upon God, the Father of all. Moreover, Jesus is not presented as manifesting a narrow, exclusive worldview. He treated with full seriousness the spiritual views of a Samaritan woman, concerned himself with a Roman officer, and told parables in which a man of another religion – a Samaritan – was the embodiment of true spirituality. His opposition to the Pharisees and Sadducees was directed not against their religion itself but against their legalistic and doctrinaire approach to religion, which he believed was insensitive to true spiritual life. He gave dignity and respect to sincere believers whose views differed from his own. By focusing on Jesus' behaviour and teachings and on his interaction with other religions, a basis exists for a Christian openness to other faiths. Krister Stendahl has recently argued that the openness of Jesus may be seen in the fact that he came preaching God and the kingdom (Mark 1:14). In the early church when the kingdom of God did not come, language shifted to focusing on Jesus as the Lord. So, although Jesus had preached the kingdom, the church preached Jesus.[18]

The other apparently open approach found in the New Testament is based upon the doctrine of Christ's pre-existence and his title of Logos. The idea that Jesus has been actively present throughout creation has provided the basis for a Christian universalism that would see Christ as being at work in all religions. This, however, has not been the basic theme of Christology in the Western church, and even when taken seriously this theme presents the danger of reducing other religions to something less than they themselves claim to be. Krister Stendahl also points out that universal claims run the risk of leading into various kinds of crusades and patterns of imperialism: 'If my religion is universalist, then everyone must see the world as I do.' In Stendahl's view, the role of Christians in the pluralistic world is to be the 'light', to be a witnessing community, and to trust the result of that witness to the hands of God.[19]

The New Testament contains both narrow Christocentric lines of thought and more open theocentric points of focus; both exclusive and inclusive interpretations can be found in it.[20] These two poles created problems for the New Testament Christians in their relations with people of other religions.

EARLY CHRISTIANITY AND OTHER RELIGIONS

The first major conflict within the early Christian church was whether Christianity should remain within Judaism as one of the many sects of that faith. If Christianity were simply a variant on Judaism, gentile converts would have to submit to circumcision, dietary injunctions and other aspects of Jewish law. While the Jerusalem Christians were in favour of such requirements, Paul argued that for Christians to insist on Jewish law was to fail to understand the essence of the gospel. Paul's view was widely accepted and Christianity was freed from the Jewish requirements in relation to circumcision, food laws and sabbath observance. This helped distinguish Christianity as a religion separate from Judaism.[21]

As Christianity freed itself from Judaism and moved out into the non-Jewish world, it encountered Greek philosophy and religion. This led to attempts to reinterpret the gospel in terms of the categories of Greek philosophy. Christianity began to internalize the sharp distinction between spirit and matter that had come into Greek philosophy through the Orphic movement centuries before Jesus. It was perpetuated through Platonism and Neoplatonism and moulded the worship and thinking of Christian converts from a Hellenistic background.[22] In sharp divergence from the Jewish tradition, shared by Jesus and Paul, the Greek approach regarded matter, including flesh, as evil, and it regarded pure spirit as good. Hebrew thought regarded body, mind and spirit as one psychosomatic unity and did not identify evil with the flesh. From the Hebrew perspective, evil occurred when the whole body/spirit unity of a person operated under a negative motivation, and good occurred when the body/spirit unity of the personality operated under positive motivation.[23] The Greek splitting of human nature in two and identifying evil with the material aspect of existence have had a lasting and unfortunate influence upon Christianity. Matters of natural instinct, like the expression of human sexuality, came to be experienced as evil and sinful, even when conducted within the required bonds of marriage. This has caused much unnecessary guilt and suffering. Salvation from the Greek perspective required the emancipation of the spirit from the contamination of the flesh. Although this provided an attractive solution to the problem of evil, it made nonsense of the New Testament insistence on the resurrection of the body – a requirement thoroughly consistent with Hebrew thought. This Greek influence is frequently found as a recurring theme in Christian asceticism and mysticism.

In its first centuries Christianity was also challenged by Greek dualism, which exerted its influence through Gnosticism. Gnosticism was highly syncretistic and drew on a variety of sources including Orphic and Platonic dualism, Syrian conceptions, Persian dualism, the mystery cults, Mesopotamian astrology and Egyptian religion. K. S. Latourette writes, 'When combined with certain elements from Christianity, Gnosticism proved so attractive that, while no accurate figures are obtainable, the suggestion has been made that for a time the majority of those who regarded themselves as Christians adhered to one or another of its many forms.'[24] Gnostics believed in a gnosis or knowledge that had been revealed and was transmitted to those who were specially initiated. It professed to be universal, accommodating the truths of the various religions. Salvation, the freeing of pure spirit from corrupt matter, was to be attained by the understanding of revealed truth presented in the form of mysteries.[25] Gnostic beliefs were integrated with Christian thought by allegorically interpreting Christian and Jewish scriptures and by appealing to some teachings of Jesus that, so it was claimed, had not been written out but handed down secretly through oral tradition. Gnosticism gave many different interpretations of Jesus. For example, some held that he was really pure spirit and only appeared to be associated with the flesh.[26] Gnosticism minimized the historical element in Christianity and attempted to divorce the wisdom of Jesus from his life, acts, death and resurrection.

The claims of the Gnostics and others (the Marcionites and the Montanists) compelled those Christians who did not agree with them to clarify and systematize the gospel. This response took three forms:

1) identifying authoritative lines of succession among bishops; 2) determining which writings were by the apostles or clearly contained their teachings, thus forming the canon of Christian scripture; and 3) formulating clear, brief statements of Christian doctrine (e.g. the Apostles' Creed), so that even a common person would know the essentials of the faith and be protected against deviations such as Gnosticism. Thus the response to the Gnostic challenge resulted in a sharpening of Christian identity. Gerard Vallee has pointed out that the desire of Christianity to show itself to be open and relevant leads inevitably to a crisis of identity. He argues that though the small New Testament community sought to build bridges to the Jewish community and the host Greek and Roman world within which it lived, these attempts at demonstrating openness and relevancy brought certain dangers:

- encounter with Judaism: danger of remaining a sect; danger of losing its Christological distinctiveness;
- encounter with the gentiles: danger of losing its monotheistic distinctiveness;
- encounter with gnostic groups: danger of losing its identity as a historical religion; danger of becoming elitist and esoteric;
- encounter with Graeco-Roman cults: danger of idolatry and syncretism;
- encounter with the Roman empire: danger of playing down its distinctive religious character; danger of overadaptation;
- encounter with Hellenistic philosophy: danger of being dissolved into philosophic doctrines; danger of losing its historical character;
- encounter with Roman law: danger of losing its prophetic and eschatological character; danger of structural assimilation.[27]

The writings of the early church fathers were a response to these dangers and as such a placing of limitations upon the openness of Christianity in the face of a pluralistic challenge.

CHRIST, THE LOGOS AND THE EARLY CHURCH FATHERS

In the second and third centuries various views were expressed by the church fathers as to the relation of Jesus to God. A common view in this regard – and one that is enjoying renewed attention in the modern encounter of Christianity with other religions – centred on the identification of Christ with the Logos.[28] Justin Martyr, with influence from Philo, held that the Logos was a kind of 'second God' incarnated in a historical person, Jesus, for the salvation of human beings. Although this incarnated Logos was not different in kind from God the Father, it was a second God. Irenaeus, on the other hand, held that the Logos, which became incarnate in Jesus Christ, was the divine agent of revelation. Against the Gnostics' view of Jesus as only apparently being a man, Irenaeus stressed that

> Jesus Christ was both man and God, fully man and from the beginning the incarnation of the Logos, that in Jesus, God Himself suffered for men (who deserved nothing from Him), and that at the same time Jesus as man at every stage of his life ... perfectly fulfilled what God had intended man and his entire creation to be, and so, as representative of man, won for man the right to be recognized by God as having met his standards.[29]

Tertullian declared that although in substance God is one, God has three activities or personae – a unity of substance but a Trinity of manifestations. Also Logos or reason is in God and expresses itself in word. In Jesus, said Tertullian quoting the Gospel of John, the Word became incarnate.

At the great catechetical school of Alexandria, Clement held that God is knowable only through the Logos, God's mind. The eternal Logos is the perfect mirror of God and the means by which God is made known. The Logos inspired the Greek philosophers, and Jesus is the Logos, the guide to all humanity. Clement's successor at the catechetical school of Alexandria was Origen. Basing his explanation on scripture, Origen taught: 1) that there is one God, the Father, who is just and good and the creator of all things; 2) that Jesus Christ, the God-man, was the incarnation of the Logos and is coeternal with the Father although subordinate to him; and 3) that the uncreated Holy Spirit is associated with the Father and the Son. He held that persons derive their existence from the Father, their rational nature from the Logos, the Son, and their sanctification from the Holy Spirit. Following Origen came the protracted dispute between Arius and Athanasius over the nature of the identity of and relationship between God and Son. Arius argued for a distinction that gave the Son a beginning but described God as without a beginning. This interpretation, which would make Christ subordinate and second to God, was unacceptable to Athanasius, who stressed the uniqueness of Christ, the Christian revelation and that revelation's eternal identity with God. The debate between the two camps is too long and convoluted to elaborate here. Suffice it to say that the followers of Athanasius, with their stress on Christ's uniqueness and identity with God, ultimately prevailed. Although controversies continued over the relation of the divine and human in Jesus, these do not seem as crucial to the relationship of Christianity with other religions. The importance of the dispute between Arius and Athanasius is that Arius' position (making Jesus a subordinate incarnation) would have given Christianity openness to other incarnations, whereas the Athanasian view produced a closed, exclusive Christianity with Jesus as the only true incarnation.

Subsequent early thinkers in the Western Christian church, such as Augustine, turned their attention to analysis of human nature, God's grace, and the church as a saving instrument. The primary focus of Christian thought shifted from what Christ was to what he did. Augustine's thinking focused more on the nature of Christ's presence in the sacrament of the Eucharist than on any speculative inquiry into the relationship between God and Christ.[30] Although these shifts in focus were important to the internal development of Christian thought, no change in the basic Christological assumptions of the Athanasian theory was introduced. This was also the case in the Eastern (Orthodox) church.[31] In the early church the single-minded focusing of doctrinal dispute upon the relation between God and Christ had resulted, to a large extent, from a reaction to the teachings of the Gnostics and numerous other Greek and Roman religions. The strength of the resultant exclusiveness of Christianity is indicated by the fact that by 500 CE Christianity had profoundly changed the religious life of the Roman empire. The Greek and Roman religions had virtually ceased to exist. Their easygoing syncretism had given way to the tough-minded claim of Christianity that only through itself was salvation to be attained.[32] Further, the Catholic church tended to identify itself with the kingdom of God on earth. Christian thought was influenced by the concept of Logos and adopted the term and concept in order to describe the relationship between Jesus and God. In a more narrow-minded way, the early church's identification of evil with the flesh and its desires led to a rejection of certain aspects of human nature by Christianity in general and especially by Christian monasticism.

CHRISTIANITY, ISLAM AND THE MEDIEVAL PERIOD

From 622 CE Christianity was challenged by a younger and more vigorous religion, Islam. Within a century Islamic rulers had become masters of over half the Christian world. Muhammad knew of Christianity and honoured Jesus as a prophet but denied the incarnation. The fundamental difference between Islam and Christianity still exists. In the Islamic view the gulf between God and humankind is too great to be bridged by Jesus or anyone else. Some Christians in the early Muslim centuries regarded Islam as a Christian heresy; Islam denied this, holding itself to be a fresh revelation from God and the final religion.[33] The impact of Islam on the Byzantine Christian church did not produce any fresh theology; rather it signalled a slowing down in creative Christian activity.

During the medieval period Christianity once again resumed outward expansion. Missionaries were sent to Europe and Asia. Missions were established in India and China, bringing Christianity into direct contact with Hinduism, Buddhism, Confucianism and Taoism. However, true to its exclusivist tendency, Christianity seems to have shut itself off from any meaningful contact with these other religions. In the Christian view, the Jews existed in a spiritual ghetto. An anti-Semitic theology said that they could not even properly interpret their own scriptures. Islam was seen by Western Christians as a political and religious enemy to be put to the sword. In spite of a few brilliant exceptions, such as Nicholas of Cusa and the early Dominican and Franciscan missionaries, the consensus was that the full extent of Christian universality and of God's kingdom on earth had been reached.

THE MODERN CHRISTIAN ENCOUNTER WITH OTHER RELIGIONS

Several factors in contemporary experience are causing many Christian theologians to re-examine seriously the closed, exclusivist attitude that has prevailed since the time of the early church fathers. For the first time Christian scholars have available to them factual information on the other world religions. In addition, there is the existential experience of cultural and religious pluralism – all over the world religious believers of different traditions are living side by side as citizens of the same country. No longer can Christians view Hindus, Buddhists and Muslims as heathens who live in far-off lands and need to be converted by Christian missionaries. Today, believers of these religions live as neighbours to Christians in the formerly Christian-dominated cultures of Europe and North America. Eastern religions in particular are evidencing considerable appeal for Westerners through sectarian movements such as transcendental meditation and Zen Buddhism.[34] In Western universities, religious studies departments are drawing large numbers of students and providing them with the opportunity to study each of the world religions in their original language and in an open academic atmosphere. All of these factors are putting pressure on Christian theologians, perhaps for the first time since Chalcedon, to re-examine seriously the traditional exclusiveness of Christian doctrine. Within the Roman Catholic church, some of the pronouncements of the Second Vatican Council have opened the way for a more positive attitude towards other religions.[35] In Protestant circles the World Council of Churches has, since the 1970s, given increasing importance to dialogue with other religions.[36] The World Council of Churches has released Guidelines on Dialogue that are generating commentaries and studies within each of its member churches.[37] Outside the formal activities of church institutions, the scholarship of the past two decades shows an increasing focus on the issue by theologians and religious studies scholars.[38]

Early modern Christian thinkers grouped themselves according to two opposing interpretations of Jesus Christ: one side represented by Kant's focus on the idea or principle of Christ as an eternally present incarnation; the other side represented by Schleiermacher's rejection of the metaphysical and ontological aspects of Chalcedon and his desire to ground himself in human experience. Immanuel Kant, in his analysis of Christ as a manifestation of reason universally inherent in human experience, represents an idealizing Christology. For Kant the historical Jesus was not a necessity.[39] Schleiermacher reacted against Kant's abstracting and universalizing tendencies and inaugurated a new humanistic approach. He interpreted the meaning of Christ from the fundamental perspective of Christ's humanity. Schleiermacher assumed a universal religious consciousness that he described as a feeling of absolute dependence.[40] He grounded Christian faith in the universal human phenomenon of religious experience rather than in abstract reason or authoritative sources. This turning inwards to subjective insights and away from outward authority was a radical change from previous approaches. Since Schleiermacher, Christology has tended either to develop further or refute his position. Although neither Kant nor Schleiermacher had a deep knowledge of other religions, they did deal with the problem of Christianity's exclusivism. Kant, through reason, and Schleiermacher, through the subjective feeling of absolute dependence, grounded Christianity in human universals that opened the doors to religious relativism.

The founding of Christian claims on history was given a severe blow by David Friedrich Strauss's book *The Life of Jesus Critically Examined*.[41] Because of his scepticism about the historical reliability of the Gospels – a scepticism that modern, scientific biblical scholarship has in some ways continued to augment – Strauss rejected historical facts as a basis for Christian knowledge.

In the twentieth century yet another theme was added to the notion of religious relativism – that of evolutionary progress. Ernst Troeltsch understood religious history in an evolutionary perspective, as a universal human movement towards perfection.[42] Because the whole of human history comprises the total evolutionary movement, other religions and movements cannot be excluded. Absolutism is rejected, and revelation is seen as a progressive movement towards the Absolute, which can never be completely attained. God's revelations in the Hebrew scriptures and in Jesus are only stages in the general history of revelation. For Troeltsch, Jesus Christ cannot be identified with God but must take his place alongside the founders of other great religions. Jesus provided the needed requirements for the evolution of the Christian religion. Jesus Christ is the means by which Christians grasp the essence of religiosity. Absolute validity cannot be claimed for Christianity or any other religion. Truth can only be truth for me, for my culture, for my religion. Yet in spite of this relativism there is, for Troeltsch, the sense of a potential Absolute as the common goal of the evolutionary process in all religions.

> [Religions] are products of the impulse towards absolute objective truth, and take effect in the practical sphere under constant critical self-purification and effort at self-improvement . . . All seem impelled by an inner force to strive upward towards some unknown final height, where alone ultimate unity and the final objective validity can lie. And, as all religion has thus a common goal in the Unknown, the Future, perchance in the Beyond, so too it has a common ground in the Divine Spirit ever pressing the finite mind onward toward further light and fuller consciousness, a Spirit which indwells the finite spirit, and whose ultimate union with it is the purpose of the whole many-sided process.[43]

For Troeltsch each religion is a different cultural manifestation of the struggle of the human spirit from the divine source to the divine goal.

At the opposite end of the spectrum are the views of Karl Barth. Barth reacted against Troeltsch by presenting an uncompromising and exclusivist view of God's self-revelation in Jesus Christ. Barth describes his basis for the theological evaluation of humanity as the subject of all religions:

> It will be man for whom (whether he knows it or not) Jesus Christ was born, died and rose again. It will be man who (whether he has already heard it or not) is intended in the Word of God. It will be man who (whether he is aware of it or not) has in Christ his Lord.[44]

Although Barth is adamantly exclusivist in his Christology, he does not accept a simple one-to-one identity of true religion with the Christian religion of the Christian church. Both of these are under the same judgement for failings as any other religion or religious institution. But to the extent that the Christian religion or Christian church through grace lives by grace, it is the locus of true religion.[45]

At first glance Barth would seem to open his definition of true religion to any religion that 'through grace lives by grace', but it is quickly evident that Barth restricts grace to association with Jesus Christ. Barth carefully distinguishes grace from fanatic piety, Hegelian and Kantian rationalism, and relativism or historical scepticism. Barth dismisses these as the worst forms of intolerance and argues that true tolerance towards other religions can be found only in the forebearance of God's grace as manifested in Jesus Christ. Barth's theology in this regard is based on two points that he finds in Christian scripture: 1) that religions are futile human attempts to know God and that only through revelation can God be known; and 2) in the revelation of Jesus Christ we experience the grace by which we are reconciled to God.[46] For Barth revelation and grace dialectically oppose religion and religions. Christian religion and the Christian church are sinful and therefore are not true religion. But by abandoning its own claims to superiority or absolute truth and by God's grace manifesting the revelation of Jesus Christ, Christianity may be judged by God as the right and true religion.[47]

Barth offers an analogy of the sun illuminating the earth as a way of understanding Christianity in relation to other religions:

> Like the sun, Christ's light falls on one part of the earth and not on the other, enlightening one part and leaving the other part in darkness, and this without ever changing the religion itself. All depends on the light of

Christ shining here and not there on the 'act of divine election.' The only difference between Christianity and other religions is that Christianity stands in the sunlight, the others in the shadow.[48]

Barth's theology takes with utmost seriousness the sinfulness of human nature which corrupts all religions including Christianity. He is very critical of any notions of superiority or pride within Christians or the church in encounters with other religions. Only God's grace in Christ can help, and, as it happens, its locus is in Christianity and not in any other religion.

RECENT DEVELOPMENTS

In the past few decades Christian theologians have taken various positions along the spectrum between the religious pluralism of Troeltsch and the Christian exclusivism of Barth. Troeltsch's absolutizing of relativism and Barth's absolutizing of faith have produced a dialectical morass from which contemporary Christian theologians are desperately attempting to escape. The outcome has been a theological medley. There appears to be no clear, single solution. In analysing this wide range of theological responses, the terms 'theocentrism' and 'Christocentrism' will be used as headings under which to classify and survey many of the contemporary positions. The dialogical model will be examined as the approach that seems to hold the most hope for further development.

THEOCENTRIC APPROACHES

Theocentric approaches to other religions focus primarily upon God rather than Christ. Typically the theologians who hold this perspective point to passages in the Hebrew scriptures where God's covenant with Abraham and Noah is understood as applying to the whole of humanity and where God elects several peoples, not just Israel.[49] Attention is also drawn to the theocentric statements of Jesus. He habitually spoke of God as the Father and placed himself below God, as when he states, 'My Father is greater than I' (John 14:28). Jesus' role as the one who points to and reveals God is highlighted, and attention is drawn away from Jesus' statements equating himself with God, for instance, 'I and my Father are one' (John 10:30). The emphasis is placed on Jesus pointing to God rather than to himself. In passages from the Epistles, the priority of God as the one who has exalted Jesus is repeatedly highlighted, as when eternal life is described as 'to know thee as the only true God, and Jesus Christ whom thou has sent' (John 17:3). God is not only previous to Jesus Christ but is also after him at the eschatological end: 'When all things are subjected to him, then the Son himself will also be subjected to him who put all things under him that God may be everything to everyone' (I Cor. 15:28). The proponents of this approach see it not as ignoring the divinity of Christ but as recognizing the greatness and freedom of God – of avoiding focusing so exclusively on Christ that it becomes impossible to have any positive relationship with other religions.

It is certainly true that shifting the centre of focus from Christ to God opens the way for dialogue with Judaism, Islam and many forms of Hinduism. But one point, not yet recognized by the theologians taking this approach, is that centring on God is a serious obstacle to Buddhists. Let us now sample some of the theocentric theologies.

Orthodox Theology

A viewpoint that is frequently forgotten in contemporary debate is that of the Eastern churches, of the Orthodox Christians who are concentrated in such places as Greece, Russia and Ukraine. Orthodox theologians seem more comfortable with religious pluralism than many of their Western counterparts. This is not surprising in that Orthodox Christians have for many centuries lived as pluralists within Christianity, developing a self-awareness that Western Christianity has to a large extent repressed.

Orthodox theology,[50] with its emphasis on the Holy Spirit, sees the continuity of God's revealing truth in all nations before as well as after the incarnation of the Logos in Jesus Christ. The contribution of Greek philosophy to inclusive Christian theology via Justin, Clement and Origen is favoured over the narrower formulations of Tertullian. Paul's analysis of the Athenians' worship of the unknown God as being Christian without knowing it (Acts 17:23) and the invocation of the Logos at the beginning of John's Gospel prepared the way for a positive attitude towards non-biblical truth. Thus Socrates' teaching that 'it is evil to return evil for evil'[51] could be recognized as more humane and godly than the Torah's command that 'your eye shall not pity; it shall be life for life, eye for eye, tooth for tooth' (Deut. 19:21). Rejecting the more exclusive and militant formulations of the Christian West, Orthodox theologians attempt to absorb and consecrate the good, no matter where they find it, as part of truth.[52] No one can limit God's presence. It is not given to Christians or anyone else to judge where God is not. As Peter confessed, 'I now see how true it is that God has no favourites, but that in every nation the person who is God-fearing and does what is right is acceptable to him' (Acts 10:34–5). For the Orthodox, this in no way denies Christ's claim that he is 'the way, the truth, and the life' (John 14:6). Christ is not limited by space or time; his Spirit lives, speaks and acts everywhere in human history. The Holy Spirit manifested in the early Christian church (Acts 2:1–4) is God's Spirit who inspires and uplifts *all* people. It is this doctrine of the omnipresence of the Holy Spirit that is the basis for the positive approach of Orthodox Christians to other religions.

The theocentric orientation of Orthodox thought is also seen in its attitude towards social responsibility and worship. In Byzantine society, for example, all authority in both church and the world was referred directly to God.[53] Both the priesthood and civil authority were seen to proceed directly from God. In worship God is directly accessible to the Orthodox worshipper in the personal experience of the divine.[54] Thus from the Orthodox perspective all of life is thoroughly God centred. This opens the way to a sense of spiritual community with the members of other theocentric religions.

Orthodox Christians point to the fact that for many centuries millions of them have lived as peaceful suffering servants in the midst of Islam. They point to the fruits of Western exclusivism – for instance, the Christian crusades against Islam – as empirical evidence of the error of that theology. Orthodox Christianity sees its past as one of living in the midst of pluralism, and its future within the context of other creeds as being no different. The theological objective of Orthodox Christianity is the absorption of the human being into God through worship. Their Christology and its relation to other religions is summarized as follows:

> Christ is never mere man or God but always the *theanthropos* (God-man), seeking to elevate human beings to *theosis*. As long as other religions have the same goal, the elevation of humanity to divine life, they are perceived by the Orthodox as instruments of God in God's world.[55]

Paul Tillich

Paul Tillich,[56] a Protestant theologian, develops a position that, like the Orthodox view, argues for openness based on the omnipresent action of the Holy Spirit. He wants to safeguard the transcendence of God over any finite manifestation – thus his phrase 'God above God' and the theocentric emphasis in his theology.[57] Tillich sees in Christianity an ongoing tension between the particular and the universal. The particularity is of course centred on the appearance and reception of Jesus of Nazareth as the Christ. This is the criterion for all Christian encounters with other religions and for all self-judging of Christians. Tillich explains this as follows:

> What is particular in him is that he crucified the particular in himself for the sake of the universal. This liberates his image from bondage both to a particular religion – the religion to which he belonged has thrown him out – and to the religious sphere as such: the principle of love in him embraces the cosmos, including both the religious and secular spheres. With this image, particular yet free from particularity, religious yet free from religion, the criteria are given under which Christianity must judge itself and, by judging itself, judge also the other religions.[58]

Thus Tillich sees an openness in Christianity in the tension between judging the encountered religions and accepting judgement from them. This was the vital power of Christianity in its early centuries – its ability to be a centre of crystallization for all positive religious elements after they had been subjected to the criterion of Jesus as the Christ. Such openness and receptivity were gradually lost with the strengthening of hierarchical authority until 'the tradition ceased to be a living stream; it became an ever-augmented sum of immovably valid statements and institutions'.[59] This stagnation and self-absorption of Christianity, which resulted in a rejection of pluralism, lasted through the medieval period and the Reformation. With the rise of modern secularism Christians became open to a more creative encounter with other religions. Tillich gives examples of the way in which this more open Christianity both judged other religions and accepted judgement from them. This attitude, he says, puts an end to Christian attempts to convert Jews, Muslims, Hindus or Buddhists and instead invokes self-criticism and dialogue. The goal is neither the mixing of religions nor the victory of one religion but rather it is to penetrate, through self-critical dialogue, ever further into the depths of one's own religion. In the depth of every religion, says Tillich, 'there is a point where particularity breaks through to spiritual freedom – and to a vision of the spiritual presence in other expressions of the ultimate meaning of man's existence'.[60] Because Tillich conceives of God in very abstract philosophical terms,[61] his theology may prove more acceptable as a basis for dialogue with Buddhists than the approaches of other contemporary theocentric theologians.

John Hick

John Hick is a British philosopher of religion cum theologian. Of late his viewpoint is much discussed in English-speaking circles. Hick takes for one of his titles a phrase from the *Bhagavad-Gītā*, 'Whatever path men choose is mine.'[62] Hick formulates his position in reaction to the Christocentric approach dominant in contemporary Western theology today. Theologians like Karl Rahner, who regard the devout Muslim, Hindu or Jew as an 'anonymous Christian', are criticized by Hick as still working within the old dogma that holds Christ rather than God at the centre. From that perspective only Christians can be saved and 'so we have to say that devout and godly non-Christians are really, in some metaphysical sense, Christians or Christians-to-be without knowing it'.[63] The intention, says Hick, is not doublespeak but the charitable extension of grace to religious persons who had formerly been regarded as beyond the pale. In his view, such a move has the psychological function of being a bridge between the no longer acceptable exclusivism of the past and a new open view that is emerging. But, says Hick, sooner or later Christians shall have to get off this bridge on the other side. His own position is offered as one in the new realm – completely on the other side of the 'anonymous Christian' bridge.

Hick develops his position by analogy to Ptolemaic and Copernican astronomy. Just as in Ptolemaic astronomy the earth was seen as the centre of the solar system with all the other planets revolving around it, so in Ptolemaic theology Christ is seen as the centre of the universe of religions. Other religions are seen as revolving around Christianity and being graded according to their distance from it. Hick notes that such a Ptolemaic approach could just as well be used by any other religion. A Hindu, for example, could say that sincere Christians are implicit Hindus, that other faiths provide various grades of ordinary paths to truth but that Hinduism is the extraordinary path, that Hinduism is not a religion but the eternal truth judging and superseding all religions (as in Barth), and so on. This stance can be taken by a theologian of any religion, but in reality it is only an interim position while we prepare our minds for Copernican theology. Just as Copernicus realized that it is the sun, not the earth, that is at the centre, so also 'we have to realize that the universe of faith centers upon *God*, and not upon Christianity or any other religion. He is the sun, the originative source of light and life, whom all the religions reflect in their own different ways.'[64] If this is so, then it is to be expected that God, as reflected in the different civilizations, manifests in different revelations or religions. But even though the various revelations differ, we may believe that everywhere the one God has been at work 'pressing in upon the human spirit'.[65]

Hick defends his position by reinterpreting traditional Christology. The biblical claims regarding the uniqueness of Christ (e.g. 'I and the Father are one', 'No one comes to God but by me') he dismisses, on the authority of New Testament criticism, as being additions by the early Christian community rather than the words of Jesus. It is worth noting that recent biblical studies do not uniformly support Hick's interpretation. For example, after a careful review of New Testament scholarship James Dunn concludes that 'in the earliest NT formulations the idea of pre-existent divine sonship of Jesus does not yet seem to have crossed the threshold of thought, is neither affirmed nor denied, and that of the statements formulated some can be seen from a later perspective to accommodate the thought of pre-existence and incarnation while others sit only awkwardly with it'.[66] Attention is called to this problem because it is on the basis of his understanding of biblical scholarship that Hick concludes that Jesus did not think of himself as God.[67] Hick then builds on this a theory that statements about the incarnation of Jesus must be understood as mythological.[68] Incarnational statements, says Hick, are simply figurative ways of saying that for Christians Jesus is the living contact with God. When this is seen, it frees us from having 'to draw the negative conclusion that he [Jesus] is man's one and only effective point of contact with God'.[69]

The Kantian background of Hick's theology is readily apparent. God is an a priori idea that is structured by human experience. However, a potential problem is Hick's use of the term 'God' as a priori in a way that seems unacceptable to the Buddhist and to Advaita Vedānta Hindus. This would call into question whether Hick's Copernican revolution is acceptable to all religions. While Hick may have stepped off the bridge of 'anonymous Christianity', he is, from the viewpoint of certain Eastern religions, still stuck on the 'bridge of theism'. Hick has recognized this problem and in chapters 5 and 6 of his book *God Has Many Names*[70] he uses the term 'God' not to refer to the personal deity of the theistic faiths, but to the infinite reality variously apprehended through varying forms of religious experience. In an article titled 'The Theology of Religious Pluralism', Hick helpfully clarifies his position:

> I have tried to use it [the term 'God'] in such a way that it is proper to ask whether God is personal. But I accept that this usage can easily be misunderstood. I therefore prefer to speak of 'the Real,' and to distinguish between human experience of the Real as personal (taking such concrete forms as Jahweh, Shiva, Vishnu, the Heavenly Father, etc.) and of the Real as non-personal (taking such forms as Brahman, the Tao, the Dharma, Nirvana, Sunyata, etc.).[71]

Wilfred Cantwell Smith

Wilfred Smith was a theologian and historian of religion. He was one of the few Christian theologians who had frontline experience with other religions, having taught in India in 1941–5. Returning to Canada, he was appointed professor of comparative religion at McGill University and within a short time organized the McGill Institute of Islamic Studies. In 1964 Smith became director of Harvard University's Center for the Study of World Religions, a centre that explicitly set out to enter into dialogue with the Harvard Divinity School and with Christian theology in general. At both McGill and Harvard, Smith brought together students and faculty from the major religions and had them develop and test their theologies among one another. For himself Smith set forth the goal of 'constructing theories that would prove acceptable both to Jews and to Buddhists, both to Muslims and to Christians, as well as being cogent within the academic tradition'.[72] Smith was aware that these were somewhat unusual requirements for doing theology, but he recognized that the religious experience of the world is entering a new phase – that of religious pluralism. A basic requirement of this new phase is that all of us are asked to understand religious traditions other than our own. No longer is it adequate to construct theology within the isolation of one religious tradition. Just as in the past Christian theologians found it necessary to construct theology in the light of Greek philosophy or scientific developments, so the challenge today to Christian theologians, as they develop their theology, is to be conscious of their position as members of a world society in which there are other theologians – equally intelligent, equally devout, equally moral – who are Hindus, Buddhists, Muslims. Theologians must be aware that the readers of their theology 'are likely perhaps to be Buddhists or to have Muslim husbands or Hindu colleagues'.[73]

Smith begins his theological statement by pointing out that there are moral as well as conceptual implications of the Christian revelation. On the moral level the revelation of God in Christ required reconciliation and a deep sense of community: 'We must strive to break down barriers, to close up gulfs, to recognize all men as neighbours and sons of God the Father, seeking Him, finding Him, being sought by Him and being found by Him. At this level, we do not become truly Christian until we have reached out towards a community that turns all mankind into one total "we".'[74] When theological statements are formulated, they must not allow Christians to perpetuate the 'we' and 'they' attitude that the exclusivism of the past has frequently generated. Such an attitude is marked by arrogance rather than the humility that Christ taught, and is simply immoral. As Smith puts it, 'it is not morally possible actually to go out into the world and say to devout, intelligent, fellow human beings: "We are saved and you are damned"; or, "We believe that we know God, and we are right; you believe that you know God, and you are totally wrong."'[75] The converse also holds true, namely, that it is unacceptable to hold that if anyone else's faith turns out to be valid, then Christianity must be false. From the Christian point of view, says Smith, this kind of exclusivist logic is morally unacceptable. When one meets or hears of a Hindu, Muslim or Buddhist leading a pious and moral life that seems to be as close to God and in that sense as 'adequate' as any Christian way of life, 'then the Christian should be overjoyed, enthusiastically hopeful that this is true, even though he might be permitted a fear lest it not be so ... It will not do to have a faith that can be undermined by God's saving one's neighbour; or to be afraid lest other men turn out to be closer to God than one had been led to suppose.'[76]

On the conceptual level Smith begins by stating that any formulation of Christian faith must include some doctrine of other religions. It must also include the positive point of previous Christian theologies, namely, 'that in Christ, God died for us men and our salvation, and that through faith in him we are saved'.[77] The problem is to reconcile a truly Christian charity with doctrinal adequacy. Smith rejects exclusivist Christologies as violating Christian charity. His own proposal is to affirm 'that a Buddhist who is saved, or a Hindu or a Muslim or whoever, is saved, and is saved only, because God is the kind of God whom Jesus Christ has revealed him to be'.[78] He further states,

> If the Christian revelation were *not* true, then it might be possible to imagine that God would allow Hindus to worship Him or Muslims to

obey Him or Buddhists to feel compassionate towards their fellows, without His responding, without His reaching out to hold them in His arms. But because God is what He is, because He is what Christ has shown Him to be, *therefore* other men *do* live in His presence. Also, therefore we (as Christians) know this to be so.[79]

Smith's position is thoroughly theocentric, but it is based on a God who is revealed through Christ. Through Christ we know that God reaches out in love to all. As finite creatures of God's creation, we are not to set boundaries to that love.

Smith has effectively carried his theological position into an analysis of how we use the term 'religion'. In his classic work, *The Meaning and End of Religion*, Smith points out that the use of exclusivist theology results in the religion of other people being viewed as idolatry and turns their gods into false deities. By way of example he cites a statement of the Christian theologian Emil Brunner, 'The God of the "other religions" is always an idol.'[80] Similarly, for many Muslims, Jesus as the Christ is an idol. Such examples of narrow-minded exclusivism exemplify the religious arrogance that, for the follower of Jesus, is unacceptable. The end of all religion is the goal to which it leads, namely, God. Smith writes, 'God is the end of religion also in the sense that once He appears vividly before us, in His depth and love and unrelenting truth all else dissolves; or at the least religious paraphernalia drop back into their due and mundane place, and the concept "religion" is brought to an end.'[81] As a Christian, Smith felt that this understanding of religion is required if we are to do justice to 'the world in which we live and to what we know of God as Christ has revealed Him to us'.[82] All religion, whether it be Christian, Muslim, Buddhist, Hindu or some other, is to be understood as a vital and changing divine–human encounter. Thus the role of the Christian missionary must be understood in a new way. Rather than seeking to convert the other to Christianity, the missionary must now participate in the divine–human encounter of the other religion for the purpose of aiding its evolutionary development. From this new perspective the missionary will be welcomed by the religious leaders of other traditions. As examples Smith cites the role of C. F. Andrews in the life of Gandhi, and the impact that Martin Buber, a Jew, has had on modern Christianity. Modern Christians, says Smith, have learned from Buber about God, about themselves and about the Christian tradition. Furthermore they 'welcomed him, applauded him, asked him to come back and give them more'.[83] In Smith's eyes Buber provides the model for the modern missionary.

Behind this new vision of Christianity and the other religions is Wilfred Cantwell Smith's understanding of how it is that we come to obtain knowledge. In his view it is in the meeting between persons, and not in the solitude of the theologian's study, that we come to knowledge of God, our world and ourselves. We cannot know each other except in mutuality: in respect, trust, equality and love. In religious knowledge, as in all human knowledge, we must move from thinking of the members of another religion as distant and other to thinking of them as equal members of a worldwide religious community. Using some of the relationships among pronouns as metaphors, Smith says that we must move from talk of the other religion as an *it* to talk of a *they*, which evolves into a *we* talking of a *they*, and presently a *we* talking of *you*, then a *we* talking with *you*, and finally *we all* talking together about *us*.[84] For Christians, then, knowledge comes not through the isolated study of the revelation of God through Jesus Christ but, conversely, by understanding God through Christ, an understanding gained through the participation in the world community of religions. The problem, as Smith recognized, is how to enlarge one's vision of truth without losing loyalty to one's own finite hold upon it.[85] Smith's answer is that it is only as we achieve a corporate self-consciousness that we will have true knowledge of ourselves and each other.

> Our solidarity precedes our particularity, and is part of our self-transcendence. The truth of all of us is part of the truth of each of us. It is self-consciously we who differ.[86]

Christian theology must not be a view from one religion or community out upon the others. This has been the error of the past. True Christian theology, says Smith, arises when we see and know ourselves as participants in the one world community that includes all other religions.[87]

Smith's theology is thoroughly theocentric and contains the assumption that each human community, each religion, is evolving toward an ultimate convergence of its knowledge and experience with that of all other communities and religions. Although this approach provides an excellent basis for helping Christians and others to identify areas of common experience, it does not answer the question of how to avoid losing hold on one's own unique revelation while enlarging one's vision of truth so as to accommodate all other truths. On this point Smith's position will pose problems for a fundamentalist within Christianity as well as within any of the other religions. Additionally, Smith's assumption that the corporate religious self-consciousness is of God will surely be unacceptable to Buddhist thinkers.

Paul Knitter

Knitter accepts much of John Hick's approach but contextualizes it and attempts to move it forward as a Roman Catholic scholar who is very open to other religions. As general editor of the 'Faith Meets Faith' series published by Orbis Books, Knitter has done much to foster both interreligious dialogue and the scholarly debate around religious pluralism. In his first book, *No Other Name? A Critical Survey of Christian Attitudes Toward the World Religions*, Knitter clearly connects the pluralist notion of truth, developed by the philosophers, with the challenge of religious pluralism. Truth can no longer be defined according to the scientific notion of certain knowledge through the understanding of cause–effect relations. This means that scientific knowledge is not truth but only on the way towards truth. On the personal level truth is not the pursuit of certainty but of ever-enlarging understanding. And this 'understanding' will be open to constant change and revision.[88] Like Smith before him, Knitter sees the cherished rationalist principle of non-contradiction, the either/or exclusion model of religious truth, as no longer acceptable. Truth, says Knitter, must now be seen as relational: 'what is true will reveal itself mainly by its ability to relate these other expressions of truth and to grow through these relationships'.[89] Aware of the danger that this approach might slide into 'relativistic pap', as he puts it, in which all positions are given equal and non-critical hearing, Knitter offers the helpful suggestion that pluralists can learn some useful criteria from liberation theology.[90] 1) Liberation theologians enter the hermeneutical circle – the process of trying to listen to and interpret scripture or tradition – with a 'hermeneutics of suspicion'. They are suspicious of how interpretations of scripture and doctrine can become ideologies or means of promoting one's own interests at the expense of others. Inclusivist Christocentric approaches, for example, are open to colonialist or imperialist distortions like so many First World development models. 2) Liberation theology privileges the poor rather than searching for an abstract unifying concept (e.g. Hick's 'the Real'). Although there may be no common ground or essence that we can evoke as the basis for dialogue, we could perhaps agree on a common approach, namely, to opt for the poor and the nonperson – the victims of this world – as a shared locus of our religious experience. Thus, rather than God or a *theocentric* approach as the starting point for religious encounter, a *soteriocentric* (or liberation from all kinds of bondage – hunger, sexism, racism, poverty, etc.) approach may move interfaith dialogue from intellectual discussion (valuable though that might be) to praxis – working together to help the world's marginalized. This, suggests Knitter, could offer the religions a basis for grading themselves in a pluralistic world. In this approach, unlike theocentricism or Christocentricism, no system of revelation (e.g. Torah, Gospel, Qur'ān, Veda) is absolute. Rather, the perspectives on *soteria*, on salvation from bondage of all kinds (of which the Christian's kingdom of God through Christ is only one) could clarify and critique each other. Knitter develops this line of thought further in his 1996 book, *Jesus and the Other Names*, which we will consider later in this chapter.

These scholars provide a fair sampling of the theocentric approach to other religions. But before moving to some of the Christocentric theologians, a footnote on a recent biblical contribution may be in order. Krister Stendahl, professor of New Testament studies at the Harvard Divinity School, recently gave three Bible studies that employed a theocentric position. Adducing both Old and New Testament sources, Stendahl interprets them as a 'witnessing particularism within a universal perspective'.[91] The Bible, says Stendahl, speaks of God's attempts to 'mend creation'. To do this God sent Noah, the prophets and then Jesus, who preached God's kingdom as a mended creation. But when the kingdom did not come, Christians turned their attention from the kingdom to Jesus as Lord (king). The Christian tendency towards exclusiveness, says Stendahl, is rooted in the fact that, although Jesus preached the kingdom, the church preached Jesus. Stendahl's exegesis of Peter's statement about Christ that 'there is no other name under heaven given among men by which we must be saved' (Acts 4:12) is that it is a confession, and he adds that religious confessions should be understood as 'love language'. Stendahl offers an example. If a husband says that his wife is the only one for him, and is telling the truth, then that is good and true. But if he were witnessing in court under oath and was asked by the judge whether he could be sure that nowhere in the world could there be another woman about whom he could have come to say the same thing, then he could not take such an oath. In that setting, says Stendahl, the same words take on a different meaning, just as would Peter's confession if treated as an axiom of dogmatic theology. Thus, although Peter is speaking before temple authorities, his language is confessional; it is love language; it should not be understood as a statement of dogmatic theology. In our particular religious experience, we are at the level of witness, confession and love language. Such primary religious experience is not a sound basis for an absolute conceptual claim. In a pluralistic world it is important for Christians to find their right and particular place as faithful witnesses to Jesus Christ, leaving the result of the witness in the hands of God. Stendahl finds guidance in this regard in Paul's letter to the church in Rome. In it Paul reflects on how his mission to the gentiles fits into God's wider plan (Rom. 9–11). Although he would like the Jews to accept Jesus as the Christ, he criticizes the gentile Christians for their attempts at converting Jews (Rom. 11:13). Paul seems to say two things: he has noted an attitude of conceit and superiority in the gentile movement; and salvation of the Jews is to be left in God's hands. Throughout this passage, notes Stendahl, the stress is on God, not Christ. The problem that Paul discerned was that Christians were witnessing to Jesus in conceit, in a manner that equated God's way solely with their mission. They did not understand their mission as a particular witness of their particular community in a world of communities, and in that, said Paul, they were wrong. They became proud, they did not 'stand in awe' (Rom. 11:20).

CHRISTOCENTRIC APPROACHES

Christocentric approaches to other religions ground themselves in Christologies that hold Jesus Christ to be the unique incarnation of God. As such he is the universal revelation for all humanity. Older Christocentric views in the Christian West often consigned other religions to spiritual darkness and their followers to damnation. These views have become increasingly unacceptable in the light of growing contact with other faiths. Consequently, contemporary Christocentric theologians have been labouring to avoid the unacceptable implication of the older views without having to implicitly renounce them. This is in accordance with the traditional theological method of reinterpreting a dogma rather than saying it was wrong. Various tactics have been adopted to reinterpret Christocentric theology in ways more acceptable to religious pluralism. Implicit faith is distinguished from explicit faith; baptism by desire is distinguished from literal baptism; the latent church is distinguished from the manifest church; salvation through Christ in the life to come is distinguished from gaining salvation in this life.[92] Theologians such as John Cobb employ the old Christological notion of Christ as the incarnation of the Logos.[93] Christ is seen as the normative incarnation of the Logos for all religions. Wolfhart Pannenberg adopts an inductive approach which lays great emphasis upon the objective historicity of Jesus as the ground of faith. Pannenberg moves from the historical Jesus to a recognition of his divinity, with the incarnation emerging as a conclusion.[94] However, such a temporally oriented Christology still leads Pannenberg to hold to the finality and universality of Christ. Although God is experienced by members of other religions, they do not really know God; because saving knowledge comes only with Christ, the experience of God in other religions cannot save.[95] The Roman Catholic theologian Karl Rahner has presented perhaps the most sophisticated and influential attempt to work out an acceptable Christocentric approach to other religions. But before examining Rahner's position let us begin at the other end of the spectrum and take note of the exclusive Christology of evangelical theologians.

Evangelical theologians

Evangelical theology is based on the authority of the Bible and on statements such as that by Peter that at the name of Jesus every knee should bow and every tongue confess that he is Lord (Acts 10:36). The Christology of the Lausanne Covenant of 1974 may be taken as representative of evangelical Christology:

> We also reject as derogatory to Christ and the Gospel every kind of syncretism and dialogue which implies that Christ speaks equally through all religions and theologies. Jesus Christ, being himself the only God-man, who gave himself as the only ransom for sinners, is the only mediator between God and man. There is no other name by which we must be saved. All men are perishing because of sin, but God loves all men, not wishing that any should perish but that all should repent. Yet those who reject Christ repudiate the joy of salvation and condemn themselves to eternal separation from God. To proclaim Jesus as 'the saviour of the world' is not to affirm that all religions offer salvation in Christ. Rather it is to proclaim God's love for a world of sinners and to invite all men to respond to him as Saviour and Lord in the wholehearted personal commitment of repentance and faith. Jesus Christ has been exalted above every other name; we long for the day when every knee shall bow to him and every tongue shall confess him Lord.[96]

In this kind of exclusive Christocentric thought, evangelical theologians avoid abstract, universal concepts such as the Logos and instead focus on the historic and unique event of Jesus – his life, death and resurrection. Also stressed is the commission recorded in Matthew, chapter 28, verses 18–19: 'All authority in heaven and on earth has been given to me. Go therefore and make disciples of all nations.' Although the expectation that all people will one day be converted to Christianity no longer prevails, the command of Jesus to make disciples of all is not lessened. Instead it is understood as a requirement to sow the seed of the gospel in each nation so that the 'wheat' and the 'tares' may grow together until the harvest at the end of the world (Matt. 13:30).

The evangelicals do allow that other religions may have some natural knowledge of God, but they add that in itself that knowledge is insufficient for salvation. As the Lausanne Covenant states, 'We recognize that all men have some knowledge of God through His general revelation in nature. But we deny that this can save, for men suppress the truth by their unrighteousness.'[97] Thus evangelicals take a low view of other religions. In their reading of the Bible, Cornelius was a prayerful, benevolent, sincere man who nevertheless did not have salvation until after Peter preached the gospel to him.[98] Although it is true that God is active in the other religions through his presence in nature (Rom. 1:19–20), people of those religions reject God until God is made known to them in Jesus Christ. For evangelical theologians, dialogue with other religions does not teach them anything additional about God, for that knowledge is most fully present in Christ; but dialogue does lead to a broader understanding of human nature and human experience, and this provides a more effective basis from which to preach the gospel.

Because of their conviction that the truth is most fully present in Jesus Christ, evangelicals have put little emphasis on learning about other religions. Only recently has the idea of interreligious dialogue evoked any comment from evangelical circles. In England the Evangelical Alliance has established a commission to clarify issues of interfaith dialogue. In the East rather more activity has been taking place. In India, for example, an evangelical dialogue with Muslims has been going on since 1963.[99] One evangelical theologian who wrestled with the challenges of pluralism is Clark Pinnock.

Clark Pinnock

Quoting Bible passages such as the statement that Christ did not die for our sins only but for the sins of the whole world (I John 2:2) and 'O God our Saviour, [you are] the hope of all the ends of the earth' (Ps. 65:5), Pinnock starts with the acknowledgement that 'Central to the Bible is belief in the comprehensive and all-embracing character of divine sovereignty and grace. God's love for the world is both broad and inclusive.'[100] How then does one explain, from a Christocentric perspective, that it is through God's revelation in Jesus Christ that this universal salvation of the world occurs? Put together the two Christian statements seem to exclude saving power from the other religions. Pinnock deals with this problem in a way that avoids a narrow exclusivism of the sort that states only those who accept Jesus as Lord are saved – and therefore Jews, Muslims, Hindus, Buddhists and Baha'is are not. By contrast, Pinnock sees the Holy Spirit as present everywhere in the world among all peoples and all religions, working to prepare them for the gospel of Christ. Although all salvation is exclusively Christian, and although everyone must pass through Jesus to reach God, still there are several paths one may follow. For example, a sincere Jew, Muslim or Buddhist has the Holy Spirit at work in them preparing them to receive the grace of conversion and explicit knowledge of God through Christ in this life or after death. Pinnock talks of encountering saintly persons of other religions. This is because, due to God's universal love, the Spirit of the Father and the Son may be found working for good everywhere – including the other religions, if circumstances permit. This follows logically from the doctrine of the Trinity within Christian belief. Nor does being historical prevent Jesus from being the saviour of the world. In his resurrection Jesus is working through the Spirit to draw everyone to himself. Therefore, we cannot act as if these 'not-yet' Christians of other religions are rivals or enemies if our God has made them his friends. There can be no wedge driven between what God does in creation and in redemption, claims Pinnock.[101]

Pinnock acknowledges the influence of the Second Vatican Council on his development as an evangelical theologian. The emphasis on the Holy Spirit and openness to the world led him to his current inclusivistic Christocentric position. However, Pinnock's aim is to demonstrate that this approach is not only theologically coherent but also well founded in scriptural exegesis and thus commendable to the evangelical tradition.

In this regard Pinnock cites, for example: the Old Testament story of Melchizedek's encounter with Abram (Gen. 14:17–24) as showing God at work among the Canaanites; and the New Testament story of God using Cornelius, a godly gentile, to teach the apostle Peter that there is no partiality in God's dealings with people (Acts 14:17). If God is thus at work in other religions, concludes Pinnock, then Christians must exhibit a generous openness to the possibility of God's presence there – be it in the devotional poetry of Hinduism, which celebrates a personal God of love, or the trusting surrender to grace seen in Japanese Buddhist Jodo Shin-Shu practice. Yet not everything in religions attributed to the Spirit should be uncritically accepted. Christians must test all claimed manifestations of the Spirit in other religions (and in Christianity) against the revelation of God in Jesus Christ. The Paraclete is the Spirit of Jesus, and thus his revelation of God is the ultimate criterion of truth in all religions.[102]

Karl Rahner

Karl Rahner's theology is a systematic effort to affirm the exclusiveness and universality of Christ while at the same time respecting God's universal salvific will.[103] Rahner writes, 'If, on the one hand, we conceive salvation as something specifically *Christian* . . . and if, on the other hand, God has really, truly and seriously intended this salvation for all men – then these two aspects cannot be reconciled in any other way than by stating that every human being is really and truly exposed to the influence of divine supernatural grace.'[104] It is the universal grace of God for all humankind that deeply moves Rahner and drives his desire somehow to reconcile Christocentric theology with non-Christian religious experience.

Rahner establishes his position in terms of four theses: 1) Christianity understands itself as the absolute religion intended for all persons and cannot therefore recognize any other religion as equal with itself; 2) until the moment the gospel enters the historical situation of an individual, a non-Christian religion can contain for that individual not only a natural knowledge of God but also supernatural elements of grace (a free gift from God on account of Christ); 3) therefore Christianity does not simply confront the member of another religion as a mere non-Christian but as someone who must be regarded as an anonymous Christian; and 4) the church will not so much regard itself as the exclusive community of those who have a claim to salvation but rather as the historical vanguard and explicit expression of Christian hope that is present as a hidden reality in other religions.

Through these four theses Rahner accommodates both the universal saving grace of God and the exclusiveness of Christ as the explicit and full criterion for it. If, because of historical or geographical circumstance, a person has not been exposed to Christ, then that person can experience God's grace – which is understood as the a priori foundation of all religions – in another religion. The other religion, as a revelation of God's grace, can lead to salvation. Seemingly a paradox is reached: salvation can be gained only through Christ (thesis 1), but salvation can be reached via another religion. The resolution of the paradox is that if salvation is reached via another religion, then it must be an experience of anonymous Christianity. Rahner is careful to safeguard the superiority of Christianity: the individual who is exposed to God's grace through Christianity has, other things being equal, a greater chance of salvation than someone who is merely an anonymous Christian, a member of another religion.[105]

Rahner realizes that Jews or Hindus will think it presumptuous of the Christian to regard them as Christians who have not yet come to understand their true identity or self. Yet, says Rahner, 'The Christian cannot renounce this presumption... It is a profound admission that God is greater than man and the Church.'[106] In Rahner's view, allowing for the reality of God's grace in other religions gives the Christian a basis to be tolerant, humble and yet firm towards all non-Christians.

From within Christianity, Rahner's doctrine of anonymous Christianity has been accused of being both elitist and relativistic. But in Rahner's mind, 'The anonymous Christian is not condemned to a defective form of Christianity; it exists at the same supernatural, radical and human level as that of the explicit Christian. The universal possibility of salvation is ontologically grounded in the creative act of God and made historically present in the Christ event.'[107]

Perhaps the theologian best carrying on the tradition of Karl Rahner is Gavin D'Costa. In his writings D'Costa offers a powerful critique of John Hick and other pluralist, theocentric scholars,[108] before restating and developing Rahner's position. While D'Costa commends Hick for his genuine protest against the Christian condemnation of other religions, his attempt to be accommodating to all the religions, says D'Costa, ends up being accommodating to none. Hick's doctrine of God is removed from any religious context and becomes a free-floating theocentricism or, in his more recent writings, a 'realitycentricism' (to accommodate non-theistic traditions like Buddhism). From a Christian perspective these moves required Hick to decentre the incarnation of Christ by interpreting it and the criterion claims of other religions as mythological. This, D'Costa contends, pleases no believer. It amounts to Hick having substituted one arrogance (that all religious claims are mythological) for another (that one religion has the exclusive truth). Rahner, thinks D'Costa, handles all of these challenges much more satisfactorily, and without asking anyone (Christian, Jew, Muslim, Hindu, Buddhist or Baha'i) to give up their own religious criteria – or to mythologize them. Following Rahner, D'Costa finds that Christ is the definitive truth criterion for Christians and approves efforts to use the criterion of Christ to trace elements of continuity and discontinuity, truth and error within other religions. The implications of this approach for interfaith worship, missionary activity, theological debate with other religions over truth claims, and ecclesiological practice within the church are touched on but not given full examination.[109]

A recent and innovative effort within the Roman Catholic Christo-centric tradition is the book *Toward a Christian Theology of Religious Pluralism* by Jacques Dupuis, S.J.[110] Dupuis, like Knitter, has spent the past decade engaging liberation theology with the religious pluralism debate. Dupuis' goal is to develop a theology that goes beyond Rahner's 'anonymous Christianity' yet, like Rahner, maintains Christian identity while being committed to interfaith dialogue. What is required, says Dupuis, is not an approach that levels differences in a search for a common denominator, but a frank admission of diversity and mutual acceptance of others in their very otherness. Although the theology of Rahner and others did this, their focus, from a Christocentric perspective, was on the problem of salvation for members of other religions, or even the role of those religions in the salvation of their members. Dupuis sees himself as moving beyond that focus to a search 'in the light of Christian faith, for the meaning of God's design for humankind of the plurality of living faiths and religious traditions with which we are surrounded. Are all religious traditions of the world destined to converge? Where, when and how?'[111] It is no longer sufficient to study religious pluralism in terms of the role Christianity can assign to the other religions but rather to see religious pluralism as God's grand plan for humankind – for the possibility of a mutual convergence in the various religions (with full respect for their differences and for mutual enrichment). For Christians in India today, says Dupuis, this is understood as interreligious theology with a universal imperative. Dupuis, in thematic fashion, offers an overview of what might be glimpses into the mystery of God's plan: in history; in God's word in the many scriptures; in the revelation of God in Jesus Christ; in the decisive role the historical Christ plays in God's plan; in the role Christ plays in the other religions, viewed as channels through which the saving grace of God flows to their members; and in the role interreligious dialogue plays in the evangelizing mission of the church. Dupuis ends seeing, as part of God's grand plan, 'the universal action of the Spirit of God in the world today, as Christians engage, together with others, in promoting the Reign of God upon the earth'.[112]

All of this begins to sound worryingly triumphal in tone and leads one to long for the simplicity of Rahner and his willingness to let believers from each religion simply view each other in 'anonymous' (anonymous Christian, Hindu, Buddhist, etc.) terms so as to make possible honest and respectful dialogue. Attempting to divine God's 'grand religious pluralism' plan, as Dupuis wants to do, runs the danger of necessarily seeing it too much through one's own theological glasses, and then superimposing that bias in one's dialogue with believers of other religions, who, as in the case of Buddhists (with their negating of God and concepts such as ultimate unity), would experience immediate problems.

As is evident in the theologies of Pinnock, Rahner and Dupuis, the Christocentric approaches, like the theocentric, are shifting their focus from the exclusivity of Christ to the universality of God.

THE DIALOGICAL APPROACH

Whereas the theologians who stress Christocentric or theocentric perspectives have been attempting to reinterpret Christian theology so as to make room systematically for other religions, another group of Christian thinkers has stressed the dialogical approach. Dialogue starts from the assumption that each religion has its absolute claims which cannot be relativized.[113] No amount of reformulation will do away with the difference. But by letting our theologizing be influenced by others we will be forced to greater honesty and deeper spirituality. The prerequisite for dialogue is not the harmonizing of all beliefs but the recognition that each spiritual person has a committed and absolute conviction, and that these convictions are different. The Christian is committed to God through Christ, the Muslim to the Qur'ān as God's final word, the Hindu to the idea of many paths to the one Brahman (the absolutizing of a relativism), and so on. In the dialogical approach, each religion is seen as having an absolute that cannot be surrendered without destroying the essential identity of that faith. Such dialogue necessitates sufficient maturity of the ego 'to let the opposites co-exist without pretending that they can be made compatible'.[114] Indeed the very capacity and need for categorical assertion are understood as held in common by all religious people and as such are a ground for dialogue.[115]

Stanley Samartha

Among Christian proponents of dialogue, Stanley Samartha has made the most serious effort at systematization.[116] Growing up and living in India, where Christians are a small minority in the dominant Hindu culture, Samartha has had to live a life of dialogue. He begins by arguing that a Christian must approach dialogue from a theocentric rather than a Christocentric basis. This frees the Christian from the exclusiveness of *possession* that petrifies revelation and monopolizes truth. True Christian commitment, he says, clings to the centre of faith without closing the gates at the circumference. Some doors must be left 'unlatched in order that the gentle breeze of the Holy Spirit may enter the Christian home, sometimes from unexpected corners'.[117] The problem, in Samartha's view, is that Christians constantly misunderstand openness to mean mere relativism or neutrality.

> To acknowledge the fact of religious pluralism means that one cannot take shelter in neutral or objective ground. There is no theological helicopter that can help us to rise above all religions and look down upon the terrain below in lofty condescension. *Our* standpoint, therefore, has to be Christian; but by the same token our neighbours are also free to have their particular standpoints.[118]

In Samartha's view the obligation of Christians today is not to Christianity as a religion, nor to the cultural forms of Christianity we have inherited, 'but to God who, at the very point where he reveals himself in Jesus Christ, liberates us from our particular bondages in order to have new relations with our neighbours in the larger community'.[119] Just as God took the risk of becoming human, so Christians must not be afraid to live in the midst of religious pluralism. What is needed is not a theology of dialogue but courage for dialogue.

Samartha defines dialogue as 'an attempt to understand and express our particularity not just in terms of our own heritage but also in relation to the spiritual heritage of our neighbours'.[120] He details three theological reasons that dialogue ought to be a continuing Christian concern: 1) God in Jesus Christ has entered into relationship with persons of all faiths and all ages, offering the good news of salvation; 2) the offer, which is inherent in the gospel, of true community through forgiveness, reconciliation and a new creation leads inevitably to dialogue; and 3) because Jesus promised that the Holy Spirit will lead us all into truth, and because truth in the biblical understanding is not propositional but relational, dialogue becomes one of the means of quest for truth.[121] Although the word 'dialogue' is not found in the Bible, warm relationships and intense personal encounters are in evidence throughout the scriptures. The dialogical approach is exemplified in the way in which Jesus deals with people such as Nicodemus, the Samaritan woman, the Roman centurion and his own disciples. It is the way of dialogue, and not 'theological bulldozing', that is required of Christians in today's pluralistic world.

As to the ultimate outcome of dialogue, Samartha maintains that 'where people meet in freedom and expectation, there are moments when the particular labels that partners wear lose their importance and that which is behind and beyond them breaks through in spiritual freedom, offering a vision of the ultimate that holds them together'.[122] Though these moments are few, they are significant, and it is Samartha's hope that they will contribute to the transformation of particular religions without denying their distinctiveness.

Raimundo Panikkar

Like Samartha, Panikkar has of necessity lived a life of dialogue between Christianity and Hinduism. Panikkar's mother was a Spanish Roman Catholic and his father was Hindu. Within Roman Catholicism Panikkar's writings have been pioneering efforts in the area of interfaith relations. Panikkar starts from the assumption that 'the truths which the Christian doctrine, on the one hand, and the Hindu doctrine, on the other, propound as universal have often come to be thought of as particular and limited – if not bigoted – points of view, whereas in actuality they are both formulations, necessarily limited by cultural factors, of a more universal truth'.[123] In his writings he attempts to demonstrate the presence of religious truth in more than one religion and to show how 'the unveiling of that truth may be to the mutual enlightenment of all concerned'.[124] Panikkar has been misunderstood as being reductionistic – of reducing the experience of truth in one tradition by describing it in terms of the symbols of another tradition, as is suggested by the title of his book *The Unknown Christ of Hinduism*.[125] Rather than engaging in religious reductionism, Panikkar is acknowledging that 'when a religious truth is recognized by both parties [in a dialogue] and thus belongs to both traditions, it will be called in each case by the vocabulary proper to the particular tradition recognizing it'.[126] Thus when Christians recognize religious truth outside of their own religion, they will naturally and properly see it in Christian terms and will describe it as a discovered Christian truth. Similarly, when a Hindu sees truth within Christianity, it will be judged as being Hindu truth in Christian dress. Panikkar's thesis is that through dialogue the particular experiences of truth – Christ for the Christian, the Veda for the Hindu – may be enlarged and deepened so as to open new experiences of religious truth. Through dialogue there will be an enlarging and deepening of each particular experience of divine truth. In dialogue the relationship between the religions 'is not one of assimilation, or of substitution (the latter under the misnomer of "conversion"), but one of *mutual fecundation.*'[127] In today's pluralistic world, says Panikkar, the goal of dialogue is to stress the continuity-in-depth that may be discovered to exist between religions and communities.[128] Behind all dialogue is the divine Mystery (not necessarily the 'same' Mystery) that every religion attempts to explain. This Mystery is not a purely transcendent divine reality known through worship; it is equally immanent and active in the historical situation where we commune with others as fellow pilgrims.[129] Within each religion the central name, such as Christ, Veda or Dharma, is the symbol that reveals that Mystery. For the Christian, Christ is the revelation of that Mystery and the living symbol for the totality of human, divine and cosmic reality. Any more neutral symbol, such as God, Spirit or truth, is rejected by Panikkar as truncating reality and limiting the divine Mystery to a discarnate principle, a nonhistorical epiphany or an abstraction.[130] Panikkar rejects the simplistic theory of a neutral symbol, such as one God who exists over and above the names of the various religions. Rather the divine 'reality is many names and each name is a new aspect, a new manifestation and revelation of it. Yet each name teaches or expresses, as it were, the undivided Mystery.'[131] Panikkar offers the following metaphor:

> Each religion and ultimately each human being stands within the rainbow of reality and sees it as white light – precisely because of seeing through the entire rainbow. From the outside, as an intellectual abstraction, I see you in the green area and you see me in the orange one. I call you green and you call me orange because, when we look at each other, we do not look at the totality. We do not intend to express the totality – what we believe – but we evaluate and judge each other. And though it is true that I am in the orange strip with all the limitations of a saffron spirituality, if you ask my colour, I say 'white'![132]

Thus Christians will either bring their conception of Christ as the divine Mystery to other religions in a missionary way, or they will have to recognize the unknown dimensions of Christ in the other religions. Panikkar adopts this latter approach.

In formulating his Christology, Panikkar attempts to include all that is required by the above basis for dialogue and at the same time to avoid either a humanistic or a metaphysical reductionism of the Christian experience of Jesus Christ.[133] On the one hand, Jesus who is the Christ for Christians is historically grounded. Although he is more, he is not less than Jesus of Nazareth. This guards against any Gnostic reduction of the historical reality of Jesus as the Christ. On the other hand, the Christian cannot say that the Christ is only Jesus, for this would be to reduce the divine Mystery to being exhaustively present with Jesus of Nazareth. Christ is more than the historical Jesus, as is witnessed in the resurrection. Nevertheless, for the Christian this 'more' that might appear as the truth of Hinduism or Islam can only be known as the Christ. The essence of Christian self-understanding is that Christ is the universal redeemer, the single mediator, the only-begotten of God. The concreteness of Christ in Jesus does not destroy his universality because the reality of Christ is revealed in the personal experience of his uniqueness.[134]

In a passage reminiscent of Krister Stendahl's metaphor of 'love language' for the exclusive experience of Christian truth, Panikkar invokes the analogy of our experience of a face:

> A face is a real face when it is more – not less – than the physiognomy of the human head. It is a face when it is a face for me, with a uniqueness of its own. The face is concrete and not particular; it is that face only for me.

It is meaningless to say that you have discovered 'another' face in it. Each
face includes your discovery of it. In both cases it is a face when it speaks,
responds and is alive with the life that flows also in me.[135]

Like Stendahl, Panikkar evokes an experience of Christ that is at once
absolute, in that it is the revealed truth for the believer, and at the same
time is open to seeing that for others there will be a different experience
of the divine. Both Stendahl and Panikkar offer analogies aimed at
helping the modern Christian, who lives in the midst of pluralism, to find
a middle way between narrow exclusivism and grey relativism. Panikkar
addresses himself to Christians who are sympathetic to other religions
'but who do not wish to dilute their own religiousness or to lose their
own identity, in spite of being ready for openness and even change should
such be required'.[136] He urges Christians to recognize that in loving and
believing in Christ as the ultimate truth they are responding to the same
Mystery that other believers experience in other religions. This does not
imply the naive and uncritical notion that there is one God, 'one thing',
that people call by different names. Rather, says Panikkar, what is
suggested is 'that each authentic name enriches and qualifies that
Mystery which is neither purely transcendent nor purely imminent'.[137] In
Christian terms the way of understanding this Mystery is through the
concept of the Trinity.

In his book *The Trinity and the Religious Experience of Man*,
Panikkar attempts a restatement of Christian theology that would
'enlarge and deepen the mystery of the Trinity that it may embrace this
same mystery existent in other religious traditions but differently
expressed'.[138] For Panikkar the Trinity is a junction where the authentic
spiritual dimensions of all religions meet within Christian thought.
Panikkar rightly rejects the notion that the meeting of religions can or
should take place on some neutral ground such as those proposed by
John Hick or Wilfred Cantwell Smith. Panikkar recognizes that the
meeting of religions can take place only at the very heart of the religious
traditions themselves, and for the Christian that is the experience of the
Trinity.[139] In Panikkar's reformulation the Father is characterized as the
Absolute that is beyond every name. Its transcendence is constitutive.
Jesus taught us to call the 'unnameable' Absolute 'Father' and to know
this Father through the Son. It is the Son who acts, who creates and in
whom everything exists. It is the Son manifested in Christ who is the
Lord, and one's personal relationship with God can only be with the Son.
The Son is 'the Mystery hidden since the world began, the Mystery of

which the Scriptures speak, and which, according to Christians, was manifested in Christ'.[140] Jesus of Nazareth is not absolutely identical to this Christ but is this Christ inasmuch as he has a special relationship 'with what Paul following Old Testament usage calls the Uncreated Wisdom, what John following Philo calls the Logos, what Matthew and Luke following Judaism consider in intimate relation with the Holy Spirit and what later tradition has agreed in calling the Son'.[141] For the Christian, Christ presents the fundamental characteristics of the mediator between the divine and creation. Although others may call the mediator of the Mystery Yahweh, Krishna, Allah or Buddha, for the Christian it can only be the Christ. But this Christ must not be encapsulated in the historical Jesus of Nazareth, for Christ is today dynamically present and leading Christians forward as the Holy Spirit. The Spirit is jointly immanent to the Father and the Son and is the communication between them. The Spirit passes from Father to Son and from Son to Father in the same process. As the Spirit, the Son no longer permits the present-day Christian to remain attached to an exclusive experience of Christ. The Spirit pushes Christians beyond themselves, their church and their religion to recognize and participate in the worldwide experience of the Mystery. For Panikkar 'the only true experience of Christ is in human and cosmic *koinonia*'.[142]

Paul Knitter

Although discussed earlier in this chapter, as a theocentric theologian, Knitter's recent thought has been moving strongly in the direction of dialogue. In his book *Jesus and the Other Names: Christian Mission and Global Responsibility*, Knitter brings together concerns for the 'suffering Other' and the 'religious Other' as a basis for interfaith dialogue.[143] In technical terms he brings together liberation theology and the theology of religions. Knitter points out that too often the Christocentric focus of Christian theology has served to hide an unconscious desire to dominate other traditions – to justify the subordination and exploitation of other cultures and religions. By contrast, says Knitter, true engagement with others must be globally responsible or liberative in nature – it must be based on a shared commitment to promoting eco-human well-being.[144] Only then will the encounter of Jesus (the Christian) with the other names or religions be one in which both sides really listen to and really speak to each other. By grounding the dialogue on concerns for the human and environmental well-being of the other person (of another religion) the Christian is able to achieve a fuller understanding of what makes Jesus unique, to engage in a more committed following of him and to carry out more meaningfully his mission to the world. Knitter recounts his own evolution from missionary beginnings rooted in Christian exclusivism, to the inclusivism of Rahner's view of other religions as legitimate ways of salvation, further to the pluralist perspective of seeing all religions as having valid responses to the divine Mystery and finally to an integration of the 'suffering other' of liberation theology and the 'suffering earth' into his 'theology of religions'. Says Knitter, 'If the unnecessary suffering of humanity and of the earth is to be addressed and removed, the religions are going to have to make a combined, co-operative, dialogical contribution. To be effective, a theology of liberation must also be a theology of interreligious dialogue. To be meaningful, an interreligious dialogue or theology must include a theology of liberation.'[145] In *Jesus and the Other Names* Knitter lays out the view of Jesus, the church and the Christian mission that such a theology requires. Its foundation is a globally responsible, correlational dialogue of religions. 'Globally responsible' dialogue requires that people seek to understand and speak to each other on the basis of a common commitment to human ecological well-being. Consequently, any inter-religious dialogue is incomplete if it does not attempt to resolve human and ecological suffering. Knitter calls his approach 'correlational' in that it encourages relationships in which people speak honestly with each other and listen authentically. 'Participants will witness to what makes them distinct, trying to show and convince others of the values they have found in their traditions. But at the same time, they will truly, courageously, open to the witness of truth that others make to them. This is a mutual, back and forth, co-relationship of speaking and listening, teaching and learning, witnessing and being witnessed to.'[146] In such a correlational approach no religious participant can speak his or her truth claim from a theological position that is meant to dominate, absorb or stand in judgement over all others. It is an egalitarian model for dialogue. This approach, says Knitter, differs from a theocentric approach in that rather than searching for a common God dwelling within different religious communities, the correlational model holds up 'the "salvation" or "well-being" of humans and the Earth as the starting point and common ground for our efforts to share and understand our religious experiences and notions of the Ultimately Important'.[147]

In Knitter's mind this approach offers to Christians a way of dialogue that does not require them to water down their truth claims but rather offers a revision and reaffirmation of the understanding of God and Christ that is essential to Christian life.

There are many other advocates of the Christian approach to dialogue – for instance, John Dunne, John Taylor, Klaus Klostermaier and Donald Swearer; however, the positions of Samartha, Panikkar and Knitter are generally representative. Christ is seen as being both the exemplar of how to dialogue and the universally present Holy Spirit that makes dialogue possible. The expected outcome is not the homogenization of particular religions but the mutual deepening of spiritual experience within each particular religion.

SUMMARY AND CONCLUSION

Due to the challenge of religious pluralism, the relationship between Christianity and other religions has become a key issue for theologians. The major problem is Christianity's claim to uniqueness and normativeness arising from the doctrine of Christology. In the New Testament some statements support the concept of a unique incarnation of God in Christ, and other statements (such as those made by Jesus about members of other religions) provide a basis for Christian openness. Paul's debate with the Jerusalem Christians over requirements having to do with circumcision and other matters helped to distinguish Christianity as a religion separate from Judaism. As Christianity freed itself from Judaism, it encountered Greek philosophy and that led to attempts to interpret the gospel in the categories of that philosophy. The challenge of Gnosticism led to the formation of the canon of Christian scripture and to the composition of statements of Christian creed. Thus began the process of rendering Christian self-understanding in exclusivist terms. This process continued with contributions from a number of early Christian fathers – Justin, Irenaeus, Tertullian, Clement and Origen – and with the Greek notion of Logos having a major influence. These theological developments culminated in the long and important dispute between Arius and Athanasius over the nature of the identity of relationship between God and Son. The importance of this dispute is that Arius' position (making Jesus subordinate to God) would have given Christianity an openness to other religions, whereas the Athanasian view, which dominated the thinking of that period, produced a closed, exclusive Christianity that proclaimed Jesus as the only true incarnation. By 500 CE this exclusive and tough-minded Christianity had destroyed the previously dominant Greek and Roman religions, and the Catholic church was tending to identify itself with the kingdom of God on earth. In the medieval period, in spite of continuous contact with Islam and the beginning of missionary activity to the East, the attitude, in Western Christianity at least, was that of a narrow exclusivism.

In the early modern period exclusivist theology was challenged by Kant and Schleiermacher. Kant, through reason, and Schleiermacher, through the subjective feeling of absolute dependence, grounded Christianity in human universals and opened the way to religious relativism. The anchoring of exclusivism in the historicity of scripture was seriously questioned by Strauss and subsequent biblical criticism. Troeltsch added further support to a relativistic understanding of Christianity by introducing the notion of an unending evolutionary progress. Barth countered this gathering relativism and scepticism by dialectically separating all religions (including Christianity) from the grace experience of revelation – which he saw as coming from God exclusively through Jesus Christ. Although he attacked the pride and sinfulness of Christianity, Barth continued to see it as the exclusive locus of God's grace and revelation.

Recent developments in Christian theology include a variety of attempts to escape from both Troeltsch's relativism and Barth's exclusivism. Theocentric approaches, such as those of Paul Tillich, John Hick and Wilfred Smith, reject a Christology that identifies God solely with Christ and assume a Christology that emphasizes God, thus opening the way to other theocentric religions such as Judaism, Islam and some types of Hinduism. By contrast, Christocentric approaches, such as Karl Rahner's anonymous Christianity, attempt to retain Christ as criterion while allowing for God's grace and even saving action in other religions. Finally the dialogical approach, perhaps the most promising of all, emphasizes both the universality of God and the human need for complete commitment to the particular truth of the worshipper's religion. In the experience of dialogue the examination by other religions of one's own theologizing and the appreciation of the truths of each religion are said to result in a spiritual deepening for all.

An unresolved problem for all of these approaches is the Buddhist and Advaita Vedānta rejection of God as ultimate reality. Christian theologians, even those with considerable exposure to Buddhism and

Hinduism, seem almost wilfully to turn a blind eye to this problem. One possible exception might be found in Tillich's formulation of the 'God above God' as the 'ground of being'. Though this may be quite acceptable to Advaita Vedāntists, it must surely pose problems for Mādhyamika and Yogācāra Buddhists. Paul Knitter's proposal for a correlational approach to dialogue within the common context of the 'suffering other' and the 'suffering earth' offers new promise in this regard.

3 RELIGIOUS PLURALISM AND ISLAM

I slam was born within the context of Judaism and Christianity. In the Arabian region there were a number of scattered Jewish and Christian communities. Indeed Muhammad understood his revelation to be a continuation and fulfilment of the Jewish and Christian biblical tradition. Muhammad's respect for the biblical tradition is exemplified in his teaching that during prayer one should face in the direction of Jerusalem. It was only when the Jewish community of Medina refused to accept Muhammad as the sole leader of the one community of God that the Prophet ordered the direction of prayer be shifted towards Mecca.[1] This initial openness towards Judaism hardened because of the basic Islamic requirements of absolute allegiance to the one God, Allah, and rejection of all other gods as false idols. The unforgivable sin of idolatry was called *shirk*. Islam's definition of idolatry is consistent, thorough and extreme.

Jihād develops in part as a response to idolatry. Allah is understood as the creator of all and is thus the God to be accepted and worshipped by all. After having had time to learn of Allah (a four-month grace period), an idolator is subject to attack as a threat to Islam and a performer of *shirk*. In the early years of Islam the principle of *jihād* was relaxed in the case of Jews, Christians and Zoroastrians. Because they were also people of the biblical tradition, they were allowed to retain their faith if they submitted to Muslim government and paid a special tax. Muhammad continued to think of Jews and Christians not as idolators but as members of the tradition that was being completed through his own revelations.[2] *Jihād* has often been misunderstood. The primary definition of *jihād* is 'struggling' or 'striving'. Islamic scholars have identified four kinds of *jihād* or 'striving': 1) *jihād* of the 'heart' (spiritual striving); 2) *jihād* of the hand (physical striving, work, labour); 3) *jihād* of the tongue (striving in preaching or debate); 4) *jihād* of the sword (striving in war, hence 'holy war').[3] One effect of the concept of *jihād* of the sword was to rapidly expand Islam during the period 634–732 CE. Within one hundred years Islam had spread to Spain, southern France, Egypt, Syria, Iraq and Iran, and it also had penetrated eastwards to the borders of India. In later years the expansion continued southward into Africa and further eastwards into India, China, Java and the Philippines.

During the modern period Islam spread into North America, where it resides as a minority religious group. Since the creation of Pakistan, the percentage of Muslims in India has decreased so much that Islam faces the situation of being a religious minority there. Until modern developments of this type that gave Islam minority status in certain areas, most Muslims lived in places where they were in the majority, and this allowed the traditional notions of *shirk* and *jihād* to guide reactions to other religions.[4] However, with cultural and religious pluralism increasingly becoming the norm rather than the exception, Islam may have to look to its experiences in India, Europe and America for leads into the future.

HISTORICAL MEETINGS OF ISLAM WITH OTHER FAITHS

Jacques Waardenburg has outlined the encounter of Islam with a number of other religions.[5] He identifies six phases in the historical meetings of Islam with other faiths:

I.   Muhammad grew up in Mecca, where he met Christians, Jews, Mazdaeans and probably Manichaeans and Sabians.

II.   During their first conquests outside Arabia in the seventh and eighth centuries, Muslims encountered the following religious communities:

    a. Mazdaeans in Mesopotamia and Iran;
    b. Christians of different varieties:

        1. Nestorians in Mesopotamia and Iran;
        2. Monophysites in Syria, Egypt and Armenia;
        3. Orthodox Melkites in Syria;
        4. Orthodox Latins in North Africa;
        5. Arians in Spain;

    c. Jews in Mesopotamia, Iran, Syria and Egypt;
    d. Samaritans in Palestine;
    e. Mandaeans in south Mesopotamia;
    f. Harrānians in north Mesopotamia;
    g. Manichaeans in Mesopotamia and Egypt;
    h. Buddhists and Hindus in Sind;
    i. Followers of tribal religions in East Africa.

III. Between the ninth and thirteenth centuries, military activities brought Muslims in contact with the following groups:

    a. Orthodox Melkite Byzantine Christians across the northwest border;
    b. Orthodox Latin Christians in northern Spain, southern France, Sicily and southern Italy;
    c. Crusaders in greater Syria;
    d. Monophysite Armenians living between the Muslim and Byzantine empires;
    e. Slavs in southern Russia;
    f. Turkish tribes, at first non-Muslims in central Asia before their conversion and penetration into Muslim territory, and Mongols in Central Asia;
    g. Buddhists in Sind, the Punjab and Central Asia;
    h. Hindus in the Punjab;
    i. Followers of tribal religions in East and West Africa.

(From the ninth to the thirteenth century, peaceful relations were maintained with Christian, Jewish, Mazdaean and Harrānian minorities within Muslim territories, and trading contacts existed with Hindus in India, Buddhists in Burma and adherents of various religions in China.)

IV. Between the thirteenth and sixteenth centuries, peaceful encounters increased between Muslims (traders and especially ṣūfīs) and religions in India, Burma, Malaysia, Sumatra and Java, resulting in an expansion of Islam in these regions.

V. Between the sixteenth and nineteenth centuries, there was confrontation between Islam and Christianity. The expansion of Western sea trade necessitated outposts in the most important regions of the Muslim world. The Islamic Moghul empire dominated India, the majority of the population of which was

Hindu. The expansion of Islam into Africa, Indonesia, Malaysia and Central Asia proceeded apace with many encounters with the religions of those areas.

VI. From the nineteenth century to the present, there has been another period of confrontation, mostly political in nature, between Islamic states and the expanding West, the heir to the Christian tradition. During this period there increasingly have been movements within Islam against Christianity, Hinduism, Judaism and non-religious ideologies such as Marxism. This modern militancy within Islam may well be the Islamic response to 'militant secularism', 'militant Christianity' and 'militant Judaism'.[6] Since World War II there have been two such major military clashes: Pakistan versus India, and the Arab countries versus Israel.

Historically, Muslim attitudes toward people of other religions have been guided by the images of those religions appearing in the Qur'ān and by the attitudes taken by Muslim religious leaders and political rulers. Almost all the information Muslims have been given about other religions has been derived from the Qur'ān or approved commentaries. However, Muslims probably had a far greater knowledge of all other religions than any other group during the Middle Ages and were certainly more objective than, say, medieval Christians in their representation of other faiths. With the spread of modern educational opportunities and their increasing minority experience in today's pluralistic society, Muslims now have better opportunities than did many of their forebears to formulate a knowledgeable response to other religions.

UNITY AND THE 'PEOPLE OF THE BOOK'

Islam's sense of its own unity is founded upon a perception and an experience: first, Islam sees itself as the unifying culmination of the Hebrew Bible and Christian scriptures; second, the ṣūfī poets, especially in their encounters with Hinduism and Buddhism in India, have experienced and described a mystical unity.

Islam maintains the idea of a prophetic succession from Adam through the Hebrew Bible and the Christian scriptures to Muhammad and the Qur'ān. This gives Islam a unity that is founded on the succession of teachings in the pronouncements of the prophets and not on the historical covenant relationship that is central for Jews and Christians. From the Islamic point of view the Christian concept of incarnation is simply mistaken. There can be nothing 'more than' or 'higher than' being a prophet – a mouthpiece for God. For the Muslim

> the call of Abraham is to repudiate idolatry rather than inaugurate a dispensation. The task of Jesus is to preach righteousness, not to bring all things into subjection that God may be all in all. Islam is the inveterate natural religion: time consists in the interventions and interludes of messengers and the vicissitudes of the communities that hearken or refuse.[7]

Islam supports and perpetuates its sense of unity by maintaining that all three religions are composed of prophets of God. The teachings of these prophets simply have to be either accepted or refused. The difficulty experienced by Christians and Jews in recognizing Muhammad as the culminating prophet is simply due to their partial spiritual blindness. From the Islamic perspective, that alone does not destroy the basis for a unity underlying all three religions. Although it is true that a significant amount of Jewish and Christian doctrine is disallowed by Islam, it is nevertheless also true that the central impulse of Islam is one that can be accepted by Judaism and Christianity. Indeed, the prophetic revelation 'that one must fear and acknowledge God in the constant submission, rightness and worship of his world' is a core belief found in all three religious traditions.[8] To worship God and not idolize some aspect of human nature is the root of Islam. It is also a central theme for both Judaism and Christianity and is therefore the foundation for the Islamic sense of biblical unity.

This central theme of a foundational unity underlying all religions is clearly presented in the Qur'ān. As Fazlur Rahman has noted, in the earlier part of the Qur'ān different prophets speaking to different people are recognized, 'but their messages are universal and identical'.[9] The messages spoken by the different prophets, Abraham, Moses, Jesus and so on, all emanate from a single source called variously by the Qur'ān 'the Mother of the Book' (43:4; 13:39) and 'the Hidden Book' (56:78). Because all prophetic messages come from a single source, Muhammad felt it was incumbent on all people to believe in all divine messages. Thus Muhammad is made to declare in the Qur'ān that not only does he believe in the Torah and the gospel but 'I believe in whatever Book God may have revealed' (42:15).[10] In the Qur'ān's view, God's truth and guidance are not restricted but are universally available to all people: 'There is no nation wherein a warner has not come' (35:24); 'For every people a guide has been provided' (13:7). Fazlur Rahman observes that the word 'Book' is often used in the Qur'ān not to refer to any specific revealed book 'but as a generic term denoting the totality of divine revelations (e.g. 2:213)'.[11] This idea of one a priori revelation is linked in the Qur'ān with the notion of an originally unified humanity.

> Mankind were one single community. The God raised up prophets who gave good tidings and warning and God also sent down with them The Book in truth, that it may decide among people in regard to what they differed. But people did not differ in it [i.e. with regard to the Truth] except those to whom it had been given [and that only] after clear signs had come to them; [and this they did] out of [sheer] rebelliousness among themselves. (2:213)[12]

According to the Qur'ān, there was originally a unified humanity, which, due to its own rebelliousness, became divided. Some Muslims see this divisive state as fostered by the various versions of the 'one Book' that were introduced by the different prophets. Why prophetic revelations should act as a force for disunity does not seem to be answered, except to say that it is a mystery that God could overcome if God so willed. The fact that God does not so will is explained as providing an opportunity for the various religions to compete with each other in goodness.

> If God had so willed, He would have made all of you one community, but [He has not done so] that He may test you in what He has given you; so compete in goodness. To God shall you all return and He will tell you [the Truth] about what you have been disputing. (5:48)[13]

The Qur'ān thus challenges all other religions to a competition in goodness and it extends this invitation: 'O People of the Book! Let us come together upon a formula which is common between us – that we shall not serve anyone but God, that we shall associate none with Him' (3:64).[14] This challenge and invitation apply to Jews and Christians, who are obviously 'People of the Book'. But, as shall be noted, there have been recent attempts within Islam to understand Hindus and Buddhists also as 'People of the Book'. The Qur'ānic logic that there is one divine Book of which the prophetic utterances of the various religions are simply different manifestations is strongly reminiscent of the Logos idea. The Qur'ān is, of course, the complete and full revelation of the one divine

Book, all other books being only partial and incomplete presentations. However, in addition to understanding this basic Qur'ānic logic, it is useful to look at the variations in the way Islam has related to each of the other religions, and it is especially helpful to examine the favoured judgement that Christianity has often been given.

ISLAM AND WESTERN RELIGIONS

The Islamic view of Judaism has been marked by the sharing of a common spiritual ancestry and a sharp divergence in the understanding of prophecy. When he arrived in Medina, Muhammad guaranteed the religious freedom of the Jewish community and called on Jews and Muslims to cooperate for peace. This positive attitude towards Judaism began to change when certain Jewish tribes in Medina sided with the opponents of Muhammad. This created a dilemma for Muhammad. On the one hand the Qur'ān contains a great deal of Judaic content that could lead Muslims to accept Jews as spiritual neighbours. On the other hand the Jews of Medina were in bitter opposition to Muhammad. Muhammad resolved this dilemma by concluding that among Jews there were two strands, the upright and the untrustworthy. The Jews that Muhammad encountered were obviously of the second strand and therefore suitable subjects for repression. As a result two Jewish tribes, the Qaynuqā and the Nadīr, were exiled from Medina. Furthermore, after the Jews of Khaybar, a prosperous oasis, helped to raise an unsuccessful army of ten thousand men against Medina, Muhammad introduced a poll tax (the *jizya*) that he imposed on the Jews. Subsequently this practice was extended and became the standard treatment of Christians and other religions.[15]

The early political and military strife between Muslims and Jews was reflected in intellectual polemics.[16] Waardenburg notes that 'although critical statements and polemical utterances occur after the Qur'ān already in the *hadīth* literature, proper information about Judaism as a religion and way of life was only later supplied by converts'.[17] During the medieval period Muslim authors wrote a number of polemical treatises against Judaism.[18] The principal argument used against Judaism concerned the doctrine of abrogation or *naskh*. According to this view a prophetic revelation occurring later in time abrogated or superseded an earlier one. God's will could be revealed successively in different ways, and therefore a series of revelations was possible.[19] The Jews, however, believed that God's will and Torah do not and cannot change, and therefore they rejected the Muslim doctrine of *naskh*. Muslim writers devoted considerable effort to attempting to convince the Jews of the necessity of *naskh* and tried to show that abrogation was already present in the Torah itself (e.g. the law of Jacob is superseded by the law of Moses). Even the Qur'ān itself generally is understood to contain specific instances of *naskh*.

Another argument between the Jews and the Muslims arose because the Qur'ān suggests that Jews had corrupted their scriptures. The theory expounded by Muslim scholars is that Moses had presented a perfect copy of 'the divine Book', which later followers corrupted.[20] These scholars cited as evidence of corruption such things as scandalous stories, failure to recognize prophets outside of Israel, and the mentioning of prophets not included in the Qur'ān. Another indication of corruption was the failure of the Hebrew scriptures to mention the mission of Muhammad and the coming of Islam; the Qur'ān clearly states that such an announcement had been made in earlier scriptures.[21] Muslim scholars also studied the transmission of the Torah within Judaism and found, for example, that Ezra had made unacceptable innovations. This scepticism by Muslim scholars regarding the status of Jewish scriptures was indirectly reinforced by the refusal of Judaism to recognize Muhammad as a prophet, the Qur'ān as revelation, and the principle of abrogation (*naskh*). Although the Jews could be identified as a 'People of the Book', Judaism had become corrupted and therefore required the purification embodied in the revelation of the Qur'ān.[22]

The polemical literature in Islam against Christianity is abundant, and many texts have not yet been edited. Favourable judgements about Christianity were given early in the Qur'ān, but by the end of the Medinan period and Muhammad's encounter with Christian Arab tribes opposing his expansion in northern Arabia, the Qur'ānic statements regarding Christianity became polemical. According to Montgomery Watt, the main Qur'ānic accusations against the Christians are that they attribute a son to God and that they venerate priests and other people besides God – therefore they commit *shirk* (idolatry) and are considered to be *kuffar* (unbelievers).[23] The early initiative in the Muslim–Christian debate was taken by the Damascus Christians who questioned the Muslim scholars on the nature of revelation and prophecy, the unity of God, and the salvation of humanity.[24] In the ninth century the Muslim theologians took the initiative and the situation changed. By then the

Muslim scholars had assimilated Greek thought and were knowledgeable about the Old and New Testaments. Thus the Muslim–Christian polemic after the ninth century takes the form of both philosophical-dialectical and biblical arguments. The Christians found that they had to agree with the principle of *naskh* (abrogation) because they themselves held that the Old Testament was abrogated by the New Testament. The Muslim scholars quoted texts from the New Testament and other Christian sources in support of the Qur'ān. New Testament texts are also cited to disprove the divine nature of Jesus. During the thirteenth and fourteenth centuries the Muslim scholars shifted their attack and sought to show that the historical parts of the Christian scriptures are forgeries but that the legislative parts of the Bible are true; however, the Christian exegesis of the legislative parts is judged to be often in error.[25]

Waardenburg has provided a concise summary of the accusations made in Muslim polemical writings against Christianity:

I. *There have been a change and forgery of textual divine revelation.* This forgery is seen not only in the corrupting of Christianity when measured against the teachings of Jesus, but also in Christians' refusal to accept Muhammad as a prophet, which is due to their neglecting the announcements contained in their own scriptures and the rational and scriptural proofs of his prophethood given by his miracles and his revelation of the Qur'ān.

II. *There have been doctrinal mistakes, in particular about things divine.* Three main doctrinal issues are involved:

  a. The Christian belief in the incarnation of Jesus is rejected. The Qur'ān denied that Jesus was anything more than a prophet, and the Muslim scholars tried to prove this using reason and arguing against the Christian distinction of a human nature in Jesus able to suffer and a divine nature free from suffering.

  b. The *Trinitarian* doctrine that God consists of one substance and three persons is rejected outright on the basis of the Qur'ān's teaching that nothing can infringe upon the oneness of God. The Muslim scholars point out that the Trinity is not found in the New Testament, and also claim that it cannot be supported by reason. In particular the idea of a Father–Son relationship within God is revolting to Muslim thought, as is the notion that God would become contingent through the action of procreation.

c. The *soteriological* doctrines of the Christians are also rejected. The doctrine of original sin goes against the Qur'ān and is seen as logically contrary to divine justice. Also the idea that people's sins (for which they are responsible) could be remitted by Jesus through atonement goes against the Qur'ānic ideas of law, justice and humanity, and it conflicts with reason.

(The basis for all of the above doctrinal errors is found by Muslim scholars in the Christian attempt to locate three eternal principles within one. From the Muslim perspective there can be only one eternal principle, God, and thus there can be no mingling of God and humanity.)

III. *There have been mistakes in religious practice* as a result of not adhering to a true account of revelation and through the use of faulty reason:

a. Christians indulge in *idol worship* by adoring Jesus or venerating Mary and the saints.
b. Christians are *lax* in their *spiritual practice*: they ignore circumcision and ritual purity as prescribed by Mosaic law.
c. Inadmissible *novelties* have been introduced by Christians since the lifetime of Jesus, e.g. sacraments, celibacy, excommunication, etc.[26]

According to the Muslim scholars it is because of these errors that Christians not only have fallen away from the true teachings of Jesus but also have refused to hear the completion of the biblical revelation given through Muhammad.

In recent times the polemic literature against Christianity has largely focused on Christian missionary endeavours.[27] The position of these writings is that Christians do not live up to their own teachings (as stated in the Sermon on the Mount), that missionaries are often agents of Western imperialism, that the Christian Bible does not stand up to the scrutiny of modern critical scholarship, and finally that Islam – when analysis of it is freed from misconceptions relating to such matters as the seclusion of women, polygamy and *jihād* – shows itself to be the religion of the golden mean and of reasonableness as opposed to the difficult mysteries of faith required by Christianity. Islam, it is argued, is much more in harmony with today's rational and scientific thought. The idea that the Qur'ān contains verifiable scientific data is often cited as something that places Islam above all other religions.

William Shepard directs our attention to Aḥmad Amīn, an Egyptian Muslim scholar who lived in the first half of the twentieth century.[28] In Aḥmad Amīn's writing Shepard sees a shift in Islamic thought to a more open attitude towards other religions, especially Christianity. Christianity is seen as the particular form that the spiritual dimension has assumed in Western culture. Although efforts of Christian missionaries to convert Muslims must be resisted, this resistance is directed more towards Western political and economic domination than towards conversion to Christianity. There is also no plea for the conversion of Christians to Islam.[29] Both Christianity and Islam should learn from each other even though Islam is the superior religion. Shepard sums up Aḥmad Amīn's position as follows:

> We may conclude that he tends to assume, particularly in relation to Christianity, a communal image of two distinct communities whose religious views are essentially compatible and which therefore stand on a par with each other.[30]

Shepard finds in all of this a 'communal model' for the relationship among religions. Islam has essentially reached the truth towards which all other religions are evolving. Christianity, it seems, has also virtually reached this goal. It is possible that various nations or cultures will reach the truth in their own way. Shepard writes, 'All of this implies the communal image, that of several separate peoples, each with essentially the same teachings in corrupted form, who may return to the truth either by accepting Islam, or by doing on their own, as it were, what Islam has already done, i.e. distilling the truth out of the preceding religions to find the universal one.'[31] The Qur'ān itself teaches that every community in every age has had its prophet.[32]

It is acknowledged that Fazlur Rahman and Aḥmad Amīn may not be representative of all Muslims, however, they offer a very positive attitude from within Islam towards other religions which is often overlooked.

ISLAM AND EASTERN RELIGIONS

Although Islam has been in contact with Buddhism and Hinduism in India since the seventh and eighth centuries, it was not until the Moghul empire (sixteenth to nineteenth centuries), that, through ṣūfism, Muslim scholars seriously began to engage Eastern religions. As the approach of ṣūfism rendered Islam more amenable to the worldview of Eastern thought, it was fortuitous that the ṣūfīs led the way East. As Fazlur Rahman puts it, 'The spread of Islam in India, in Central Asia and Anatolia and in Africa, was carried on through ṣūfī brotherhoods, and ṣūfism in all these zones made compromises with the spiritual *milieu* already existing.'[33] The ṣūfī response to the encounter with other, especially Eastern, religions not only helped significantly in the massive spread of Islam to the East but also infused a fresh vitality into the Muslim community and Muslim orthodoxy.[34]

In medieval Islam only a few Muslim scholars were acquainted with Buddhism. There was diffuse and limited knowledge of Buddha and teachings relating to such things as rebirth, Bodhisattvas and Buddhist monks. Muslim authors described the Buddhists as having lived before the coming of revealed religions to the East and as having been the ancient idolators of the East. The main Buddhist doctrines reported in medieval Islam include: the worship of idols, the idea of rebirth, and belief in the eternity of the world and thus in the notion that the world was not created. It was also held, probably as a misunderstanding of the Mādhyamika position, that Buddhists were sceptics who denied reason and logical inference.[35] None of these concepts seems to have had much impact upon Islam.

The first real interchange is evident in the influence of some Buddhist ascetic practices and teaching techniques on the early development of institutional ṣūfism. Anything that would make ṣūfī sermons more persuasive and effective was borrowed from Buddhism, as well as from other religions.[36] At a later date the impact of Buddhist ideas on ṣūfism was considerable. Aziz Ahmad summarizes this relationship as follows: Certain ṣūfī exercises like *habs-i dam* (holding back of breath) seem to have been derived through Buddhist channels from yogic *prānyama*. The ṣūfī concept of 'peace with all' (*sulh-i kul*), which became a dominant feature of Indian ṣūfism of the later seventeenth and eighteenth centuries, seems to have been borrowed much earlier from Mahāyāna Buddhism. Also, the concentration of the ṣūfī student on the teacher's image in the early stages of an initiate's education seems to have been adopted from Buddhism. And the ṣūfī use of a rosary seems to be borrowed from either a Christian or an Indo-Buddhist tradition. The Buddhist monastic centre in central Asia, named Balkh, later became the home of a number of eminent ṣūfīs. It is clear that ṣūfism willingly borrowed from Buddhism, but it is also evident that at heart the two traditions remain far apart.[37] As R. A. Nicholson puts it, 'The Buddhist moralizes himself; the ṣūfī becomes moral only through knowing and loving God.'[38]

Islam's interaction with Hinduism is much more significant than its encounter with Buddhism. One of the early comprehensive treatments of Hinduism within Islam was written by the medieval scholar al-Bīrūni (c. 1000 CE). Waardenburg notes that al-Bīrūni opened the eyes of educated Muslims to Indian and Greek science and philosophy and held that both could be integrated into one higher intellectual worldview. The content of this higher insight, maintained al-Bīrūni, was that: 1) both Hindu and Greek philosophers arrived at the truth of one God, in conformity with the teachings of the prophets; 2) this kind of universal religious thought was known only to the literate elite, whereas the illiterate masses both within and outside Islam fell prey to the innate human disposition to idolatry; and 3) both Greeks and Hindus knew God as the One and sought spiritual unification (*ittiḥād*) leading not only to scholarly knowledge but also to insight of the mind.[39]

A hundred years after al-Bīrūni divided Hindus into the educated and the uneducated, ash-Shahrastānī compared Hindus with the Sabians and ranked them in terms of degrees of idolatry:

> The Vaiṣṇavas and Śaivas are like the Sabian *aṣḥāb ar-rūḥaniyyāt*: they venerate Viṣṇu and Śiva as Spiritual Beings or mediators who were incarnated and brought laws albeit without a scripture, so that they cannot be called idolators in the real sense of the word. Those adoring Āditya and Chandra (sun and moon considered as deities) are star worshippers (*'abadat al-kawākib*) which is a grade lower but still not idolatry. Only those who adore and prostrate themselves before real idols are real idolators (*'abadat al-asanā*) of the lowest rank, like the Arabs of the Jāhiliyya.[40]

Because the Sabians are understood by ash-Shahrastānī to be followers of the ancient Greek figure Hermes (identified with the Qur'ānic Idris or Enoch), the Sabians are loosely grouped with Jews and Christians as People of the Book. Thus, by equating Hindus with Sabians, ash-Shahrastānī attempted to interpret much of Hinduism so that it would be acceptable to and compatible with Islam.

Two articles by Yohanan Friedmann are noted by Waardenburg as providing further evidence that medieval Muslim scholars had a positive attitude towards Hinduism.[41] Friedmann shows that the Muslim Hanafī and Mālikī schools of law did not treat Hindus according to *sharī'ah* prescriptions for the *mushrikūn* (polytheists): conversion, departure or death. Friedmann also identifies six Muslim thinkers living between 1000 and 1781 whose attitudes to Hinduism were positive in varying degrees. For example, prince Dārā Shikōh (born *c.* 1650), in looking for a bridge between Hinduism and Islam, suggests 'that all holy books including the Vedas stem from one source, that they constitute a commentary on each other, and that the advent of Islam did not abrogate the religious truths contained in the Vedas or supersede the religious achievement of the Hindus'.[42] The last of these thinkers is the ṣūfī Jān-i-Janān (born 1781) who divided Hindus into two groups: those who lived before Muhammad's mission pleased God with their religion; however, Hindus born after Muhammad are guilty of being astray if they do not convert to Islam once it has been preached to them.[43] A persistent criticism of the Hindus is that though they honour the unity of God they remain misguided because of their denial of prophecy. An Egyptian ṣūfī master, Abd al-Karīm al-Jīlī (born 1304), writes, 'They [the Hindus] testify to His [God's] Oneness in Being, but they deny the prophets and messengers completely.'[44] Al-Jīlī also provides an interesting example of how Islamic views were sometimes superimposed upon Hinduism:

> They [the Hindus] claim to be the children of Abraham – upon whom be peace – and say that they possess a book [the Veda] written for them by Abraham – upon whom be peace – himself, except that they say it came from His Lord. In it the truth of things is mentioned and it has five parts. As for the four parts they permit their reading to everyone. But as for the fifth part they do not allow its reading except to a few among them, because of its depth and unfathomableness. It is well known among them that whoever reads the fifth part of their book will of necessity come into the fold of Islam.[45]

Al-Jīlī, like other ṣūfīs, separated out Hindu daily practice and searched for Hindu metaphysical notions that could be identified with the doctrine of divine unity in Islam. He sought to approach Hinduism by penetrating its esoteric truths so that they might reveal the presence of the one God behind the veil of the many.

The translation of Hindu literature is an aspect of the Islam–Hindu encounter that has yet to receive careful scholarly attention. Early in the encounter between Islam and Hinduism, al-Bīrūni translated Patañjali's *Yoga Sūtras* into Arabic.[46] But it was the translations of Hindu texts into Persian during the Moghul period that had the most significant impact. The Moghul prince Dārā Shikōh (1615–59) was responsible for the translation of the *Bhagavad-Gītā*, the *Yoga Vāśishṭha*, and the *Upaniṣads*. (It was from these Persian translations that the Latin translations were made – which subsequently were read by the philosopher Schelling and the poet Blake.) Dārā was a ṣūfī of the Qādiriyyah order, and in his translations he attempted to place Hindu ideas into the framework of ṣūfism so as to create a bridge between Hindu and Islamic metaphysics. Dārā believed the *Upaniṣads* to be the 'Hidden Books' to which the Qur'ān refers (56:78), and he argued that it is thus one of the sacred books Muslims should know, just as they know the Torah, the Hebrew Bible and the Gospels.[47] He believed the *Upaniṣads* contain the essence of unity.[48]

Dārā Shikōh was the great-grandson of the Emperor Akbar (1556–1605), whose unique approach to religions demands special attention. Although Akbar was born into a ṣūfī culture, the Indian ṣūfism that pervaded that culture had lost its dynamism.[49] Early in his life Akbar began exploring other religions and evidencing considerable eclecticism.[50] He married Hindu wives (permitting them to continue Hindu worship) and engaged in debate with scholars from other religions. In 1578 Akbar met Tāj-al-dīn Ajodhanī, a heterodox ṣūfī strongly influenced by Abd al-Karīm al-Jīlī. According to one Islamic scholar, 'This contact, instead of restraining Akbar within the fold of traditional Islam, seems to have unintentionally smoothed his path to a heretical application of al-Jīlī's conception of the Perfect Man to himself.'[51] About the middle of his life Akbar announced the formation of his own religion, the Din-i-Ilāhī. The tenets were simple: one was to pray three times a day; no meat was to be eaten; rebirth and *karma* were accepted; gentle words were recommended for daily communication; and forgiveness, toleration and kindness towards all living creatures were stressed. Furthermore,

> The sun was worshipped as the body of the Divine, and unification with God was the ultimate goal. There was no priesthood, no clergy. Akbar alone was the Holy Magnifying Glass through which the rays of the sun were focussed onto humanity. He was, in essence, a god on earth. '*Al-lahu Akbar*' was stamped on his coins; and since '*Akbar*' also means 'great,' the phrase could be read either as 'God is great' or 'Akbar is God.'[52]

Akbar's ideas and religion resulted in part because nearly a thousand years had elapsed since the birth of Muhammad and because messianism was rife within Indian Islam. Equally important was the interest of Abu'l

Fazl, a close associate of Akbar, in comparative religion.[53] Fazl's curiosity about other religions undoubtedly helped Akbar decide to build the Emperor's House of Worship at Fathpur Sikri. There academic discussions were held among scholars of all the major religions, often with Akbar chairing the debate.

Aziz Ahmad concludes that there is little evidence of direct Hindu influence on Akbar. In spite of the constant Hindu presence, due to the religious practice of his wives, only a few isolated features of Hindu ritual seem to have attracted him, and not the Hindu religion itself.[54] He celebrated *rākhi* (the wearing of a band on one's arm), participated in the festival of *dipāvali*, drank Ganges water and wore the *tilak* (a sacred mark placed on the forehead) and sometimes the sacred thread. Probably the most far-reaching Hindu influence in the palace was the sacred fire of his Hindu wives. But Akbar's tendency towards sun worship seems to have originated more in his contact with Zoroastrianism or heterodox Muslim ṣūfism – although it must be remembered that Hinduism had earlier influenced the latter. Ahmad concludes that Akbar showed a surprising indifference to Hinduism; however, his liberal treatment of the Hindus, although probably in part politically motivated, is remarkable. He abolished the *jizya* or poll tax. He permitted Hindus who had converted to Islam to revert to Hinduism and justified this action on the Qur'ānic teaching, 'Let there be no compulsion in religion.'[55] However, he did interfere with Hindu practices, such as *sati* (widow burning), that he considered unjust. He supported Hindu arts and sciences and sponsored the translation of Hindu scriptures into Persian. In education he introduced courses in Sanskrit and opened the way for the equal participation of Hindus with Muslims in high civil service offices. Akbar's religious views remain a dilemma for scholars. Ahmad notes, 'European historians generally regard him as an apostate from Islam, while modern Hindu historians consider him a liberal Muslim.'[56] Perhaps the most helpful evaluation of Akbar is given by M. G. S. Hodgson:

> The universalist sort of culture and moral life which Akbar fostered, and which was largely accepted as the basis for court life by Muslim and Hindu officials alike, was not in itself inconsistent with Islam. Indeed, it was cast in Islamic terms, and attracted its most explicit support chiefly among Muslims rather than among Hindus. But it presupposed an alternative interpretation of Islam, as it bore on life and culture, which excluded the more particularistic, communalistic, interpretation of the Islamic mission in the world which had always been upheld by the Sharī-ah-minded.[57]

MILITANT RESPONSES IN MODERN ISLAM

In recent years Muslim confrontation with the West has given rise to militant responses within Islam. In reaction to earlier attempts to modernize and liberalize Islam by disregarding those accumulated traditions that were felt to be no longer relevant, more recent movements have returned to the insistence that Islam must be the norm by which all aspects of life are measured. The ultimate goal of such thinkers and movements appears to be the reconstitution of a vibrant Islamic society.[58] An example of this is found in the writings of Sayyid Qutb, whose popular interpretations of the Qur'ān support a revolutionary Islam. Although he started his career as a proponent of westernization, Qutb became totally disenchanted with the West after the formation of the state of Israel. In the denying of the Palestinians of their rights and homelands, he saw modern Western hypocrisy and the betrayal of liberal values. During his stay in the United States from 1949 to 1951, he encountered American bias against Arabs. This led him to renounce his earlier works and begin writing on Islamic revolution as the divine imperative. In Egypt this eventually led to Nasser ordering his arrest and execution.[59]

What is of special interest is that Qutb's interpretation of the Qur'ān contains long sections on Christians and Jews. Both religions are identified with 'the West' that has for centuries attempted to undermine Islam. In Sura 2, verse 120 ('The Jews and Christians will never be satisfied with you until you follow their religion') and Sura 2, verse 109 ('Many People of the Book desire to turn you away after you have believed because of covetousness in themselves'), Qutb sees Allah warning Muslims against following the ways of the Jews and the Christians. Further evidence of the truth of these warnings is found in the painful experiences of Muslims under Christian colonialism and Jewish Zionism. Qutb sees a deep-rooted struggle between the ideology of the Muslim community and that of Christians and Jews. In Qutb's thinking this struggle between Islam and the other religions has been going on for a long time, as is witnessed to by the warnings of Allah in the Qur'ān. Although the Jews and Christians may periodically struggle against each other, they will always manage to unite against Islam. In recent times this attempt to subvert Islam has taken the forms of seizure of strategic lands and economic and educational colonization. In reaction Qutb says that Muslims must remember that Allah has prohibited the reception of guidance from any source other than Allah. Qutb argues, 'Muslims have been singled out by God as the best community. They must assume the role of leadership.'[60] The goal of Islamic revolutionaries such as Qutb is to eliminate Western (Christian and Jewish) influences that are seen to be aimed at destroying the Islamic order by altering its social, political and economic structure under the guise of westernization. Such westernization is judged to be a subtle technique for the conversion of Islam to the Jewish or Christian way.

Militant responses in modern Islam end up opposing not only Jews and Christians but also other Muslims who have liberalized or westernized. Thus, 'the enemy is no longer "out there"; rather the enemy is the Muslim community that lives life ignoring the Islamic *sharī'ah*'.[61] This is the context out of which the fragmentation of modern Islam arises. It also provides the doctrinal basis for battles between Islamic countries such as Iran and Iraq. Modernization as such is not rejected, but technology and modernization are distinguished from westernization, which is detested and rejected.

Before leaving the question of modernization and its impact on Islam, let us briefly examine the quite different responses of two significant Muslim thinkers: Sayyid Ahmad Khan (1817–98) and Abul Ala Mawdudi (1903–79). In her fine study, McDonough describes how both men lived in India and exerted strong influence on the shape of modern Islam in present-day India and Pakistan.[62] Mawdudi's narrow 'fundamentalist' response now has wide influence throughout Islam. Sayyid Ahmad Khan's response was very different, arguing for an open, educated, rational but pious approach to modernity. Different as they were, however, both men were motivated to find and communicate a new ethical basis for life suitable to the pluralistic challenges of modernity. Both were original thinkers who arrived at very different conclusions as to how Muslims should think and act in the modern world, yet both believed themselves to be faithful to the most basic wisdom of Islam. For them, the change required by modern Muslims, who cannot simply repeat the patterns of life and thought of their ancestors, is to return to the basic values of Islam's far distant past.

Sayyid Ahmad Khan was born and raised in an aristocratic family in Mughal Delhi. A magistrate by profession, Sayyid also functioned as a diplomat and was made a Fellow of the Royal Asiatic Society for his archaeological researches in Delhi. A great believer in rational thought and the importance of education, Sayyid held that Muslims were free to interpret for themselves from the Qur'ān what God required of them. The social, economic and political affairs of the community should be dealt with by institutions in which all participated. As McDonough puts Sayyid's position, 'The transformation of society should come about through the free co-operative effort of its citizens ... problems would differ from age to age.'[63] His concern was with the process rather than with specific answers. But he did not believe that one had to live in a Muslim state to be faithful. Indeed he worked to ensure that Muslims could live a vital life as Muslims alongside Hindus, Sikhs, Christians and the other religions that would constitute an independent India.[64] Sayyid's vision of modern improvements to the social order is optimistic. He sees movement away from Muslim and other forms of medieval despotism to be progressive because people will be able to live under constitutions that protect them from such despots. The democratic participation of all citizens will help to protect them from abuse. The progress of Muslim civilization is part of a wider change within history away from tyranny. For Sayyid, Muslim progress required learning from Western-style studies. To make this possible he set up the Mohammedan Anglo-Oriental College at Aligarh. Muslim students from all over India enrolled. Hindu students were also welcomed and their dietary customs respected. Muslims in both India and Pakistan view Sayyid Ahmad Khan as the father of their modern outlook on education.

Abul Ala Mawdudi offers a marked contrast to Sayyid. He was not from the Muslim elite. Mawdudi's father had been pulled out of the Aligarh school, established by Sayyid, because of his own fears of too much foreign influence. Educated at home by tutors, Mawdudi was essentially self-taught. His first profession was as a religious journalist and writer. His book *Towards Understanding Islam* was widely used as a text in schools. McDonough concludes that much of Mawdudi's fame and influence came from the vigour and persuasive power of his writings.[65] He found traditional Islam unsatisfactory and devoted himself to personal study of the Qur'ān and the Prophet's *sunna* in order to discover the true system of Islam, which he then taught to others as a renewal of faith. A Constitution was established for his followers and they elected Mawdudi as their Amir or leader. He governed with the help of a consultative council but he was the final arbiter of all matters for his followers. His understanding of the Qur'ān and *sunna* required that his followers abstain from dealing in interest, alcohol, dance and music. Western influence was to be avoided, since it would betray the true interests of Muslims. After India achieved independence, Mawdudi and many of his followers went to Pakistan, where they have opposed all governments as being insufficiently Islamic. Throughout his life Mawdudi continued to write books which have been influential in many parts of the Muslim world. For example, his writings are said to have influenced Hasan al Banna, the founder of the radical Muslim Brotherhood of Egypt. This Muslim Brotherhood made an attempt on Nasir's life and continue to agitate against all leaders who they consider betrayers of the true Islamic system.[66]

Modern Western civilization and other religions are seen by Mawdudi as hostile to the Islamic truth he teaches, and to be fostering the moral corruption of the modern world. Only a radical transformation to true Islam can halt this corruption. Rather than the approach of reason, science and individual democratic choice favoured by Sayyid, Mawdudi argues for a system based on the selection of a few moral men in authority whom everyone else would follow in the revolution that is needed to restore a true Islam as the religion of the whole world. Clearly this leaves little room for religious pluralism of the sort Sayyid encouraged. And whereas for Sayyid women and girls were encouraged to become educated and active in society, Mawdudi teaches that the feminine virtue is modesty – that women should receive some degree of education to enable them to become adequate wives and mothers, but their lives must be spent within the home. 'Males are to practice their moral duties by protecting the females of their family and by guarding themselves against sexual impropriety of any kind.'[67]

Many modern Muslims see Mawdudi's approach as conducive to a form of *jihād* against the modern Western forces of religious disintegration that they fear. Against such a threat the appeal of submission to the authority of those conceived of as morally upright leaders is popular in fundamentalist positions in all religions. By contrast, Sayyid, who was also a fighter for the renewal of Islam and of people's lives, put more trust in the power of education and the good choices of individual persons than in submission to those in either religious or political authority. He urged Muslims to implement forms of government in which individuals would be protected from all kinds of tyranny. Mawdudi, like many revolutionary leaders, believed that God has a plan, that Mawdudi and his followers know it, and that rigorous state control of society is needed to actualize God's plan. As McDonough points out, this is in one sense a very modern way of thinking: God is like an engineer with a plan to be implemented,[68] or, to put it another way, the religious goal is 'management by objectives or deliverables'. In her comparison of these two thinkers, McDonough finds Mawdudi's approach of terrifying the population into seeing the moral and religious worth of his position is out of keeping with the general thrust of Muslim ethical thought. It does not respect the dignity of persons. Rather, Muslim ethical thought, McDonough argues, is egalitarian and encourages the development of a sensitive conscience within the individual. This latter is much more the approach of Sayyid in his attempts at religious and social reform in the modern world.[69]

CONCLUSION

The encounter of Islam with other religions dates back to the prophet Muhammad. Throughout this history the basic attitude has been that the other religions are deviations from the one primordial religion, of which Islam is the full revelation. During the medieval period certain categories were developed by Muslim scholars to understand other religions. Buddhists were sceptics; Hindus were rationalists who denied prophecy; Christians were tritheists; and Jews were corrupters of prophecy. Often these judgemental categories were assumed before the factual evidence relating to the religion in question was investigated. Indeed, because Islam was the full revelation and therefore the norm of all religion, there was little need within Islam to study and understand other religions on their own terms. And since Islam, until modern times, was mainly lived in a self-enclosed Islamic state where Islam was the religion of the majority, there was little cultural or political pressure to do otherwise. Throughout the centuries the basic Islamic approach to other religions was to search for some fundamental structures that were harmonious with Islam but which lay hidden beneath the other religion's deviations from true Islam.[70] Other religions were at fault because they had lost or corrupted the original revelation or had fallen into doctrinal error. Although this scheme worked well for dealings with the biblically based religions of Judaism and Christianity, it produced some far-fetched results when used to analyse Buddhism and Hinduism. Nowhere is the Buddhist refusal to accept God taken seriously, and in one case the Veda is interpreted as a piece of biblical prophecy that should produce conversion to Islam.

A major obstacle for understanding other religions was the lack of accurate information. Analysis of Judaism and Christianity by Muslim scholars was often based not on those religions themselves but on the tenets of Judaism and Christianity as they are described and evaluated in the Qur'ān. Much information came from converts and more from the polemical discussions. Information about Hinduism and Buddhism was very limited during the medieval period and often was distorted so as to fit familiar categories, for instance the identification of Brahman with Abraham.[71] However, in general, Islamic scholars, on encountering strange or new religions, did not dismiss them as mere idolatry (a move that the important sin of *shirk* must have rendered quite tempting) but rather treated them as deviations from the one true religion and therefore deserving of respect. In recent centuries, especially with the expansion of Islam to the East and the modern migration of Muslims to Europe and America, Muslims have been getting to know other religions on their own terms rather than as they are presented via the Qur'ān and *hadīth*. In India and in the West, Muslims find themselves in the unfamiliar position of being members of a minority group within a culture that is dominated by another religion. This may have the effect of calling forth a sharper delineation of Islam from other traditions so as to enable the minority Muslim community to retain its identity. A study in Canada indicates that the educational emphasis in mosques is shifting from passive receptivity to an active rejection of that which is against the Islamic tradition and as such is against the will of God.[72] One European Muslim leader states, 'The greatest task that besets us in America and Europe is not only to conserve our ideological and cultural identity, but also to develop true Islamic character in the individual and establish dynamic Muslim community at the social level.'[73] Muslims in America are now very involved in interreligious dialogue, politics and community affairs. Many more Muslims want to be engaged in the host cultures and societies, and thus 'have a place at the table'. Muslims who live as a minority group also see the development of strong Islamic communities within the host culture as being crucial if the goal of reforming society according to Islamic principles is to be furthered. In Europe and America the method of achieving this goal is still described as resisting assimilation into the host culture while absorbing and reforming it so that it may conform to the religious ideas of Islam – the one true primordial religion. Though this vision may still be clear, the practical problems of living in a modern, secularized and basically Christian society pose serious and, as yet, unsolved problems for Islamic law (*sharī'ah*).

In India and the Far East the ṣūfī influence has produced an essentially mystical response to the encounter with other religions. The traditional Islamic doctrine of divine unity is taken as foundational and the concept of the Logos is appropriated to account for diversity. According to this interpretation, which was first offered by Ibn 'Arabī and later by al-Jīlī, the founder of each religion is an aspect of the universal Logos, which is identified with the revelation of Muhammad.[74] The ṣūfīs not only assert the unity of revelation but also consider themselves as the guardians of Islam and of all other religions. The ṣūfī master Jalāl al-Din Rūmī describes this viewpoint using an image very familiar to Hindus:

> Though the ways are various, the goal is one. Do you not see that there are many roads to the Kaaba? ... So if you consider the roads the variety is great and the divergence infinite; but when you consider the goal, they are all of one accord and one.[75]

Ṣūfism sees itself as providing the key necessary for opening the door to a true encounter with other religions. The ṣūfī vision provides Islam with a way of recognizing the truth present within other traditions because it sees divergent paths as the way to the *Kaaba* – the experience of unity with the one God. Because Islam has the full revelation and experience of the *Kaaba*, its role is to be the guide for the other traditions on their upward journey. Islam remains the norm, but sincere believers of other faiths are embraced as spiritual neighbours and are helped along their own path toward the final goal of the *Kaaba*. Although this view has been very helpful to Muslims living in minority communities in host cultures such as Hindu India, it has posed unresolved problems for orthodox Islamic law and doctrine.

With the exception of Akbar, there is little evidence that Muslims in the past really understood Buddhist, Hindu, Jewish or Christian religion. Instead they saw images presented in the Qur'ān or developed in their own cultural experiences and filtered through Islamic rules and problems.[76] In most instances these images were formulated in the sociopolitical context of an Islamic state or empire. In the future, with Islam increasingly having to experience itself as a minority within a foreign host culture, these traditional views of other religions undoubtedly will be modified. Modern education will offer Muslims an opportunity to understand each religion in terms of its own culture, history, worldview and claims to truth. This will have an effect on Islamic self-perception. The religious pluralism of the modern world will force Islam, finding itself in much the same position as the other traditions, to come to grips with the rather provincial character of some of its past views of other religions. Among some of the modern revolutionary movements, of course, there has been a diametrically opposite response to religious pluralism – that of militant Islamic fundamentalism of the sort fostered by the thought of Abul Ala Mawdudi. Within such movements there is obviously little inclination to be open to other religions.

4 RELIGIOUS PLURALISM AND THE BAHA'I FAITH

O f the new religious movements in the modern world, the Baha'i
Faith is sufficiently independent and widespread in its international
membership of about six million people to be regarded as a world
religion. Its international spread is described as second only to that of
Christianity.[1] Although the Baha'i Faith originated in the Islamic context
of Iran, it quickly spread to North America and Europe and now has a
majority of its membership in developing countries such as India. Baha'i
scripture proclaims all established religions to be divine in origin and that
no religion is superior to the others, since they all come from God. The
various religions are understood to be successive and progressive, with
the Baha'i revelation reaching the highest level so far achieved in human
experience – but with more advancement expected towards the universal
realization of one common revelation.[2] In contemporary discussions of
religious pluralism, Baha'i writers see their tradition as rejecting both
exclusivist (only one religion, ours is true) and inclusive (ours is the
whole truth, but other religions share some of that truth) approaches,
and adopting the modern pluralist position that all religions embody
equally valid human responses to the divine.[3]

The Baha'i Faith arose in the 1860s as a movement within Babism
(founder, the Bab, 1819–50), a messianic sect of Shi'a Islam which began
in Iraq and Iran in 1844. The Bab, in his book, *The Bayan*, argued for the
social and religious reform of Iran in preparation for the coming of the
promised deliverer – a new prophet or manifestation of God who would
reveal the teachings for the coming age. Baha'u'llah (1817–92), the
founder of the Baha'i Faith, claimed that he was the promised deliverer,

foretold by the Bab, the one for whom all the religions of the world were waiting.[4] Claiming to be a 'new manifestation of God' in the long line of prophets (Abraham, Moses, Zoroaster, the Buddha, Jesus, Muhammad), Baha'u'llah and his followers were judged to be a threat to orthodox Islam, which holds that Muhammad was the 'Seal of the Prophets' and thus the bearer of God's final revelation. This resulted in a history of persecution of Baha'is and exile of Baha'i leaders from Iran to Iraq, Turkey and finally to Acre and Haifa in present-day Israel. Baha'u'llah spent the last twenty-four years of his life creating the principles and institutions of the new religion, which included: the unity of God, the unity of the world religions, the unity of humankind and the need for a world language and a form of global governance. He advocated parliamentary democracy, disarmament, greater spending on education and the poor, and a world security system in which if any country attacked another the rest of the world's nations would intervene to achieve peace.[5]

Since the Baha'i Faith arose from the context of Shi'a Islam, it is not surprising that there are many similarities in Muslim and Baha'i belief. God is one and utterly transcendent. God reveals his will through a series of messengers or prophets, whom the Baha'is call 'manifestations of God' and whose role is to guide the spiritual progress of individuals and to mould society as a whole. In the previous chapter we noted the Islamic teaching of a foundational unity underlying all religions. Baha'is agree with this teaching but offer additional refinements. According to the Qur'ān, messages spoken by the different prophets all emanate from a single source called 'the Mother of the Book' (43:4; 13:39) and 'the Hidden Book' (56:78). Since all prophetic revelations come from a single source, Muhammad taught that all divine messages should be embraced. The Qur'ān specifically addresses Jews and Christians as 'People of the Book', inviting them to come together with the followers of Muhammad's revelations to serve God (3:64). But ṣūfī thinkers, through their contact with India, made efforts to widen 'the People of the Book' so as to include Hindus and Buddhists. The logic of the Qur'ān is that there is one a priori revelation in heaven, which all messengers or prophets convey to their different peoples (religions) perfectly. Differences between the religions are attributable not to any fault of the original message (e.g. as given by Moses in the Torah or Jesus in the Gospels) but to errors in the way that followers (Jews and Christians) have transmitted the original revelations. Only in the case of Islam has the revelation, namely the

Qur'ān, been passed on free from errors or interpolations creeping in. Baha'is are in basic agreement with Qur'ānic teaching in this regard, but offer two important refinements. First, whereas the Qur'ān limits 'the People of the Book' to Jews and Christians, Baha'u'llah clearly extends this notion to include all religions:

> There can be no doubt whatever that the peoples of the world, of whatever race or religion, derive their inspiration from one heavenly Source, and are the subjects of one God. The difference between the ordinances under which they abide should be attributed to the varying requirements and exigencies of the age in which they were revealed. All of them, except a few which are the outcome of human perversity, were ordained of God and are a reflection of His Will and Purpose.[6]

For Baha'u'llah it is clear that the Islamic embrace of Judaism and Christianity should be extended to include the prophets and revelations of all religions, which are all understood to manifest the same God. Later we will note that from a Buddhist perspective it is problematic to include them in this system, since God, for them, does not exist but is an obstructing ego-generated illusion. The second significant difference from Islam is also mentioned in the above quotation from Baha'u'llah. Unlike Muslims, Baha'is see the succession of prophets (religions) and their revelations as progressive in nature. This is different from the Qur'ānic logic of an original revelation (the Mother Book in heaven) given perfectly and fully by each prophet to his people, and from which the followers fall away. Differences between revelations, in the Baha'i view, occur because God tailors the revelation to suit the varying circumstances of the people to whom the prophets speak, and over time this forms a progressive succession, to which Baha'u'llah is the most recent contributor. As Baha'u'llah puts it in the above quotation, 'The differences between the ordinances [scriptures] under which they abide should be attributed to the varying requirements and exigencies of the age in which they were revealed.'[7]

Shi'a Islam also had a tradition that an Imam or inspired spiritual leader will emerge at the end time to usher into the world a reign of justice. According to the Iranian Shi'a tradition, the line of Imams ended in 873 CE when the twelfth and last appointed Imam withdrew into hiding to escape being put to death and communicated with his followers through a series of intermediaries (called *bābs* or gates to the hidden Imam). There were four *bābs* up to 941 CE when the last one died without naming a successor. According to the tradition, at the end time the hidden Imam (the *Mahdi*) will arise and again provide a direct channel from God to humans. The Baha'is arise out of this tradition in Iranian Islam in which the Bab claimed to be the promised deliverer, the Imam *Mahdi*, and also anticipated the coming of a further messianic figure whom he referred to as 'He whom God shall make manifest'.[8] Baha'u'llah, the founder of the Baha'i Faith, claimed to be that new manifestation – a claim that Shi'a Islam has rejected. Appropriate to his claim as the new manifestation of God, Baha'u'llah in 1867 began writing a series of letters to the secular and religious leaders of the world declaring himself to be the One promised in the Torah, the Gospels and the Qur'ān and calling on them to arise, champion his faith and adopt a progressive series of world reforms.[9] Around the same time, as he formulated his world mission, he completed the *Kitāb-i Aqdas* (the Most Holy Book) which today serves as the core revelation of Baha'u'llah for Baha'is.

In the year before his death in 1892, Baha'u'llah passed the leadership of the Baha'i community to his eldest son, 'Abdu'l-Baha (1844–1921), who was to be the sole authoritative interpreter of Baha'u'llah's teachings and the source of authority in all the affairs of the faith. 'Abdu'l-Baha was not to be regarded as a prophet or divine messenger but rather as a perfect example of his father's teachings. 'Abdu'l-Baha focused on expanding the Baha'i movement beyond the Middle East to North America and Europe. The first recorded reference to the Baha'i Faith in North America occurred at the 1893 Parliament of Religions held in connection with the Chicago World's Fair. Groups of Baha'is gradually grew up throughout the United States and Canada. For them, the high point was a journey to Haifa and Akka in what was then Palestine to meet the master 'Abdu'l-Baha and receive his teaching. Responding to these developments abroad, 'Abdu'l-Baha worked hard to simplify and clarify the key teachings of Baha'u'llah for the world – focusing on the social message rather than metaphysics. Not only the individual heart but also the social order must be transformed. And, key to our concern with pluralism, the validity of all the world's religions was emphasized.[10] In 1911–12 'Abdu'l-Baha undertook a twenty-eight-month preaching tour of Canada, the United States and Europe. He was invited to speak in numerous Christian churches, labour meetings, a synagogue, a mosque and gatherings in private homes. His trip was given extensive coverage in the newspapers. He encouraged the formation of spiritual assemblies at both the local and national levels – forerunners of what later came to be called 'Houses of Justice'. After 'Abdu'l-Baha's death in 1921, leadership of the faith passed to his grandson, Shoghi Effendi (1897–1957). Shoghi Effendi continued the westernization and expansion of the faith. Educated at the American University in Beirut and at Oxford, he had a strong ability to put Baha'i concepts into English, which played a major role in the spread of this new faith in the Western world.[11] It is from Shoghi Effendi's English writings and key translations of original Arabic or Persian texts into English that translations are made into about seven hundred other languages in use in the Baha'i Faith. The Baha'i Faith has not suffered any significant schism and so there are no competing schools of theology. With this brief overview of the origin of the Baha'i Faith in mind, let us examine 1) the Baha'i theology of religious pluralism, 2) relativism as a basis for Baha'i theology, 3) the Baha'i approach to interreligious dialogue and 4) the Baha'i mission to India.

THE BAHA'I THEOLOGY OF RELIGIOUS PLURALISM

How do Baha'i thinkers relate the claims of their faith to those of other religions? For a tradition that teaches that all religions are divine in origin and no one religion is superior to others – yet at the same time engages in a world mission for converts and claims that revelation is progressive, with the revelation of Baha'u'llah being the most recent in the progressive succession of prophets and scriptures – this is a key question. Two Baha'i scholars have offered responses.

Seena Fazel wrote the article 'Religious Pluralism' for the *Baha'i Encyclopedia* (as yet unpublished, but available on the Internet – see note 2). Fazel identifies Baha'is as religious pluralists rather than exclusivists or inclusivists. Exclusivists see only one mode of religious thought (their own) as true, and all others as false. Although he admits there are instances in Baha'i scripture capable of exclusivist development, that can only be done by taking them out of context. He quotes Shoghi Effendi: 'One cannot call one World Faith superior to another, as they all come from God.'[12] Inclusivists maintain that their own religion has the whole truth while other traditions may possess some truth or constitute approaches to the whole truth. Baha'i writings are not inclusivist, since they claim no finality for their revelation and maintain a doctrine of progressive revelation. Some ambiguity is, however, admitted: 'Inclusivist trends do exist in the Baha'i writings in that the Revelation of Baha'u'llah marks "the last and highest stage in the stupendous evolution of man's collective life on this planet".[13] Fazel attempts to interpret this as non-inclusive in nature by saying, 'This should be attributed not to "any inherent superiority" or "superior merit" of the Baha'i Faith but rather to the fact that the present age is one which is "indefinitely more advanced, more receptive, and more insistent to receive an ampler measure of Divine Guidance than has hither been vouchsafed to mankind." It is the present age, not the religion of the age, that is superior.'[14] In other words, it is not that the Baha'i Faith is superior to earlier revelations such as Islam, Christianity or Judaism, but that people today are more receptive than peoples of the past and actualize more of the revelation.

The pluralist position claimed for Baha'i theology is described by Fazel as the view that the great world religions embody different perceptions and conceptions of, and correspondingly different responses to, the divine, and that within each religion salvation is occurring. However, an apparent contradiction to this position is Baha'u'llah's reported statement that there will come a time when all nations should become one in faith and all diversity of religion should cease.[15] Fazel deals with this contradiction by quoting the explanation of Shoghi Effendi that the different religions are like 'stages in the eternal history and constant evolution of one religion'.[16] The founders of the religions shared in one common revelation which they manifested with increasing intensity. As the evolving capacity of human understanding more fully realizes the common revelation that is at the core of each religion, the realization will dawn that there is only one religion. Thus the Baha'i Faith need not become imperialist in its approach to other religions. Rather, the principle adopted is one of freedom of religion and full respect for those following other paths – since in the end all will reach a common goal. An example of this freedom of religion is the way Baha'i families raise their children giving them the choice to remain Baha'i or leave the faith when they reach the age of fifteen.

Inherent in the Baha'i view of the common core that underlies all religions is the vision of a future in which religious conflict will disappear and universal peace will be established. Consequently, the Baha'i Faith urges the leaders of all religions to submerge their theological differences in a spirit of mutual forbearance that will enable them to work together for the advancement of human understanding and peace. Baha'is see themselves functioning as a 'propelling power' in this process of fostering peace between religions. Baha'is are prepared for this role by the teaching of Baha'u'llah that they are to relate to the followers of other religions in a spirit of friendliness and fellowship. The shunning of members of other religions is forbidden, as is any approach involving conflict. Baha'is are to go to churches and mosques of other religions for worship, since in each of these places the name of God is spoken. Likewise leaders of the religions are called on to go to each other's churches and speak together of the fundamental principles that undergird all religions.

In his article on religious pluralism, Fazel concludes that this topic has yet to be widely discussed in Baha'i scholarship. He calls for 'a theory that fully acknowledges the vast range and complexity of the differences apparent in the phenomenology of religion while at the same time enabling us to understand the major streams of religious experience and thought as embodying the different awarenesses of one ultimate truth'.[17] Such a theory, suggests Fazel, will be based on the basic Baha'i principle that religious truth is relative.

RELATIVISM AS A BASIS FOR BAHA'I THEOLOGY

In his teachings, Baha'u'llah says God is so exalted beyond the capacities of mortal humans that it is impossible to describe God or even hint at the nature of God's essence. Consequently it is impossible for humans, even the brightest scholars or theologians, to capture God's glory in words. All descriptions, then, are limited by the viewpoint of the person making them. Understood this way, all theology is partial and relative – hence the theory of metaphysical or cognitive relativism which effectively deals with conflicting truth claims between the religions. (In chapter 6, we shall see that Mādhyamika Buddhism pushed this insight to its logical conclusion.) Baha'i writings employ the concept of relativism to explain the differences between religions. First, as noted above, there is the idea that human beings have a limited capacity to conceive of and describe God – although there is also an idea within Baha'i thinking that with evolution our abilities in this regard are steadily improving. Second is the notion that human society is evolving over time and gradually becoming more receptive to divine revelation. Thus some of the differences between religions can be explained by the changing contexts in which they were born. Shoghi Effendi, for example, explains that the central themes of the Christian, Islamic and Baha'i faiths have differed because of the societies these religions originated in: 'The fundamental distinction between the mission of Jesus Christ, concerning primarily the individual and the message of Baha'u'llah is that the latter is directed more particularly to mankind as a whole. The conception of the nation as a unit is the central theme of the Faith of Islam inasmuch as the evolution of society required it at that time.'[18] Baha'u'llah looks at the Faith of Islam as an evolving spiritual maturity and receptivity of humankind and uses the example of feeding children: 'Words are revealed according to the capacity so that beginners may make progress. The milk must be given according to measure so that the babe of the world may enter into the Realm of Grandeur ... The Revelation of which I am the bearer is adapted to humanity's spiritual receptiveness and capacity.'[19] What is unclear in Baha'i thought is whether this evolving human spiritual capacity can ever reach the point of a perfect reception of the revelation as the Eastern religions of Hinduism and Buddhism claim. But even in these traditions the state of perfect reception of the divine is a mystical one that transcends the descriptive capacity of human words, thus agreeing with Baha'u'llah's contention that it is impossible to describe God. Consequently, even the best efforts of an evolved theology seem doomed to remain relative.

Baha'i scholars Juan Cole and Moojan Momen have given this topic careful study. Cole understands the Baha'i doctrine of the relative and incomplete nature of all religious truth in a positive fashion.[20] In the Baha'i view all religions are equally valid in that they embody equally valid human responses to the divine. The Baha'i scriptures teach a pluralist theology of religions as a key part of the primary Baha'i belief in the unity of all religions. The different religions reflect different stages in a single process, namely, the progressive unfolding of religious truth. Differences between the various religions are regarded as a function of the different social conditions and receptive capacity of individuals that prevailed at the time and place that these religions first appeared. Thus the relative but valid nature of the 'truth' contained in each religion. In the Baha'i view religious truth is not absolute but relative and divine revelation is progressive, not final. All established world religions are divine in origin, identical in their aims, complementary in their functions and indispensable in their value to humankind. It is admitted that some small religions and cults may be false. 'The Baha'i criterion for the truth of a prophetic message is that it offers believers ethical and spiritual guidance, that it be long-lasting in its impact, that it encompass large numbers of persons, and that it inspire both a new organized religion and ultimately a civilization.'[21] It is in this context that a key difference between the Baha'i Faith and Islam is identified: 'The Baha'i faith differs from mainstream Islam, not only in recognizing further prophets after Muhammad and adhering to a new, liberalized religious law, but also in recognizing the truth of South Asian and other non-Abrahamic faiths and in accepting the general validity of the existing Bible along with other holy books for use as scripture. This theological pluralism differs from syncretism in that the various religions are affirmed in their world-historical specificity from the standpoint of a new and independent tradition, with its distinctive rituals, laws and theology.'[22] The unity of religions as taught by Baha'is is seen to be present in the deeper archetypes, spiritual experiences and ethical expressions that are held in common rather than in the specific and varying details of liturgy, history or doctrine. The truth talked about is not so much the philosopher's truth, with its criterion of non-contradiction, but the archetypal and metaphorical truth encountered in religious texts. For example, says Cole, in the historical context of Shi'a Iran in the mid-nineteenth century with its messianic expectations, Baha'u'llah 'underwent mystical experiences that led him gradually to see himself as the archetypal return of Husayn [the last of the Shi'a Imams] and of Christ, and as the promised one of the Bab'.[23] Each new prophetic figure is seen as a manifestation of the Logos (*kalimatu 'llah* or Word of God) and each offers a new revelation (suited to the needs of the day) that is an advance upon the preceding religious civilization. The progressive nature of this revelation should be seen not as a straight line through history (versus the cyclical notions common in Eastern religions) but rather as something like a spiral – a progressive revelation that picks up and completes past themes as it moves on to new, more complete manifestations of the divine. Cole offers an illustration of this process in his close reading of the scriptural text in which God commands Abraham to sacrifice his eldest son. He shows how this text is differently presented in the Torah, the New Testament, the Qur'ān and by Baha'u'llah. This illustrates both the different perceptions of the archetypal truth of the text and the progressive unfolding of the revelation through the succession of prophets and religions. It is in this way that Baha'is understand the differences recognized in the concept of religious pluralism to be positive and non-contradictory in nature.

Moojan Momen, in his article 'Relativism: A Basis for Baha'i Metaphysics', examines Baha'i teaching in terms of the worldviews of the

Eastern religions (Hinduism and Buddhism in particular).[24] The problem is that whereas the Western religions assume a dualistic separation between humans and God, in much Eastern religious thought (e.g. Advaita Vedānta in Hinduism and Mādhyamika in Buddhism) such dualism is explicitly rejected in favour of monist notions in which the true self of the individual is identified with the divine. Also in Buddhism there is no notion of a creator God or an authoritative revealed scripture. As Baha'i teachings arose out of an occidental Western religious context, it is not surprising that the dualist perspective of significant separation between God and humans and nature pervades most Baha'i writings. But, given the fact that the majority of Baha'i believers now come out of an Eastern religious background, how can the Baha'i perspective be reconciled to include the monistic approaches of the Eastern religions – remember that Baha'is maintain that the teachings of all religions are valid. Momen answers by first pointing out that in most Baha'i writings those being taught were living in an occidental context. So, for example, Baha'u'llah uses the classical theological viewpoints of Islam, Judaism and Christianity to express himself because these were the viewpoints to which his listeners were accustomed. But there are passages within Baha'u'llah's writing that Momen quotes as supporting a monist position of the Eastern type; for example: 'Turn thy sight unto thyself, that thou mayest find Me [God] standing within thee, mighty, powerful and self-subsisting.'[25] But for theological resolution of the problem Momen goes to Baha'u'llah's teaching that, due to the limitations of our finite human minds, all theological viewpoints (including the dualist and monist positions) are necessarily relative. But within the relativity of our human knowledge of the divine, essences or archetypal forms of the divine can be identified as valid truths. In the dualist case, humans are fundamentally different from the divine. In the monist perspective, humans are in essence nothing but an emanation or manifestation of the divine. 'Abdu'l-Baha suggests that the proofs and evidence given for these two positions are equally correct. The two groups are 'viewing the same object [the divine] from different viewpoints and so are arriving at different and even contradictory conclusions. The differences in the viewpoints arise from differences in the fundamental natures (i.e., the attributes predominant within the soul/psyche complex) of the observers. The fundamental nature of one individual inclines him to see Reality in a monist mode.'[26] The author notes that 'Abdu'l-Baha's solution of the dualist/monist problem in theology corresponds to the relativity theory of modern science, in which what is observed has reality only relative to the observer.

'Abdu'l-Baha goes even further in the negative theology direction.[27] No matter how hard a person strives for knowledge of the divine, he says, the only achievement will be better knowledge of one's own self. He employs the metaphor of a compass: 'No matter how far the compass travels, it is only going around the point at its center and, similarly, however much men may strive and achieve within the realms of spiritual knowledge, ultimately they are only achieving a better and greater knowledge of themselves (or of the Absolute manifested within themselves), not of any exterior Absolute.'[28] This is indeed very close to the monism of much Eastern thought. Yet the Baha'i position wants to include both the dualist (there are fundamental differences between the human and the divine) and the monist (there is no fundamental difference between the human and the divine). To do this, say the Baha'is, we must give up the rational laws of non-contradiction and the excluded middle. 'Abdu'l-Baha's position seems to be that no absolute answer can be given to the question of the relation between the human and the divine. Both answers are equally correct from their relative viewpoints, even though they appear to be contradictory. The apparent contradiction arises only because of our limited capacity which prevents us from seeing them both as correct. This can be intuited but not known conceptually or logically. Hence the Baha'i position that God is unknowable conceptually. As 'Abdu'l-Baha puts it, 'The Essence of the Divine Entity ... is beyond thought.'[29]

What are the consequences of the Baha'i embrace of theological relativism? First it puts Baha'is in a strong position to relate positively to believers of other religions, for all traditions are seen to be true if only relatively so. Similarly, it means that the revelation of no tradition, including that of the Baha'is, should be judged more valid than any other. This poses a bit of a challenge to the Baha'i doctrine of progressive revelation, which seems to suggest that Baha'u'llah's revelation coming last in the order of the prophets is superior to those revelations that came earlier. However, relativism is seen as applicable to metaphysical truths in each religion, whereas the concept of progressive revelation applies mainly to the social teachings of each faith. The two ideas are therefore viewed as referring to different aspects of the religions' teachings. Momen helpfully shifts the focus of the discussion away from possible conflicts between revelations and their order in time, to relationships. He suggests that in the relative approach to theology our focus is no longer on descriptions or definitions of the divine but on what our relationship with the divine should be, and on the consequences of that relationship. 'The emphasis has shifted from structures to processes and relationships. And therefore ethics comes to the forefront of consideration.'[30] This may offer an explanation for the lack of Baha'i theology on pluralism and its greater focus on social and personal ethics. It is more important, say Baha'is, that actions and intentions are in accordance with divine requirements. When that is the case then one's theology is not so important, since it will be valid only for a particular person with a particular psychological make-up and cultural background.[31]

THE BAHA'I APPROACH TO INTERRELIGIOUS DIALOGUE

Seena Fazel has studied the implications of the Baha'i imperative to foster interreligious dialogue.[32] Baha'u'llah calls on his followers to engage in intimate association and fellowship with believers of all religions so as to promote unity and concord.[33] The purpose of the Baha'i revelation, says Baha'u'llah, is to foster the love, fellowship and unity of all people. Interreligious dialogue on all levels, from institutional to individual, is an important method to be used in fostering unity and peace. While in North America in 1912, 'Abdu'l-Baha stressed the need for theological dialogue: 'All must abandon prejudices and must each go into each other's churches and mosques, for, in all of these worshipping places the Name of God is mentioned.'[34]

Fazel finds five reasons in Baha'i writings as to why interfaith dialogue is emphasized. 1) Knowledge of other religions can aid understanding of Baha'i writings, which are infused with the religious symbolism and imagery of other revelations – especially Islam. This knowledge of other religions can best be gained through dialogue that takes place on a significant rather than superficial level. Dialogue will also enable the Baha'i Faith to work out its theology of other religions. 2) Dialogue can act as a tool to actualize the main aim of the Baha'i Faith, namely, the transformation of world religions so that their sequence, wholeness and unity can be realized. For example, 'Abdu'l-Baha on his trip to America in 1912 challenged a rabbi by saying Jews should reconcile their differences with Christians. And in meetings with Christians he urged them to celebrate the uniqueness of Christ without falling into exclusivism. It is through reaching a deeper understanding of one's own revelation in the context of dialogue that religious differences may be understood and world peace achieved. 3) Dialogue will foster the inner transformation and renewal of the Baha'i Faith. Fazel suggests that a current limitation of the Baha'i Faith is that it is founded too exclusively on concepts arising from the Western religions of Judaism, Christianity and Islam. Baha'i needs tò broaden its base of self-understanding by adapting itself to the worldviews of Eastern and aboriginal religions – and this can be achieved through dialogue. 4) Interreligious dialogue is integral to the realization of the Baha'i goal of world peace. The Baha'i founders put forth a vision of unity in a global community, and this can be fostered through dialogue with the leaders of other religions. 5) An important by-product of interreligious dialogue for Baha'is is that it will help to achieve recognition of the Baha'i Faith as an independent world religion with a contribution to make to the challenges facing humanity today. Such dialogue creates friendships and alliances that help to overcome obstacles to the Baha'i Faith emerging from obscurity and becoming an important player on the world stage. This is a circular situation. Because of its relative smallness and newness, the Baha'i Faith is not always included in interfaith exchanges. By participating in more dialogue with other religions, the Baha'i Faith will achieve more visibility and increase its status in the eyes of many academics and religious leaders – and consequently be invited to participate in more interfaith dialogue events.

Fazel concludes his study by identifying two key benefits of Baha'i engagement in interreligious dialogue. First, Baha'is will gain a deeper understanding of the other religions (and simultaneously of their own). Second, in searching out the deeper mystical unity that underlies all religions, Baha'is may learn from others how to nourish a deeper sense of mystical unity within their own community. Baha'is have tended to focus strongly on the ethical and social teachings of their faith, and they need to recover the essential mystical aspect of their religion and its founder. This would lead to a deeper sense of spirituality and community in Baha'i devotional life. Acquaintance with these qualities in other religions could help Baha'is to become sensitized to these qualities in their own tradition.

CONCLUSION: THE BAHA'I MISSION TO INDIA

We have seen above how the Baha'i Faith intellectually relates itself in very positive ways to the other world religions. By way of conclusion it may be of interest to examine briefly how the Baha'i Faith has put these theological ideas into practice in its expansion into India. William Garlington notes that in the early 1960s Baha'i missionary work in India took a new turn.[35] Earlier missionary efforts over nearly a century had been directed towards urban, well-educated elements of Indian society and required that believers demonstrate knowledge of Baha'i beliefs, laws and administrative structure. By 1960 Baha'i membership in India numbered about one thousand people. However, by 1964 the figure had risen to over 100,000 and by 1973 it was close to 400,000. This sudden increase was due to a change in Baha'i activity to focus on people of low and unscheduled caste in rural villages. The test for membership was simplified to a declared belief in the prophet-founder of the Baha'i Faith, Baha'u'llah.[36] Whereas historically the Baha'i community in India had been more closely allied with Islamic and Zoroastrian cultural elites, the missionaries now decided to use Hindu symbols and the popular devotional practice of *bhajan* singing as a means for spreading the Baha'i Faith.

A *bhajan* is a rhythmic devotional song of a sort long popular in India. It is performed in a group setting; one devotee stands and sings the various verses and the entire group joins in unison to sing the words of the refrain. Since the Baha'i Faith accepts Hinduism as a revealed religion, it was deemed acceptable to use Hindu concepts such as 'Krishna' (the human incarnation of God in the Hindu scripture the *Bhagavad-Gītā*) and to identify them with Baha'u'llah in the words of the *bhajan*. Theologically this move involves identifying the Baha'i concept of a prophet or manifestation of God with the Hindu concept of an *avatāra* or incarnation of God. Although the Baha'i tradition prefers to speak of 'manifestations' rather than 'incarnations' of God, there is evidence that as early as the 1920s Baha'is in India identified Baha'u'llah as an *avatāra* or incarnation. This would seem acceptable to the Baha'i notion that God's revelation needs to be understood in the psychological and cultural context of the believer. Certainly, among the masses in India, the notion of God taking human form – especially as Lord Krishna – to give grace to the believer is very common. Therefore if one wants to use Indian thought forms to communicate the Baha'i message, the identification of Krishna with Baha'u'llah is likely to be effective.

In the Baha'i writings, says Garlington, we find the names of Krishna and Buddha as legitimate manifestations of God.[37] They are both found in Baha'i *bhajans*, where they are identified with Baha'u'llah. For example, one *bhajan*, referring to Baha'u'llah, says, 'He manifested the righteousness of Krishna.'[38]

Another Hindu *avatāra*, Rama, who does not appear in the writings of Baha'u'llah, 'Abdu'l-Baha or Shoghi Effendi, also appears in the Baha'i *bhajans*, usually in close connection with other *avatāras*. One *bhajan* says, 'He [Baha'u'llah] brought the holy promise of Rama; He brought the justice of Krishna.'[39] Garlington notes that the incorporation of Rama as an *avatāra*/manifestation was a natural outgrowth of the teaching mission and may well have been sanctioned by Ruhiyyih Khanum (widow of Shoghi Effendi and a prominent Baha'i) during her trip to India in 1964, when she made reference to Rama alongside other established prophets.[40] Hinduism also has the notion of an *avatāra* yet to come, Kalkin. Baha'i *bhajans* have used the name of Kalkin, joined with the Baha'i idea of manifestations to come, as a way of giving hope to the low castes and tribes of rural India. All of this seems in line with the Baha'i embrace of other religions within the notion of progressive prophetic revelation. One *bhajan* verse effectively sums it up:

> How can I cause awareness of the Gita's prophecies?
> How can I spread the knowledge of the Bible stories?
> In the Qur'ān it says, 'show the light to the world.'
> The essence of all of these I call the path of Baha'i.[41]

Garlington observes that for Baha'is, out of the many scriptures of Hinduism, it is the *Bhagavad-Gītā* that has been taken to be the supreme revelation text of that tradition.

Another problem Baha'i teachers encountered in India, with its long history of Muslim–Hindu hostility, was that the name Baha'u'llah itself carries a Muslim connotation ('Allah' being the Islamic term for God). Thus in many Baha'i *bhajans* the Hindu Sanskrit term 'Bhagavan' ('Lord') was substituted for the Arabic 'Allah'. In popular Hindu usage 'Bhagavan' is used to refer both to God and God's *avatāras* or incarnations (e.g. Krishna). Garlington reports finding *bhajans* reflecting this dual usage: 'Bhagavan has said that he will return in every age to restore righteousness' and 'We must spread the news of Bhagavan Baha.'[42] Garlington notes, 'Baha'u'llah thus becomes Bhagavan Baha, a title no doubt more congenial to the Hindu villager's ear and perhaps more befitting of the kalkin *avatāra*: "Oh sing the praises of Bhagavan Baha, Oh sing the peace message of Bhagavan Baha, Oh manifest today the shelter of Bhagavan Baha".'[43]

In concluding his analysis of the considerable Baha'i success in India since the adoption of the new approach in the 1960s, Garlington comments that this approach is culturally inclusive, rather than triumphalist, in the way the *bhajans* have communicated the essential Baha'i beliefs.[44] This approach is not just strategic for the Baha'i mission but embodies the Baha'i concepts of the validity of all revelations and all prophets. Willingness to extend the concept of prophet/manifestation, so central to the Baha'i tradition, so that it can be identified with the Hindu incarnation of God, the *avatāra*, shows that the Baha'i principle of relativism can be seen in practice. Although this clearly demonstrates that the Baha'i approach to other religions is significantly different from that of Islam (where such a move could not take place), it does raise the question of why a missionary thrust such as the mission to India is necessary. It could call into question the Baha'i Faith's description of itself as a 'pluralist' rather than 'inclusive' religion in its approach to other traditions. One could also ask how such missionary activity is reconciled with the Baha'i theology of interreligious dialogue, which would seem to propose trusting conversation aimed at deepening the spiritual experience of each participant within their own tradition, rather than the goal of conversion. Should Baha'i success in India continue, Baha'is may one day find themselves in the situation that Christians in India currently experience – of being criticized by Hindus (often of the more fundamentalist kind) who see missionary activity that leads to conversions, especially among the poorly educated lower castes, as a sheep-stealing exercise. As Christians have discovered, such charges, when made publicly in the media, can result in a significant setback to dialogue between the religions involved. For Baha'is, the question may become: are greater numbers as a result of missionary conversion activities more important than progress in interreligious dialogue in actualizing the Baha'i vision for the world? Or is there a way to do both honestly and sensitively? This is a challenge for future Baha'i theology and practice – as it is for every religion that engages in both missionary conversion activity and interreligious dialogue.

5 RELIGIOUS PLURALISM AND HINDUISM

Unlike the Western traditions, Hinduism does not have an easily identifiable beginning. Although records of its early history are not available, it seems clear that the Hindu religion developed in the same fertile soil that nourished Jainism and Buddhism. All three religions share the presuppositions that *karma* (the mental trace or seed left behind by each thought or action that predisposes one to a similar thought or action in the future; volition; action), *samsāra* (the world of phenomena, which is incessantly in motion or flux and of which rebirth is an aspect) and *jīva* (the empirical self; the individual soul) are *anādi* (beginningless) and that by following a particular spiritual path (*mārga*) release can be realized.[1] Each religion posed a different understanding of the divine or absolute to be experienced at the end of the spiritual path. In the Brāhmanical tradition, reality was conceived of as 'pure being', by which was meant that reality was a pure unchanging substance, a concept expressed in the *ātma* doctrine of the *Upaniṣads*. The Buddhists took the opposite position, the *anātma* doctrine of the Buddha, and perceived of reality as momentary (*kṣaṇika*), unique (*svalakṣaṇa*), unitary (*dharmamātra*) and in constant flux. Jainism seems to have taken the middle path between these two opposing views by describing reality as giving equal reality to its substance and to its modes – to 'being' and 'becoming'. T. R. V. Murti suggests that the Jaina view 'may be said to constitute the third stream of Indian Philosophy – lying mid-way between the two extremes'.[2] It was un-Brāhmanical because it accepted a changing *ātman*; and it was un-Buddhistic because it accepted a permanent entity (*ātman*) as well as change. Murti suggests that the Jaina tradition, in its middle position, found favour with neither of the other traditions and as a result has had comparatively little influence on the development of Indian philosophy.[3] But the Brāhmanical and Buddhist traditions to a large extent shaped each other through mutual opposition and debate.

P. T. Raju argues that two similar opposing trends can be found at the beginnings of Western thought: the Orphic, concerned with the human being's inner spirit, and the Olympic, concerned with outward nature.[4] The two are balanced in Plato, but the latter becomes dominant in Western thought through Aristotle while the former is passed on through the minor tradition of Plotinus and the mystics. Although it has yet to be established whether these two trends of thought were born in India and carried to the West, or vice versa, or whether they spontaneously arose in both places, the two trends do seem fundamental to religious experience. Hinduism, as understood through the Brāhmanical tradition, claims for itself revelation of the identification of the inner self – the unchanging pure being (*ātman*) – with ultimate reality, the absolute, the divine.[5] The *Upaniṣads*, which are mostly assigned to periods pre-dating Mahāvīra and Buddha, contain discussions on *jīva*, *karma* and *saṁsāra* but focus on knowledge of the inner spirit and the means of its realization. The result of this inward search is the Hindu belief in one divine reality that can phenomenalize in many different forms. The Hindu typically sees the different sects within Hinduism and the other religions as different manifestations of the one, external, divine reality. Because all manifestations lead back to the same source, there should be no conflict among traditions. Cooperation, community and mutual respect should prevail among all believers. Let us examine the way in which this philosophic perspective has functioned in the encounter of Hinduism with other religions.

THE CLASSICAL PERIOD

According to the Hindu view, all aspects of the world come from a common ancestry. 'There is of necessity some sort of equivalence between sounds, forms, numbers, colors, ideas, as there is also between the abstractions of the subtle and transcendent worlds on one side and the forms of the perceptible universe on the other... The whole of Nature (*prakṛti*) is but the symbol of a higher reality.'[6] From the viewpoint of the perceiver it is rather like looking at a piece of sculpture from different angles. The whole form can be grasped only when the sculpture has been looked at from different perspectives: the front, the back, the sides. Although each of these views is different from the others and although some aspects of what is seen and described from the different angles may seem incompatible, even from these contradictory reports a reliable overall description of the sculpture can be reached, which could not be obtained from only one angle. In the Hindu view the various religions are understood as different and sometimes conflicting perspectives on the one divine reality. In fact divinity is sometimes described as 'that in which opposites coexist'.[7] According to this logic Hinduism should be tolerant and open to other religions because the more aspects of the divine we can perceive, the more complete our understanding will be. Even within Hinduism broad tolerance is required to include all denominations (e.g. Vaiṣṇavism and Śaivism) and all points of view (*darśana*), from the experimental or logical perspective of the Nyāya-Vaiśeṣika to the supra-mental psychology of Saṅkhya-Yoga and the dialectical and metaphysical outlook of Vedānta. Within these Hindu viewpoints, the conceptions vary – according to the presuppositions of the various schools – from atheistic to pantheistic, to deistic, to monistic and to mystical. Each of these is true within its own perspective; that is, each viewpoint is a logical conclusion based on the presuppositions of its own perspective. The fact that the truths expressed by each viewpoint may conflict is to be expected because each viewpoint is only a partial perspective of the divine. The aim of scholars within each view is to expand their understanding to the utmost limit in a particular direction. The builders of the various *darśanas* within Hinduism are described as seers of divine reality (*ṛṣi*). All *ṛṣis* see the whole of reality but due to the necessity of human finitude they have to choose one form (out of the many possible forms) through which to convey their revelatory vision to others. For classical Hinduism, other religions could be understood as additional visions of the same divine reality; new *ṛṣis* such as Moses, Jesus, Muhammad and Buddha could be seen as describing new and varying perspectives of the one divine.

Religious seekers start with whatever path matches their sensibilities and is within their reach. Since all paths are different views of the divine, it would not seem to matter which path is selected. Theoretically, all paths eventually reach the same goal. Alain Danielou writes, 'Persecution or proselytization of other religious groups, however strange their beliefs may seem to him, can never be a defensible attitude from the point of view of the Hindus.'[8] However, classical Hinduism does seem to exert a qualifying clause. Although each of the religions moves one towards the goal of release from *karma-samsāra* and union with the divine, only with the aid of the revelation of the Vedas can one go the entire way to complete release. Raju offers a reasonable explanation as to how this Vedic criterion came to be the norm for Hinduism:

> Vedic religion, after the development of its own inwardness, spread by inwardizing and incorporating all other religions with which it came into contact. All of them took pride in tracing their origins to the Vedas and the Upaniṣads. Some of them, Śaivism, Saktism and Vaiṣṇavism, had their own scriptures called the *Āgamas*, to which they give even now as high a place as to the Vedas. Yet they later began writing commentaries on the original Upaniṣads and wrote their own Upaniṣads and added them to the list. Thus both in the past and present, no religion can be alien to the Indian, provided it emphasizes the truth of inwardness. The Vedic or the Upaniṣadic tradition in philosophy is the tradition of the truth of inwardness.[9]

The growth and spread of Jainism and Buddhism produced a Hindu intensification of 'inwardness', as Raju puts it, of the *ātma* tradition in opposition to the *anātma* tradition of Buddhism. The inward emphasis of Vedic religion did not result in a lack of attention to outward forms. Within the Vedic tradition, social duties were required, and the way to tread the path of inward realization was carefully marked out through the order of castes and the *āśramas* or stages of life. The duties accorded to each caste and allotted to each stage of life were meant to discipline the individual and lead by stages to the goal of inner spiritual realization. Thus within Hinduism both a structure to maintain and regulate society and the opportunity for inner spiritual realization were provided. To a large extent the Hindu social and ceremonial ordering of society was adopted by Indian Buddhism.

The challenge of Buddhism not only produced an intensification of the Hindu *ātma* emphasis but, in line with Brāhmanical philosophy, all that was considered new and good in Buddhism was quietly absorbed. Gauḍapāda (seventh century CE), the teacher of Śaṅkara, wrote his *kārikās* on the *Māṇḍūkya Upaniṣad* and in them incorporated the best methods of Buddhist philosophy while retaining the Vedic content.[10] Śaṅkara systematized the developments of Gauḍapāda and others into the Advaita Vedānta school. Śaṅkara also travelled the length and breadth of India debating with Buddhists[11] 'and apparently leaving behind monastic orders [again borrowing from Buddhist practice] in the north at Badrinath, in the south at Sringeri, in the east at Puri, and in the west at Dwaraka'.[12] However, Hindu practice differed significantly from the Buddhist (and Christian) in that each branch monastery maintained autonomy. Buddhist monastic practice, modified for increased autonomy and flexibility, has played an increasingly central role in Hinduism through the medieval period to the present day. As David Miller argues, it may make more sense to think of medieval and modern Hinduism in terms of a *sampradāya* or monastic teaching tradition with a *guru* as its core rather than to conceive of it as sectarian groups classified according to particular deities.[13]

The absorptive tendency was also evident in the development of the new form of *bkakti* or devotional Hinduism. Buddha was absorbed and made one of the *avatāras* or incarnations of Viṣṇu. The account of this event in the *Viṣṇu Purāṇa* reads as follows:

> When the mighty Vishnu heard their request [the request of the gods to be protected from the Daityas (Asuras) or evil ones], he emitted from his body an illusory form, which he gave to the gods, and thus spake: 'This deceptive vision [Buddha] shall wholly beguile the Daityas, so that, being led astray from the path of the Vedas, they may be put to death; for all gods, demons, or others, who shall be opposed to the authority of the Vedas shall perish by my might, whilst exercised for the preservation of the world. Go then, and fear not; let this delusive vision precede you; it shall this day be of great service to you, oh gods!'[14]

The *Viṣṇu Purāṇa* goes on to recount how Viṣṇu, in the form of Buddha, succeeds in seducing all the Daityas from their study of the Vedas and their proper social duties by promising them a secret path to liberation and teaching the equal truth of contradictory tenets. When the gods see that the Daityas have given up the Vedas, the only true religious armour, a battle begins. The gods gain an easy victory, and the Daityas are destroyed.[15] The followers of the Vedas are purified and renewed and the heresy of Buddhism – having served its divine purpose – perishes within India. A similar interpretation is offered in the *Agni Purāṇa*.[16] Buddha is absorbed into the Hindu tradition, but the representation and interpretation of Buddhist believers are certainly not positive. The negative interpretation of these believers may be linked to the persecution of Buddhists. A. L. Basham gives historical examples of this persecution – in the sixth century, for example, the Huṇa king Mihirakula destroyed Buddhist monasteries and killed monks.[17] Until recently, however, the Hindu response to other religions has been marked in general by peaceful absorption rather than the harsh opposition characterized in the above *Purāṇic* account.

The *Purāṇic* account of Buddha as *avatāra* again highlights the key position of the Vedas in Hinduism. Hindus consider the Vedas to be eternal, impersonal (not composed by any person or god) and the most perfect revelation of divine truth. From the Vedas comes all knowledge of *dharma* (law, especially moral law or duty; righteousness, the inner principle of religion), and without the Vedas release (*mokṣa*) is not possible.[18] This raises the question of how Hindus view the scriptures of other religions. In the case of the Jainas and Buddhists this question is not hard to answer. Since both Jainas and Buddhists reject the concept of scriptural revelation and treat the teachings of Mahāvīra and Buddha as examples to be tested out and proven for oneself, it is quite natural for the Hindus simply to reject such teachings in relation to the revealed Vedas.

During the classical period there is an interesting case of pluralism within Hinduism itself in relation to the Vedas. How are different texts such as the Epics and *Purāṇas* to be related to the Vedas? The Hindu tradition solved the problem by giving such texts the status of secondary revelation – of re-revealing the truth of the Vedas in a form more suited to the increased *karma* of the age. The Epics and *Purāṇas* add nothing new, but, as in the *Bhagavad-Gītā*, they represent the original Vedic revelation in simpler forms such as stories and historic events. The overriding principle seems to be that of continuity based on the Vedas, a continuity that runs through changing times and conditions.[19] The way this principle operates in Hinduism is that scholars write commentaries that elucidate teachings inherent in earlier texts so as to establish an unbroken series that reaches backwards in time and necessarily ends (or begins) at the Vedas. Perhaps this principle of continuity can somehow be applied by Hinduism to scriptures of other revealed religions (i.e. Christianity and Islam).

Another perspective on the response to pluralism can be found in the classical Hindu treatment of evil. In her study of evil in Hindu thought, Wendy O'Flaherty notes that early Vedic religion largely ignores (rather than denying) the more tragic aspects of life.[20] Dating from a later period, the *Upaniṣads* pay more attention to the evil and suffering in life. Next, the Epics and *Purāṇas* attempt to integrate the evil in life with the positive goals of the Vedic view of life. O'Flaherty sees this changing approach to evil as having developed in interaction with Buddhism.

The Vedic approach, with its doctrine of *svadharma*, assumes that all roles, good and evil, are necessary for the variety that constitutes society as a whole. Although the individual has no choice of roles, society is arranged in such a way that the contribution of each person is important to the total mosaic, and some of these individual roles, as parts of the whole, necessarily involve suffering and evil. O'Flaherty suggests that Buddhism, the *Upaniṣads* and *bhakti* challenge the above approach by emphasizing individual moral responsibility and an individual spiritual goal (release from *karma-saṁsāra*) rather than the *svadharma* of the earlier view. She writes, 'Under the influence of Buddhism, the Upaniṣads and the bhakti cults, the individual is given a choice of action, freedom from the structures of caste; instead of creating his life from *objets trouvés*, he may choose his medium and free himself from karma.'[21] Of course the choice is not entirely free. In Buddhism the choice is conditioned by past *karma*, and in *bhakti* theory God is often seen as choosing the worshipper; yet in both of these systems individuals can consciously change their lives in terms of action.

The one aspect of Hindu doctrine that O'Flaherty leaves out of the above analysis is the notion of 'stages of life'. Part of the distinction made between the Vedic and the free-choice approach may be removed to some extent by seeing *svadharma* as a required duty during the first two stages of life. When the duties of the student and householder stages have been met (and here there seems little room for individual free choice), then in the last two stages one has individual freedom to pursue spiritual development towards release. It does not yet seem clear whether the idea of the individual freedom of the last two stages comes from Buddhism, is original to Hinduism, or is a shared development. O'Flaherty is correct in her observation that in the *svadharma* context evil is defined as the threat of impurity, defilement, mixing of castes, and so on.[22] She is also right in pointing out that the *svadharma* notion of wholeness never allows evil (impurity) to become an autonomous principle or to be dispensed with, for it is always regarded as functioning in the service of purity. This classical perspective does seem to contrast with the *bhakti* viewpoints that developed in response to Buddhism and the Buddhist challenge to the caste system. As O'Flaherty writes,

> The *svadharma* view of orthodox Hinduism is an ethical system based on the pluralism inherent in the social system of caste (the whole goal is the preservation of social and moral balance); the *bhakti* philosophies deny

the validity of the caste system in favour of a more universalistic and apparently more individualistic ethical system, whose goal is salvation.[23]

Taken as a whole, Hinduism does not see these different philosophic perspectives as exclusive but rather as different viewpoints on reality. Thus it is possible for Hinduism to imply that evil in human life is necessary and desirable and yet to assume at the same time a universally valid good towards which all humankind should strive. As O'Flaherty states, '"Evil" must be accepted, but "good" must be sought; these views together provide a working solution to the problem of evil, a framework in which mankind as a whole, and each individual, may function in the face of an ultimately insoluble problem.'[24] True to its fundamental philosophic and religious insight of diversity as the manifestation of unity, Hinduism demonstrates its ability to cope with the problem of evil in relation to good – perhaps the most difficult paradox in life. Analysis of the problem of evil leads the seeker back to the basic and unifying source. As one text says of this quest and source,

> There are many religions – that of the Vedas, Sāṅkhya, Yoga, Pāśupatas, Vaiṣṇavas – and one person chooses this path, another person another path; because of the variety of preferences, favouring a straight path or a winding, you are the goal for men, as the ocean is the goal for all rivers.[25]

However, the idea that all paths lead to the same goal was present more in theory than in practice in classical Hinduism. Debates between rival philosophical schools were very serious affairs, for matters of right or wrong knowledge regarding how to reach liberation were seen to be at stake. In the minds of these philosophers, each school with its different path to liberation was exclusive of the others. You were either right or wrong in your knowledge and interpretation of the Vedas. Debates occurred not only through commentaries but also in public, and, according to tradition, the loser was required to accept the victor's point of view – to 'convert' to the opponent's path to realization of the divine.

HINDUISM'S ENCOUNTER WITH ISLAM

Arabs visited India long before the birth of Muhammad, and small coastal Muslim communities seem to have existed from the eighth century CE. Basham states that the Māppilā (Moplah) community of Malabar is descended from people who settled or were converted there before the Muslim invasion of India. But there is no clear evidence of any influence of Islam on Hinduism until after the Muslim conquest.[26] It was the second wave of Islamic expansion that brought the first Muslim invaders into India to do battle with Hindu forces. In 711–12, Muslims captured and established rule over Deval, a port near modern Karachi, and Aror, north of Hyderabad.[27] However, it was not until the ninth and tenth centuries that the full Muslim invasion was launched and powerful Islamic dynasties obtained control of a large part of India. Ṣūfīs, the missionaries of Islam, soon arrived to take up residence at court, and the encounter with Hinduism began in earnest. On the Islamic side the immediate effect was an infusion of new life from Hindu mystical religion into the ṣūfī tradition, which had been experiencing a period of stagnation. There does not seem to have been any comparable immediate effect on the Hindu side. Even though Hindus were given high places in the Islamic bureaucracy and Hindu scholars were summoned to dialogue with Muslims, Hindus apparently kept their religion apart from Islamic influence. The society seems to have been dominated by a pattern of cultural and religious segregation.

Like Buddhism and Jainism before it, Islam attacked Hinduism by breaking down caste. Muslims proclaimed, 'Before Allah all men were equal; in the sphere of religion there was no privilege of birth.'[28] This anticaste emphasis did reinforce and provide a point of contact with the Hindu *bhakti* movements. From the thirteenth to the eighteenth centuries a long succession of *bhakti* saints and prophets strove for the purification of Hindu religion. Many of them were converts from Islam to Hinduism.[29] Another point of mutual reinforcement between *bhakti* Hindu movements and the Islam of India was the production of vernacular religious literature. One such *bhakti* poet-prophet was a low-caste Hindu called Nāmdev (*c.* 1300). The fundamental tenets in Nāmdev's teaching were the worshipper's dependence on God and the necessity of personal repentance. An early experience of sin and forgiveness gave Nāmdev great confidence in the universal presence, forgiveness and love of God. Nāmdev found much in his religious approach that parallelled Islam, including rejection of the futile devotional service to religious idols. Referring to an idol, he asks, 'Why bathe it when God was in the multitudinous species of the water; why weave a garland of flowers which the bee had smelled, when God was already in the bee?'[30]

The rejection of caste, the use of the common language, and Nāmdev's stress on sin, repentance and the rejection of idolatry lay the groundwork for attempts at drawing together Hinduism and Islam. Two notable attempts demand mention: that made by Kabir from a basically Hindu perspective, and that made by Akbar from a basically Muslim perspective. Like Nāmdev, Kabir (c. 1500) was another poet and singer of *bhakti*. Born the son of a Muslim weaver, Kabir was raised in a Muslim house and was constantly surrounded by Islam.[31] The most authoritative record of his teaching is entitled the *Vījak*, which was apparently dictated by Kabir to a disciple named Bhagwan Das.[32] Like Nāmdev, Kabir shunned outward symbols of religious life including caste, idols and pilgrimage austerities, and he taught in a common language, Hindi. Kabir was influenced by teachers of both the Hindu and Islamic communities, and he had very close contact with the ṣūfīs.[33] He was a tireless critic of empty formalism in either religion. In Kabir's view, 'The same God is sought after in all religions which differ only in naming Him.'[34] This makes all religious quarrels – those between Hindus and Muslims and those among all other religions – futile. Kabir's religious prescription is that every person must give up ego and vanity and consider the other as one's own self.

Another aspect of Kabir's appeal was that he did not believe in ascetic denial, but, rather, that by living a natural life, in a pure manner, one can carry on one's *sādhanā* (spiritual discipline leading to release or enlightenment). God and the universe, he says, are within one's own self.[35] And the way to know that God who is within is to repeat God's name until one 'becometh as he'.[36] Like Islam, Kabir's vision sees everywhere the action of a divine revealer using the Logos or Word as an educative and devotional instrument. Kabir, in line with the Grammarian Bhartṛhari's philosophy of language,[37] takes the Word to be the foundation of all spiritual experience and the chanting of the Word to be a spiritual discipline. J. Estlin Carpenter writes that 'Kabir says: "Listen to the Word, the Truth, which is your essence."'[38] Kabir's emphasis upon the Word provides a natural bridge between Islam and Hinduism. Both traditions treat the scriptural Word as divine, eternal and powerful. But in terms of language, in terms of his use of a vernacular, Kabir's Hinduism is more like ṣūfism than like the orthodox Grammarian tradition that used classical Sanskrit. As Kabir puts it, 'Sanskrit is the water of the well, while the spoken languages (*bhāṣā*) are water of the running stream.'[39] Anchoring himself in the Sanskrit tradition, influenced strongly by Islamic ṣūfism, Kabir gave a fresh expression to Hinduism in the Hindi tongue of northern India.

In contrast to Kabir, Akbar seems to have had little in the way of a lasting encounter with Hinduism. Kabir was predominantly Hindu; Akbar was basically a Muslim. Akbar's wives practised their Hindu rituals unimpeded, and distinguished Hindu scholars instructed the emperor, but apparently neither had a significant impact on Akbar. Hindu scholars, joining in the general adulation of the emperor, found prophecies of his kingship in the *Laws of Manu* and proclaimed him an *avatāra*.[40] Akbar attempted to transcend the conflicts and inadequacies of both Islam and Hinduism by creating his own religion, the Din-i-Ilāhī or 'Divine Monotheism'. Akbar's religion gained few converts and did not last beyond his death. However, Tulsī Das, a poet of Akbar's reign, had a very strong effect on the Hinduism of northern India. As a boy, Tulsī Das learned Persian and thus received some influence from Islam. His major contribution to modern Hinduism was to revivify it, in the face of the Islamic challenge, by rewriting Vālmīki's *Rāmāyana* in Hindi as the 'Lake of Rāma's Deeds'. For all practical purposes this became and remains the scripture of the majority of Hindus in northern India.

P. T. Raju claims that the Muslim invasion's main legacy to Hinduism was enervation.[41] When the Muslims destroyed Buddhist universities and libraries, much orthodox Hindu literature also perished. However, vernacular books held by Hindu scholars tended to be more diffused and better hidden and thus the simple vernacular *bhakti* religion became dominant.

HINDUISM AND THE SIKHS

Nānak (b. 1469), the founder of Sikhism, wrote in Hindi and criticized the caste system and idol worship.[42] He expounded a system of worship that was a synthesis of ṣūfism, Vaiṣṇava *bhakti* and ideas associated with the Nath *yogis*.[43] The strongest interaction between Sikhism and Hinduism occurred during the period 1708–1849 when the Sikh religion experienced a period of decline. The absorptive power of Hinduism asserted itself in response to the inner weakness of Sikhism. During this period there was a tendency among Sikhs to abandon their customs and symbols and to adopt orthodox Hindu practices.[44] Some Sikhs even proclaimed themselves to be a special variety of Hindu.[45] However, during the nineteenth century there was a Sikh resurgence, two aspects of which have been the sending out of missionaries and the conversion of Hindus. Within the Punjab itself, Sikh and Punjabi Hindus share a common history of persecution, social patterns and religious tradition. N. G. Barrier adds that 'Ārya Samājists with whom educated Sikhs initially identified and co-operated insisted that Sikhs were Hindu.'[46] But a decade after the introduction in 1877 of the Ārya Samāj in the Punjab, Sikh cooperation turned to hostility. Quickly the Ārya Samāj became identified as the primary enemy of Sikhism. Battles over Sikh–Hindu relations, which have political overtones in the Punjab, continued into the twentieth century.[47]

Nānak, more clearly than Kabir, did attempt to fuse and transcend both Hindu and Muslim elements in his teachings.[48] But the background of his wisdom seems primarily Hindu.[49] God is at once the formless Absolute (*nirguṇa*) and the manifested reality (*saguṇa*). Following Kabir, he emphasizes the confession of sin and repentance. Humane and vigorous activity is demanded of all. Certainly Hinduism had much influence upon Sikhism. Perhaps the major impact of Sikhism on Hinduism was that it helped to break down the Hindu system of barriers of race and caste.

HINDUISM AND CHRISTIANITY

There is much speculation about the early encounters of Hinduism with Christianity.[50] According to the fourth-century Christian historian Eusebius, St Thomas was allotted a mission territory reaching across north-west India as far as the Indus, although no definite trace of Christianity can be found in that region. Catholic tradition, however, continues to connect Thomas with India, and Gregory, the Bishop of Tours from 573 to 593, mentions that Thomas's relics had rested in an elaborate church and monastery in India. Marco Polo (*c.* 1290) locates this church in Mylapore, just south of Madras. Little is known of the connections of this church with St Thomas, but excavations across the Adyar river from the church turned up a piece of granite adorned with a cross and inscription. A similar cross and inscription have been found in a church at Travancore in Kerala. The Persian language of the inscription suggests the existence in the seventh or eighth century of a Persian, perhaps Nestorian, Christian community in India. During that time, however, there seems to have been little, if any, Christian impact upon Hinduism.

It was with the arrival of British and Portuguese traders in India in the seventeenth century that the way was paved for Christian missionaries from Europe.[51] As early as 1573 Akbar had summoned Jesuit Christians from Goa to appear before him and take part in theological debate, but it was not until the Moghul empire collapsed and the British took control to protect their trading interests that the Christian missionaries arrived in force. British rulers wanted to govern the Hindus according to Hindu law and religion, and so they established the Asiatic Society of Bengal for the study of Indian philosophy and literature. Christian missionaries also began taking an interest in Hindu thought – mainly to be able to criticize it and gain converts.[52] The cumulative effort of these and other activities produced the Hindu Renaissance, which aimed at reforming and rationalizing Indian religion in various ways.

Rāmmohun Roy (1772–1833) set out to recover from obscurity the ideas of Vedic Hinduism, which had become neglected in favour of shallow idol worship. Roy was deeply interested in the religious teachings of the Christian missionaries. He read the New Testament and extracted those ethical teachings that he felt were universally consistent with the laws of nature. With the intention of improving the hearts and minds of his fellow Hindus, he translated these extracts into Sanskrit as the *Precepts of Jesus*.[53] Because he had rejected the divinity of Christ, Roy caused an uproar among the Calcutta Christian missionaries. After more than three years of debate with the Christians, Roy began to write in 'vindication of the Hindu religion against the attacks of Christian missionaries'.[54] In public letters he effectively argued that Hinduism is not inferior to Christianity (as the missionaries were suggesting) but that the mysteries of each religion equally transcend human understanding so that one cannot be preferred to the other.[55]

Roy's programme of incorporating the ethical teachings of Jesus into Hinduism resulted in a campaign against the Hindu practice of *sati* (widow burning) – a practice that finds no basis in the *Dharma Śāstra* or Hindu law code. In opposing the practice, Roy argued against the attitude, prevalent in the Hinduism of his day, that women were 'subject to passions', 'unworthy of trust' and 'lacking in intelligence'. He pointed to the ability of women, if given the opportunity, to succeed in education, spiritual discipline, virtue and so on.[56] Roy's views on women exemplify the way in which he 'carefully distinguished between English errors, and defended Hinduism against the criticism of missionaries as he challenged the orthodox to abandon its excrescences'.[57] In order to defend Hinduism against Christian charges that it was a pagan and idolatrous religion, Roy and his colleagues set out to reform it. The Brāhmo Samāj was formed for this purpose. Its goal was to 'purify Hinduism and immunize it against the Christian ideas and practices'.[58] This strategy, initiated by Rāmmohun Roy, was passed to Keshub Chunder Sen and then to Dayānanda Sarasvatī. But before moving on to examine each of these Hindu reformers, it is worth noting the role played by Roy in the introduction of English into Hindu education.

It was Roy's view that the only way to modernize Hindus was to make English the language used in their education. He opposed British attempts to impose traditional Sanskrit education and instead argued effectively for teaching modern Western knowledge through the medium of English.[59] The subsequent emphasis on English and lack of stress on Sanskrit have had an impact on Hinduism that has yet to be evaluated. Certainly it turned the minds of young Indians to the West and away from the traditional wisdom of Hindu Sanskrit texts.

Keshub Chunder Sen (1838–84) was willing to go much further than Rāmmohun Roy in appropriating Christianity. Indeed in the last years of his life he did something reminiscent of Akbar – he experimented in synthesizing elements from the major world religions. W. T. De Bary writes, 'Although he borrowed devotional and yogic practices from Hinduism, he drew even more heavily on Christian teachings and practices.'[60] Sen went to such extremes that he was virtually excommunicated from Hinduism, and his conversion to Christianity seemed imminent for years. Whereas Roy had accepted only the ethical teachings of Jesus, Keshub embraced Christ as the fulfilment of Hinduism's devotional strivings. He propounded that Christ, the apostles and the gospel were Asiatic in nature and concluded that 'in Christ, Europe and Asia, the East and the West, may learn to find harmony and unity'.[61] Furthermore, Keshub thought that Christianity, Hinduism and Islam could coalesce. He thought that the resulting new religion would both sustain India and lead to a worldwide spiritual community. The Hindu religious genius, in continuity with the Old and New Testament revelations, would, he felt, be able to reconcile all conflicting religions.

> How the Hindu absorbs the Christian; how the Christian assimilates the Hindu! Cultivate this communion, my brethren, and continually absorb all that is good and noble in each other. Do not hate, do not exclude others, as the sectarians do, but include and absorb all humanity and all truth.[62]

While Chunder Sen was preaching the one extreme of a Christian–Hindu–Islamic universal religion in Bengal, an opposing viewpoint was being taught by a stern ascetic Hindu in northern India. Dayānanda Sarasvatī (1824–83) was also an ardent reformer, but he wanted to root out all non-Vedic influences upon Hinduism: 'Standing foursquare on the authority of the Vedas, he fearlessly denounced the evils of post-Vedic Hinduism.'[63] Early in life Dayānanda learned Sanskrit, and at age fourteen, revolted by the idol worship around him, he ran away from home and became a *sannyasī*. He was taught complete reverence for the Vedas and disdain for all later texts. He devoted his life to lecturing on the exclusive authority of the Vedas.

Dayānanda's approach was to debate with those he disagreed with. Hindus were attacked for their practices that, Dayānanda argued, could not be supported from the Vedas: for instance, idol worship, untouchability, arranged marriages, the subjugation of women, and the restriction of the study of the Vedas to brahmins. Caste, he said, should be decided functionally in accordance with one's merits. Speaking like a biblical prophet, Dayānanda attacked the immoral living of a prince – an action that cost him his life. Because of the fervour of his reforms and preaching, he was called 'the Luther of India'. His followers are called the Ārya Samāj, a group that became especially strong in the Punjab, and now, with the emigrations from India to many countries, has spread around the world.[64]

Dayānanda's approach to other religions and other groups within Hinduism was aggressive and militant. This marked a considerable change from the traditional Hindu attitudes of passive tolerance for all other beliefs. Dayānanda's approach to Christianity was to engage a minister in debate and to demonstrate the logical inconsistencies of Christian belief.[65] Dayānanda devoted careful attention to Islam, reading the Qur'ān in translation and formulating his objections to each passage. The conclusion of his study was that 'God was presented in the Qur'ān as a being whose qualities were unworthy of human worship'.[66] Islam, he argued, lacks a valid basis, whereas the Veda was the firm foundation for true religion.

> Such teachings [Islam] deserve to be utterly discarded. Such a book, such a prophet and such a religion do nothing but harm. The world would be better off without them. Wise men would do well to discard a religion so absurd and accept the Vedic faith which is absolutely free from error.[67]

One branch of Dayānanda's followers, under the leadership of Pandit Lekh Ram, devoted their energies to open conflict with Islam. Their goal was to obtain Hindu converts. A system of specially educated paid preachers (*up-deshaks*) was established for the purpose of proselytism.[68] Dayānanda's militant response to other religions, especially Islam, has helped to fan the hostility between Muslims and Hindus and has also been a contributing factor in the development of Hindu nationalism.[69] Apparent adoption of some Christian practices is evident in the move of the Ārya Samāj away from the traditional Hindu tolerance of other religions to the *śuddhi* or conversion movement of the 1920s.[70] This led to the outbreak of Hindu–Muslim communal riots, which continue to recur in northern India.

If Dayānanda attempted to relate to Christianity by taking over its fundamentalist and missionary thrust, Sarvepalli Radhakrishnan made the opposite move of seeking out the universalist aspects of Christianity that would be contiguous with the Vedāntic teachings of Hinduism. Radhakrishnan represents the response of orthodox Hinduism to the challenge of Christianity and the modern West. He argues that Hinduism and the Vedas are still the ultimate truth of religion, but a truth that can be universally accepted by all. He has been described as a 'liaison officer' between India and the West.[71] Certainly his appointment to the Spalding Chair of Eastern Religions and Ethics at Oxford and his lectures there in 1936–8 have made a considerable contribution to the West's understanding of Hinduism.[72] Perhaps because of his time at Oxford, Radhakrishnan is very aware of the challenges of modern religious pluralism. As he states, 'Neither a contented fatalism nor religious expectancy nor reversions to the past can give meaning to a world which is in search of its soul.'[73] The foundations of the past no longer seem secure; everything is changing. This should not depress us. Great periods of human history have always been marked by doubts and the infusion of foreign influences, including influences from other religions. Consequently, suggests Radhakrishnan, perhaps the difficulties of the modern West, which was inspired by Christianity, can be helped by the infusion of some wisdom from the East. In particular it is the Indian rational approach and emphasis on individual experience – rather than belief in an objectified deity – that is especially suited to the needs of modern-day religion.[74] He states,

> Real religion can exist without a definite conception of the deity but not without a distinction between the spiritual and the profane ...
>
> Religion is not so much a revelation to be attained by us in faith as an effort to unveil the deepest layers of man's being and get into enduring contact with them.[75]

With this Vedāntic conception of religion as a basis, Radhakrishnan presents an approach that he feels can be acceptable to Christians, Buddhists and all other traditions. In many of his lectures given after 1938, he sought to demonstrate this approach, particularly with regard to Christianity.

In Radhakrishnan's view the different religions must develop the spirit of mutual comprehension that characterized Hinduism even in its earliest age. The Indus Valley excavations have produced evidence strongly suggesting that as early as 1500 BCE four different groups coexisted in that area.[76] In the Ṛg Veda there is evidence of conflict between many groups, Aryan, Dravidian and aboriginal, but there is also a resolution that absorbed aspects of each. This resolution and acceptance of other cults are explained as follows: 'The real is one, the learned call it by various names, Agni, Yama, Mātariśvan.'[77] The Upaniṣads give further development to the same view. Brahman is one; the different deities are merely manifestations of the various aspects of Brahman.[78] Radhakrishnan ascribes the same attributes of the one and the many to Buddha. A Buddha is one who has the vision of the whole, whereas members of the various religions are each attached to their own partial views. Within Hinduism this attitude is given explicit statement in the Bhagavad Gītā: the divine accepts those coming towards divinity in the paths of the different religions, and in his supreme vision Arjuna sees the different deities within the boundless form of the divine.[79] Hinduism, says Radhakrishnan, has practised what it has preached. Christians, Jews, Parsees and Muslims have all lived in Hindu India for hundreds of years in an atmosphere of tolerance and religious freedom. Occasional outbursts of Hindu militancy and intolerance are, as interpreted by Radhakrishnan, imitations of Islam and Christianity provoked by those very religions.[80] Because of its tolerant attitude, Hinduism itself has become a mosaic of almost all the types and states of religious aspiration and endeavour: 'It has adapted itself with infinite grace to every human need and it has not shrunk from the acceptance of every aspect of God conceived by man, and yet it has preserved its unity by interpreting the different historical forms as modes, emanations, or aspects of the Supreme.'[81] Radhakrishnan's claim is that no other religion with the exception of Buddhism, which he aggregates with Hinduism, has this genius for religious diversity and unity which makes it the prototypal answer for the modern challenge of religious pluralism. The attitude of the cultivated Hindu to other forms of religion is one of sympathy and respect.

The reason that Hinduism can be so tolerant of other religions is that it assumes religion is a matter of personal realization. 'Creeds and dogmas, words and symbols have only instrumental value . . . The name by which we call God and the rite by which we approach Him do not matter much.'[82] According to Radhakrishnan, this Hindu approach receives confirmation from the experience of mystics of all traditions. He also appeals to Christian scripture for support. He quotes the statement of Jesus, 'He that doeth the will of God, the same is my brother and my sister and my mother.' The roots of Christian exclusiveness he ties to the inherited Semitic creed of the 'jealous God' which Christians have translated into 'Christ as the only begotten son of God'.[83] For the Hindu, Christ can be accepted as an *avatāra* or incarnation but not as the *only* incarnation. Christ, Krishna, Buddha and others must all be seen as equally valid incarnations of God. In Radhakrishnan's view the validity of each religion is found in its instrumental value. It is valid to the degree that it allows its followers to achieve realization.

> If the Hindu chants the Vedas on the banks of the Ganges, if the Chinese meditates on the Analects, if the Japanese worships on the image of Buddha, if the European is convinced of Christ's mediatorship, if the Arab reads the Qur'ān in his mosque, and if the African bows down to a fetish, each one of them has exactly the same reason for his particular confidence. Each form of faith appeals in precisely the same way to the inner certitude and devotion of its followers. It is their deepest apprehension of God and God's fullest revelation to them. The claim of any religion to validity is the fact that only through it have its followers become what they are.[84]

In line with classical Hinduism, Radhakrishnan views the different religions as various historical formulations of the one formless truth. Every historical tradition is to be valued in its own right because of its ability to engage a particular racial/cultural group with the divine. Christianity is suited well to the European, for whom another tradition such as Hinduism or Buddhism is not at all appropriate. 'Religion is like the string of a violin: if removed from its resonant body, it will give the wrong tone, if any.'[85] The solution to the problem of religious pluralism is not to collapse or do away with individual religious traditions but rather to affirm and respect the faith of others. Traditions are societies' memories of their own paths and the instrumental means for release. Removing individuals from traditional roots leaves them abstracted and 'ost. The *Bhagavad Gītā*, says Radhakrishnan, has a clear understanding of this dynamic and warns against taking away the psychological comfort of people by unsettling their faith.[86]

Radhakrishnan observed the problem that just as faith in one's nation seems to kill faith in humankind, so also 'faith in one religion seems to kill faith in others.'[87] The common tendency is to attempt to impose one's own faith on others. But this only robs religion of the richness of the diversity of the various paths to God. Hinduism recognizes this truth. The route taken by the Hindu sage, for example, may be too straight and steep for the majority of Hindus; therefore there is a need for a variety of paths to the same goal. Religious liberty is required to allow individuals to choose freely the path suited to their nature and cultural background. Hinduism also recognizes the close relationship between each religion and its own culture. Religions and cultures can grow. They reform and develop themselves by interpretation and adjustment to one another. 'The Hindu attitude,' says Radhakrishnan, 'is one of positive fellowship, not negative tolerance.'[88] The spiritual attitude is one of constant striving towards higher perfection and truth. This ceaseless striving for truth may be taken as the goal for all religion.

> The greatest requirement of human life is to be loyal to truth as one sees it. Above all, one must learn to be loyal to the spirit of loyalty in other people, even when we do not share their visions of the truth . . . This world loyalty is the essence of religion.[89]

The Hindu contribution to the modern challenge of religious pluralism is to encourage the inquiring spirit and devotion to truth that is larger than any individual tradition. Thus, 'Religious life becomes a cooperative enterprise binding together different traditions and perspectives to the end of obtaining clearer vision of the perfect reality.'[90]

In looking back over the result of the Hindu encounter with Christianity, it seems evident that Rāmmohun Roy's hope has been fulfilled. Through its various reactions to Christianity in the past two centuries, Hinduism has revived and reformed itself. And now its philosophy, as expressed by Sarvepalli Radhakrishnan, is presenting itself to the other traditions as *guru* – as a guide to the future.

In recent years Hindu scholars have followed Radhakrishnan's lead and become actively involved in interfaith dialogue with Christian churches. Anantanand Rambachan, a Hindu scholar from Trinidad and Tobago and now Professor of Religion at St Olaf College, Northfield, Minnesota, offers a good example. Rambachan participates in World

Council of Churches consultations on interfaith relations. He rephrases the Hindu view in even more inclusive words than those of Radhakrishnan while at the same time more explicitly acknowledging the real differences that exist. Rambachan says, 'I am aware of the fact that my own tradition, in its worthwhile enthusiasm to affirm and give importance to the unifying elements in the world's religions, is often guilty of overlooking and underplaying the significance of differences.'[91] Rambachan restates the Hindu position, in relation to other religions, as follows. From a Hindu standpoint, God is seen as *our* God. But, while we recognize that our God can be called by various names (in the different religions), for our own devotional purposes, we choose one divine name and form as the centre of our lives. This is partly due to the limitations of language (no single word or name can fully define God) and to our finite limitations as humans. Due to these limitations each of us has the right to select the name and form, the *ishtadevata* or God of one's own choice, 'along with the recognition that others have chosen differently and that the divine may be celebrated and honored under many names and forms'.[92]

This does not mean that religious differences are merely semantic or that all paths are equally capable of leading to the divine. Rambachan notes that although Hinduism recognizes one divine or absolute as the source and destiny of all beings, Hinduism does not naively assume that all religions are equally true to that divine. He cites Mahatma Gandhi as a good example of Hinduism in this regard. 'Gandhi creatively balanced an openness to the insights of the world's religions with sharp questioning of the content of particular traditions.'[93] Religion without morality was not valid for Gandhi and the virtues of truth and compassion were equally essential. In Gandhi's view no single religion could fully contain God, and all religions reflected the limitations of the human condition. The principal limitation of Hinduism, for Gandhi, was its tolerance of untouchability. A nineteenth-century Hindu who manifested openness to other religions was Ramakrishna. But, like Gandhi, Ramakrishna was critical of all religions including Hinduism. For Ramakrishna, 'a religious way led to God only if there was sincere and earnest longing for God as the ultimate value, the renunciation of materialism and compassion for all. Some paths to God were preferable to others.'[94] It is worth noting that for both Ghandi and Ramakrishna the criteria for assessing the validity of religions included a stress on morality and compassion. Hinduism thus not only allows that there are many paths to God, but also provides normative tests for the different degrees of spiritual realization that the various religions, including Hinduism, achieve. So, concludes Rambachan, 'while the Hindu tradition clearly recognizes God to be our God, it does not legitimize everything that transpires in the name of religion'.[95]

HINDUISM AND SECULAR INDIA

Aside from the inspiring philosophizing of Radhakrishnan and Rambachan, another perspective in the Hindu response to religious pluralism can be understood by studying the Constitution of India. As Robert Baird notes, the Constitution not only contains provisions relating to religion in modern pluralistic India but is itself a religious document.[96] In contrast to the *Manusmṛti*, the Constitution ignores the doctrines of *karma* and *saṁsāra* and restricts itself to concerns relating to this life. In contrast to the class system assumed by Manu, the constitutional religious model adopts the principle of the equality of all.[97] The Constitution also defines religious liberty in such a way that it will not infringe upon the principle of equality. Religious freedom is subject to dictates created in response to concerns for public order, morality and health. It cannot stand in the way of social reform.[98] In order to distinguish between areas of religious freedom and religious restriction, the distinction between the sacred and secular is introduced. It is the duty of the secular realm to ensure equality. In the religious realm, the freedom of each tradition to follow its own beliefs is guaranteed. The task of distinguishing between these two realms is given to the Supreme Court of India. The Supreme Court rejects the definition of 'religion' accepted by the United States Supreme Court; Buddhism and Jainism are not religions according to the US Supreme Court's definition.[99] The practice adopted by the Indian Supreme Court requires first a definition of the tenets of the religion in question and then a judgment as to whether the matter at issue is secular or religious. If the matter is judged religious then the tenets of the tradition, as defined by the Court, are the criteria against which the judgment is made. Although this legal approach does allow for religious pluralism, justice depends on the ability of the court to understand and apply the tenets of all religious traditions. It also tends to reify each religious tradition into a set of established tenets – something that conflicts with Radhakrishnan's understanding of the need for change and adaptability in modern religion.

It is worth noting that Bhimrao Ramji Ambedkar, who drafted the Constitution, has in his own life posed a serious challenge to modern Hinduism. Because he was born an untouchable, he worked under the assumption that much of the injustice in India was the fault of the Hindu tradition. In Ambedkar's view Hinduism is beyond reform. He dismissed Gandhi's attempts to deal with the problem of untouchability as mysticism and mere name changing. To get himself and the untouchables a new identity and religious freedom he felt it necessary to leave Hinduism and adopt the casteless religion of Buddhism.[100] As a result, some three million followers are said to have left Hinduism in the span of ten years (1951–61).[101] The fact that three million Hindus can suddenly become Buddhists seems, on the one hand, to be a living demonstration of the long-claimed tolerance of Hinduism and of the religious freedom guaranteed in Ambedkar's constitution. On the other hand, this poses a modern challenge to Hinduism to adapt and develop in the way Radhakrishnan envisaged it would. The practice of untouchability has changed radically. The influence of caste on marriage and employment is also showing signs of change, but such a deeply ingrained notion cannot be legislated out of Hindu consciousness quickly.

There is a fundamental conflict between the presuppositions of the Constitution and those of Hinduism. The Constitution proposes that all persons be treated as equals – suggesting some kind of *tabula rasa* view of human nature. Hinduism, in contrast, understands the nature of each person to be different and to be the natural result of the individual's own action in this and previous lives. It is the cumulative traces (*karma*) of such past actions that compose the nature of the individual before the realization of *mokṣa* or release. This understanding of *karma-saṁsāra* underlies the notion and practice of caste and is a fundamental aspect of Hindu psychology. There seems no obvious way to resolve this head-on clash between the tenets of Hinduism and the theory of human nature assumed in the Constitution. Since the Constitution is now the law of India, the home of Hinduism, this challenge from within cannot be avoided and may well be the testing ground for the Hinduism of the future.[102]

The Constitution's concern for religious freedom and its distinction between the sacred and the secular are being currently challenged by the upsurge of Hindu nationalism in politics,[103] and events such as the 1994 destruction of the mosque at Ayodhya by Hindus along with the targeting of Christians for their conversion practices. In his 'Essentials of

Hindutva' written in 1922, V. D. Savarkar defined the principles of Hindu nationalism.[104] For Savarkar Hindus are those inhabitants of India who consider it both their holy land and the land of their ancestors. In his view only Hindus are the true children of India. They are entitled by birthright to rule India simply because they constitute the overwhelming majority in India, their own fatherland and holy land. As president of the Hindu Mahasabha from 1937 to 1944, Savarkar travelled and spoke throughout India applying the principles of Hindutva to various political issues. This activity roused support for Hindu nationalism especially from upper-caste Hindu political leaders and led to the denunciation of Muslims as anti-national. In the last decade of the twentieth century, this anti-Muslim approach by Hindu nationalists spread to include Christians, especially in their missionary conversion activities. Anti-Christian sentiments became especially vocal during 1999 in the lead-up to the visit to India in November of Pope John Paul II. The Hindutva principle, that India is the holy land of Hindus and thus should be ruled by Hindu nationalists, suggests that the hostility that has so far been directed towards Muslims and Christians may well spread to other religions in India. Hindutva principles underpin popular present-day support for movements such as the Vishva Hindu Parishad (VHP) and the Bharatiya Janata Party (BJP). The BJP is currently battling with the Congress Party (the party of Gandhi and Nehru) for political control of India. Gandhi's Hinduism (and that of scholars like Radhakrishnan) with its support for open religious pluralism in India is under considerable siege as the twenty-first century begins.[105] The same can be said for the secular principles of religious freedom and equality for all which Nehru wrote into the Constitution of India. Thus, the much-vaunted pluralism of Hinduism may be seriously undermined if Savarkar's ideology of Hindutva grows in strength and influence.

Mahmood has provided a helpful anthropological analysis of the roots of the Hindu nationalist movement.[106] Mahmood offers convincing evidence that the Hindu nationalist movement has a longstanding core that has always dominated Indian society. Hindutva, therefore, should not be seen as a modern political movement without historical or cultural roots. Pre-modern India, when seen in terms of its community boundaries between the pure (*arya* or higher-caste Sanskrit speakers) and the impure (*mleccha*, non-caste or low-caste, tribal and heterodox groups) or between *brahmanas* (followers of Vedas) and *sramanas* (followers of non-Vedic religions, e.g. Jainas and Buddhists), was not a land of open, tolerant religious pluralism. The us/them ethic and religious boundaries have functioned at the community level at least since the advent of Jainism and Buddhism (*c.* 600 BCE) to consolidate a core Hindu identity that, in Mahmood's view, has always dominated Indian society.[107] The strategy of the Hindu core, says Mahmood, when faced with the Jaina/Buddhist challenges (e.g. rejection of Veda and caste divisions), was a refusal even to recognize differences and subsequently to absorb or incorporate all competitors. So, when faced with more recent Sikh demands that Sikhism be recognized as a different religion, many Hindus continued to view Sikhism as simply a part of the Hindu tradition, with all of the caste and purity restrictions still applying. A hill tribe that follows animistic traditions is viewed by the caste communities on the plains of Bihar as Hindu – in spite of the fact that there is nothing Hindu about their practice or belief, and that they clearly fall into the impure (*mleccha*) group. Hindus, says Mahmood, think they are being tolerant in their benevolent inclusion of others: the Buddha as an *avatāra* of Viṣṇu, the Sikhs as a caste of Hindus, the tribals as one's fellow travellers, and so on. From this inclusive perspective, which is adopted by Hindutva, what is wrong with talking about the Hindu nation? But from outside, from a Muslim, Buddhist or Sikh perspective, such an assertion of Hindu nationalism seems to equate any real religious separateness with virtual treason.[108] This mistaken notion of Hindu tolerance, as Ainslie Embree puts it, is based on the idea that various cultural/religious identities can be encapsulated within Hindu society only if everyone agrees to the premises (those of Hinduism) on which such encapsulation is based.[109] However, a pluralism whose terms privilege one religious community above others does not work – as events in India today demonstrate. Such an approach is criticized by the contemporary Hindu philosopher Rambachan (discussed above), who insists on an honest recognition of real differences as essential to both pluralism and the deeper teachings of Hinduism. Nor do the foundational ideas of the Indian Constitution support the narrow Hindu nationalism that Savarkar's Hindutva ideology has produced.

CONCLUSION

Throughout its long history, Hinduism's attitude towards other religions has remained constant. There is one divine reality that manifests itself in many forms. The various religions are simply different revelations of the one divine reality. In this recognition of other religions as being different revelations of the One and as providing different paths by which devotees may attain release from *karma-saṁsāra*, Hinduism sees itself as being a very open and tolerant religion. But because it asserts that the Vedas are the most perfect revelation of divine truth, Hinduism also sees itself as providing the criteria against which the revelations of all other religions must be tested. Thus Hindu tolerance of other religions is directly proportionate to their congruence with the Vedas. There is no doubt that for the Hindu there is only one divine, as revealed by the Hindu scriptures, and that any other revelation (e.g. the Torah, New Testament or Qur'ān) is seen as a secondary manifestation to be verified against the Hindu revelation.

Once one steps back from Hindu metaphysics, Hinduism no longer appears so open and tolerant in its view of other religions. The Hindu approach to other religions is to absolutize the relativism implied in the viewpoint that the various religions are simply different manifestations of the one divine. The Hindu refusal to recognize claims to exclusive truth (e.g. Christianity or Buddhism) that differ from the revelation of the Veda indicates the limited nature of Hindu tolerance. In this, of course, Hindus are no different from those of other religions who believe they have the true revelation and seek to impose their truth upon others. Sarvepalli Radhakrishnan has been a most effective modern representative of this kind of 'Hindu tolerance'. Radhakrishnan's tolerance has always exclusively affirmed his own position and has protected him from the challenge of other positions.[110] Nevertheless, the Hindu view that there is one divine, which may be reached by many paths, has proven throughout the centuries to be a powerful influence upon Hinduism's interaction with the other religions. Contemporary Hindu thinkers, such as Rambachan, seek to give more recognition to real differences that exist between traditions, while retaining the Hindu stress on an underlying unity of all. But the ideas of Hindutva, and the Hindu nationalist movements it has produced, are severely testing the traditional Hindu claim of tolerance towards others.

6 RELIGIOUS PLURALISM AND BUDDHISM

The Buddhist attitude to other religions[1] has been described as 'critical tolerance' combined with a missionary goal.[2] Buddhism has spread widely from India – south to Sri Lanka and South-East Asia; north to Tibet; east to China and Japan; and recently west to Europe and North America. Although Buddhism encountered established religions in all of these regions, there is little evidence of war or persecution. Buddhism has demonstrated a remarkable degree of tolerance and flexibility throughout the course of its expansion. Unlike some other religious expansions, the spread of Buddhism has been accomplished more through the dissemination of ideas than by migration of peoples. Arnold Toynbee credits the Hindu context in which Buddhism arose as at least a partial source of 'Buddhist tolerance'.[3] Toynbee praises this Hindu–Buddhist tolerance as the prototype of a religious attitude necessary for peace in today's pluralistic world.[4] In addition to its attitude of critical tolerance, Buddhism's stress on compassion provides a natural point of contact with other religions. Its critical assessments of other religions arise from the particular Buddhist experience of *prajñā* (wisdom) as the outcome of meditation.[5] Buddhism rejects the worship of God or gods and the performance of religious rituals as a means to release. It also rejects speculations about ultimate beginnings, especially about whether the self and the world are eternal, and a number of speculations about the ultimate state of the self in the future.[6] To understand the way in which these three factors of tolerance, compassion and *prajñā* function in the Buddhist encounter with other religions, let us begin with the Buddha's own experience.

EARLY BUDDHISM AND OTHER RELIGIONS

Although Sakyamuni Buddha (c. 560 BCE) was born into a Hindu society, he lived in a period of Hinduism marked by considerable pluralism of philosophy and practice. In philosophy, it was a time during which a large number of conflicting theories were being proposed about the nature and destiny of humanity in the universe. With regard to religious practice, many varieties of ascetic self-discipline were being pursued as ways of release.[7] Some of these were undoubtedly Jaina and yogic in background. It was in this Hindu yet pluralistic world that the Buddha pioneered the path of Buddhism. A contemporary Buddhist scholar, K. N. Jayatilleke, observes that the very presence of such a variety of religious theories and practices is a tribute to the tolerance of the Hinduism of the Buddha's time. Like Toynbee, Jayatilleke suggests that the non-dogmatic attitude of Buddhism, at its inception, may be due to its sharing in the tendencies of Hindu tolerance.[8]

The Buddha was intimately familiar with a broad plurality of views and formulated his own position within such a context. Buddha accepts rebirth, although not in terms of a soul, and gives evidence for this not from reason or scripture but from empirical experience – his own ability to recall his past lives. Many of his disciples also report having been able to remember previous lives.[9] On this point Buddhism is in harmony with Hinduism and Jainism but differs distinctively from Judaism, Christianity and Islam. A similar broad range of views on topics such as free will versus determinism, moral responsibility versus no moral responsibility, and theism versus atheism were present at the time of Buddha. It is not surprising that Buddha referred to them as a tangle of views in which one could be trapped and pulled down. Such a pluralism of views is also present in today's world. The opening verse of the *Visuddhimagga* in the Pāli Canon provides an apt description of the thinking person caught in such a situation:

> Tangle within, without, lo! in the toils
> Entangled is the race of sentient beings
> Hence would I ask thee, Gotama, of this:
> Who is it can from this tangle disembroil?
> (*Kindred Sayings*, 1:20)[10]

The method developed by Buddha for getting disentangled was based on 'critical tolerance' and the empirical criterion of 'personal experience'.

Rather than proceeding by blind faith or authority (either scriptural or institutional), Buddha taught a 'provisional faith' that was then to be tested by the individual's personal experience. Such personal testing of the provisional faith would either prove or disprove it. To base religion on a dogmatic attitude or to accept any of the many possible Vedic or non-Vedic views uncritically would, in Buddha's view, be self-defeating. Thus to those bewildered by the choices and conflicts of religious pluralism, 'Buddha advocated a critical outlook, recommending that they test the validity of any particular religion or philosophy which appeals to them in the light of their personal experience.'[11] In the *Aṅguttara Nikāya* (1:18) it is stated

> There are certain religious teachers, who come to Kesaputta. They speak very highly of their own theories but oppose, condemn and ridicule the theories of others. At the same time there are yet other religious teachers who come to Kesaputta and in turn speak highly of their own theories, opposing, condemning and ridiculing the theories of these others. We are now in a state of doubt and perplexity as to who out of these venerable recluses spoke the truth and who spoke falsehood.
>
> O Kalamas, you have a right to doubt or feel uncertain for you have raised a doubt in a situation in which you ought to suspend your judgment. Come now, Kalamas, do not accept anything on the grounds of revelation, tradition or report or because it is a product of mere reasoning or because it is true from a standpoint or because of a superficial assessment of the facts or because it conforms with one's preconceived notions or because it is authoritative or because of the prestige of your teacher. When you, Kalamas, realize for yourself that these doctrines are evil and unjustified, that they are condemned by the wise and that when they are accepted and lived by, they conduce to ill and sorrow, then you should reject them.

As stated in the *Digha Nikāya* (1:3), this critical attitude should be focused on Buddhism itself:

> If anyone were to speak ill of me, my doctrine or my Order, do not bear any ill-will towards him, be upset or perturbed at heart; for if you were to be so, it will only cause you harm. If, on the other hand, anyone were to speak well of me, my doctrine and my Order, do not be overjoyed, thrilled or elated at heart; for if so it will only be an obstacle in the way of forming a realistic judgment as to whether the qualities praised in us are real and actually found in us.

For Buddhism, religion is what one finds to be reasonable and true after having taken it provisionally on faith and tested it out for oneself.

When such a faith ends in knowledge, Buddhism calls it a 'rational faith' (*ākāravatī saddhā*) as opposed to a blind or baseless faith (*amūlikā saddhā*).[12] This approach is sometimes called 'the Buddhist charter of free inquiry'.

The Buddhist approach of critical tolerance is also based on a causal conception of nature (*paṭicca-samuppāda*). This is a causal system in which there are physical laws (*utu-niyāma*), biological laws (*bīja-niyāma*), psychological laws (*citta-niyāma*), and moral and spiritual laws (*kamma-dhamma-niyāma*). These laws are like the law of gravity – they are simply there. What the Buddha does is to discover and pass on these laws to aid others in attaining the spiritual life. As the *Samyutta Nikāya* (11:25) puts it

> Whether Tathāgatas arise or not, this order exists, namely, the fixed nature of phenomena, the regular pattern of phenomena or conditionality. This the Tathāgata discovers and comprehends; having discovered and comprehended it, he points it out, teaches it, lays it down, establishes, reveals, analyses, clarifies it and says, 'Look.'

The Buddha has discovered the law of causation as the true description of reality. He passes this on to others not to be accepted on his authority but to be tested in their own critical experience. It is an approach much like that of modern science. Laws or theories discovered by one scientist must be experimentally tested and verified by other scientists before they are accepted. This conception of the Buddha as a discoverer of truth, rather than an authoritative giver of law, yields tolerance because it leaves open the possibility for others to discover aspects of truth or the whole truth for themselves (e.g. the Buddhist acceptance of *Pacceka-Buddhas*, who discover the truth for themselves).[13] Other religions may also provide ways to discover the causal law of the universe, the one truth.

The missionary motivation originated with Buddha's directive that the *dharma* is to be preached to all persons so as to encourage those who are spiritually minded to test it for themselves (*Aṅguttara Nikāya* 1:20:1). Again the process and rationale parallel science: a scientist passes on a new discovery to colleagues so that it can be tested and verified by them and so enable them to reach new knowledge.

Although all of this clearly allows for spiritual growth and salvation or release outside Buddhism, all religions are not considered to be equally efficacious guides to the truth. The word for 'religion' in early Buddhism was *dhammavinaya*, which means 'doctrine and discipline' or 'truth and practice'.[14] To fulfil the demands of this definition, a religion must practise what it preaches and live the truth of its teaching. From this perspective an ideology like Marxism could be included in the broad classification of religion. The way in which religions are judged by Buddhism is outlined by Ānanda in the *Sandaka Sutta*. Reporting the teaching of the Buddha, Ānanda says that there are four false religions (*abrahma-cariyavāsā*) and four religions that are unsatisfactory (*anassāsikam*) but not necessarily false.[15] The false religions are: 1) materialism, which asserts the reality of the material world alone and denies life after death; 2) any religious philosophy that recommends an immoral ethic; 3) any religion that denies free will and moral responsibility and asserts that persons are either miraculously saved or doomed; and 4) any religion that asserts the inevitability of eventual salvation or release for all.[16]

The four unsatisfactory but not necessarily false religions are those which in some sense maintain a concept of life after death, moral values, freedom and responsibility; they also must assert that salvation or release is not inevitable. Religions in this category include those based on: 1) the omniscience of the founder while in both conscious and unconscious periods of existence (e.g. Christian theologies taking Jesus as only apparently being a man); 2) revelation or tradition (e.g. Judaism, Christianity, Hinduism); 3) logical and metaphysical speculation (e.g. some Greek religions); 4) pragmatic scepticism or agnosticism (e.g. Stoicism). Buddhism judges the satisfactoriness of these types of religions in terms of the degree to which they approach the core requirements of the Buddhist religion itself (i.e. rebirth, moral values, freedom, and responsibility to achieve release).[17] This logic is not much different from many of the Christian theologies discussed earlier, especially the theology of Karl Rahner – other religions are means of salvation to the extent that they conform to the criterion of Jesus Christ. In Buddhism it is the Buddha's experience of truth (*dhamma*) that is the criterion. Based on the Buddha's experience, religions dependent upon the founder's omniscience, upon revelation or tradition, upon metaphysical speculation or upon pragmatic scepticism are judged as helpful but unsatisfactory in that they are grounded on uncertain foundations. The point being made in the Buddhist argument is that, whereas these foundations may be either true or false and cannot be verified, Buddhism is, in its core teaching of rebirth, moral values, freedom, responsibility, and the need to achieve salvation, a religion that can be verified by reason and experience.

It should be noted that all of the other religions reviewed in this work also claim to have the same kind of verification: reason and experience. Thus, Buddhism does not seem, on this count, to be in a qualitatively different category (i.e. the only verifiable religion), although it clearly believes this to be the case.

Since moral values are included as one of the requirements in the Buddhist criteria for true religion, it is necessary to consider the Buddhist conception of these values. The Buddhist understanding of moral value may be found in Buddhism's explanation of 'the right view of life' (*sammā diṭṭhi*).

> There is value in alms, sacrifices and oblation; there is survival after death and recompense for good and evil deeds; there are moral obligations and there are religious teachers, who have led a good life and who have proclaimed with their superior insight and personal understanding of the nature of this world and the world beyond. (*Majjhima Nikāya* 3:72)[18]

This summary of the right philosophy of life is broad enough to give general recognition and respect to the basic teachings of other religions, although there are clear differences of interpretation with regard to points such as the nature of survival after death. But it does seem clear that the early Buddhist conception of the nature and destiny of humankind is not in basic conflict with the other religions. The critical distinction that the Buddha would make – and this is a move not unlike that of Karl Barth in Christianity – is to examine all religions, including all Buddhist religions, for ways in which they have fallen short of living and realizing the core criteria of belief in survival after death, moral values, freedom, responsibility and the non-inevitability of salvation or release. The Buddhist is different from someone like Barth, a *bhakti* Hindu or a ṣūfī because these latter three believe that it is God's grace that makes possible religious attainment, whereas for the Buddhist it is human effort, not supernatural intervention, that is effective. It is the end of salvation or release that concerns the Buddhist. Consequently, if the Jew, Christian, Muslim or Hindu finds that it is necessary to believe in a God to reach salvation, that is quite acceptable. The danger of such a devotional tactic (i.e. believing in a supernatural God who gives grace) is that it may become a hindrance to one's own sense of moral responsibility and one's own efforts towards release. If such theistic beliefs do not get in the way, then there is no objection. Indeed, as we shall see, Mahāyāna Buddhism itself employs just such 'spiritual devices' as aids to release.

Since belief in God is a major point of distinction between Buddhism and the other five religions examined in this work, it is worthwhile to consider the Buddhist arguments against theism. The specific brand of theism the Buddha was reacting against was that of Makkhali Gosāla, who believed that God had predestined salvation for all. Gosāla's view was that everything has been preplanned and takes place according to the will of God; it is like the unravelling of a ball of string thrown upon the ground. Such fatalistic and deterministic theism was repulsive to the Buddha because it denied free will and moral responsibility and militated against human effort. In the Buddhist scriptures the two arguments against this kind of theism are: 1) 'if God designs the life of the entire world – the glory and the misery, the good and the evil acts – man is but an instrument of his will and God is responsible' (*Jātaka* 5:238); 2) some evils are inexplicable if the truth of such a theism is granted (e.g. if a good God is omnipotent, why does that God create injustice?) (*Jātaka* 6:208).[19] Both arguments attack the moral irresponsibility that a theism such as Gosāla's produces. But in his conversations with Hindu brahmins, Buddha also made it clear that so long as theism allowed for individual freedom and moral responsibility and produced compassionate behaviour, then it should not be treated in the same negative way as Gosāla's theism. On pragmatic grounds, belief in God is not to be discouraged so long as it is an incentive and not a hindrance to moral and spiritual development.[20] However, most Buddhists view belief in God as a serious hindrance, as a form of delusion to be let go of – as the first spoke of the eightfold path, 'right understanding'.[21]

A contemporary example of such an open approach to religions, including theistic religions, is found in the Theravāda Bhikku, Buddhadāsa of Bangkok. Stressing non-attachment and compassionate action, he declares that to the extent these are found in religions, all religions are the same.[22] If belief in God helps members of other religions achieve non-attachment and compassionate action, then God as world saviour may be judged as equivalent to *dharma* as world saviour – but Buddhadāsa does urge that God be understood in impersonal terms.[23] In a comparative analysis of Christian and Buddhist teachings regarding sin, death and non-attachment, he finds little significant difference.[24] It seems clear that, for early Buddhism and for contemporary Theravāda thinkers like Buddhadāsa, religion, including theistic belief, is to be judged according to its instrumental value for the realization of truth and the compassionate life.

MAHĀYĀNA BUDDHISM AND OTHER RELIGIONS

The tolerant but critical attitude of the Buddha towards the plurality of religious views is shaped into a rigorous philosophic approach by the Mādhyamika Buddhists. Like the Buddha, the Mādhyamika purpose in criticism is affirmative. The critical analysis of the beliefs of a religious view is not aimed at rejecting that religion or demonstrating its inferiority in relation to other religious views (including even other Buddhist views); rather the goal of Mādhyamika is the removal of ego-attachment to any religious philosophy or theology so that true spirituality can be experienced and lived.[25] Thus Buddha is seen as the physician who prescribes the correct medicine (i.e. the critical outlook) to cure the disease of ego-attachment to religious theologies or philosophies. If, as the Buddha discovered, the goal of religion is compassion, then, say the Mādhyamika, the biggest obstacle to realizing that goal is attachment to our own religious beliefs in such a way as to make them absolute. Philosophy, theology and scripture have useful roles to play as guides, as providing the contents for 'provisional faith'. But as soon as such viewpoints become attached to the ego and made absolute, they destroy the capacities for tolerance, objective criticism and compassionate action. The unending and often destructive history of philosophical/theological argument among religions and within particular religions is cited as evidence of the truth of the Buddha's insight.

Based on this understanding, the Mādhyamika Buddhist's attitude towards other religions (and the various viewpoints within Buddhism) is one of openness and indeed a 'missionary desire' to enter into dialogue. But the dialogue will be of a specific kind. Following the lead of the great Mādhyamika thinker Nāgārjuna (c. 150–250 CE), the Mādhyamika will first attempt to understand clearly the position of the other and then ruthlessly subject it to dialectical criticism until it collapses due to its own internal inconsistencies. The details of Nāgārjuna's dialectical technique of 'four-pronged negation' (cātuṣkoṭi) have been presented elsewhere.[26] Our concern is with its effect upon other religions.

Over the centuries the Mādhyamika critique of other religious views has had a considerable impact. Within Hinduism, it influenced Gauḍapāda and Śaṅkara in the systematizing of Advaita Vedānta. It seems clear that

Vedānta borrowed the critical method of Mādhyamika Buddhism. Within Buddhism itself, Mādhyamika has had the purifying effect of reminding all Buddhists that they should take neither the Buddha's words nor the formulations of any Buddhist school as absolute truth. Now that Mādhyamika texts have been translated and made available in the West, Christian, Jewish and Islamic thinkers will also begin to receive the benefit of the Mādhyamika philosophic presentation of Buddha's critical outlook. In one sense Mādhyamika would seem to be the most intolerant of approaches in that it negates, without exception, all possible views. In another sense it can accommodate and give place to all religious views so long as they don't claim to be absolute.[27] Thus Nāgārjuna's statement:

> All is concord indeed for him who to Śūnyatā conforms;
> All is not concordant for him who conforms not to Śūnyatā.[28]

Although it is an able representative of the critical outlook of the Buddha towards other religious views, Mādhyamika bears within itself the danger that it can lead its practitioners to attach their egos to the critical outlook itself and so lose touch with Buddha's tolerance and compassion and open the door to nihilism. This would be the absolutizing of the dialectic and may well be as real a temptation for the unpurified Mādhyamika as the absolutizing of a certain view is to the proponent of a particular religious position. Mādhyamika has recognized this danger and prescribes purificatory meditation along with the practice of the dialectic.

One point at which Mādhyamika Buddhism would seem to diverge from all other religions is in its insistence that the critical outlook (dialectical reason) plus meditation are sufficient for the realization of release. Judaism, Christianity and Islam all allow roles for reason but maintain that without revelation salvation cannot be reached. And, although Hinduism has a great variety of views regarding the place of revelation, there is general agreement that the Veda is necessary for release. The disagreement would seem to be rooted in the different assessments of the status of ego-attachment in human nature. From the perspective of Judaism, Christianity and Islam, ego-attachment (human-kind's sinful nature) can be controlled but never completely overcome. God's grace can control ego-attachment so as to make spiritual life and salvation possible. Hinduism maintains that the revelation of the Vedas, reason and some form of spiritual discipline destroy ego-attachment and allow for the realization of release. Buddhism, like Hinduism, radically differs from the Western religions in holding that it is possible for ego-attachment to be completely removed. But Buddhism differs from Hinduism in maintaining that revelation, though it may be used, is not necessarily required. For the Mādhyamika only the critical outlook (the dialectic) and meditation are required for the full removal of ego-attachment.

While Mādhyamika offers a critique of all metaphysical views, Buddhist and non-Buddhist, Yogācāra Buddhism may well have arisen as a reaction to the danger of understanding Mādhyamika nihilistically. Yogācāra offers a more positive formulation. Yogācāra Buddhism shifts the focus to consciousness itself and the realization of it as pure compassion. Rather than *dharma*, *ālayavijñāna* (the storehouse of consciousness) is identified as the ground of all beings and awareness. The various systems of belief can be seen as different obstructions of consciousness, which is to be purified by meditation and thus readied for the realization of *nirvāṇa* or release. The end result is not a subjective idealism, but a non-dual consciousness with no delusive dichotomy between subject and object present. Because of its inward focus on meditation and consciousness, there seem to be only a couple of aspects of Yogācāra Buddhism that can be related to other religions. The common Buddhist features of critical tolerance and compassion towards others have been maintained. The stress on 'consciousness alone' suggests the possibility of some influence from Advaita Vedānta.

As it has expanded and developed, Mahāyāna Buddhism has absorbed significant influences in India from Hinduism, in China from Taoism and in Tibet from Bon. Y. Krishnan has analysed the interaction between Hinduism and Buddhism.[29] He notes that the Buddhist development of the doctrine of *karma* as an ethical law posed a serious threat to Vedic Hinduism. The Buddhist identification of the moral aspects of *pratītya-samutpāda*, the law of causation, with *karma* meant that good conduct produces good effects and evil conduct produces evil results. Thus the good and bad experienced in life are not the result of gods or mysteries but are conditioned by one's own action through the law of causation. Consequently, such Vedic practices as sacrifice to the gods were rendered powerless in the face of this law of the universe, which operates outside the realm of the gods. It seemed that there was no way of countering, neutralizing or escaping from the effects of *karma*. Of course this also posed a problem for Buddhism, namely, that it was apparently necessary that Buddhism identify an ongoing entity able to carry *karma* from one birth to the next. The problem for Hinduism was that its system of sacrifice to the gods no longer seemed to have any power over the course of events (controlled by the law of *karma*). Thus there seemed to be no reason that such activities should be continued. According to Krishnan, it was to answer this challenge from Buddhism that the *Purāṇas* came into existence in Hinduism. The *Purāṇas* accept the law of *karma* in full, but as means for mitigating the effects of *karma* they develop the Vedic concept of *tapas* (austerity) and the new notion of *avatāras* (incarnations) and stress such practices as pilgrimage, religious observances and charity.[30] Thus various means of grace were introduced (and made available to all regardless of caste, sex, etc.) so that the Buddhist moral law of *karma* was absorbed and Vedic notions of divine power were retained, notwithstanding the apparent inconsistencies this entailed. It is Krishnan's contention that this Hindu resolution had a significant influence on Mahāyāna Buddhism:

> In Mahāyāna Buddhism, the doctrine of *puṇya parinamnā* (transference of merit) and of the *Bodhisattva mahāsattva*, who renounces *nirvaṇa* again and again to bring deliverance to suffering humanity, were patently inconsistent with the teachings of Buddha. They necessarily implied a serious modification of the law of *karma*. These were the Buddhist versions of the Hindu doctrine of grace and *avatāras* (incarnations) and were in the nature of a compromise the Buddhists were forced to make to meet the counter-attack of Hinduism.[31]

In China, thè Taoist influence on Mahāyāna Buddhism was significant. In the third and fourth centuries CE, Chinese thought was dominated by the study of *Tao-te-ching*, *Chuang-tzu* and the *I-ching*. These three works constituted what are called the metaphysical scriptures (*sanhsüan*).[32] To these was added the study of Buddhist works, and Buddha, as their author, was judged to be a sage, like the sage of the *Tao-te-ching*. Often the two sages become amalgamated. The Buddha's enlightenment, his *prajñā*, was an aspect of his role as a sage and a seer and meant that he should know and reveal in scripture the secrets of immortality and the all-embracing power of nature, secrets eagerly sought by the Taoists.[33] Chinese thinkers thus questioned the *sūtras* of the Buddha. It is not surprising that the answers they found in the texts led to quite a different understanding than the same texts had engendered in India. The Buddha for the Chinese was not an Indian, but a Chinese sage who had gone to

India to convert the barbarians. As such he was received by the Chinese with open arms.[34] This mixing of Buddhism and Taoism is seen in works such as the *Chao-lun*, in which the Indian notion of the Middle Path assumes another appearance. In the *Chao-lun*, it is not the Middle Path of Gotama the Buddha nor that of Nāgārjuna that appears, but rather a new interpretation of the Middle Path, an interpretation that expresses the identity of the two states of the universe: the impure and the pure, the true and the seeming.[35] It was in this way that the Taoist philosophy of nature was incorporated into Mahāyāna Buddhism in China and later was carried into Japan as well as other East Asian countries.[36] In terms of popular religion, the figure of Amida (Amitābha) became the focus for both Indian and Chinese religious imagination and produced a cult of devotion similar to Hindu *bhakti* piety. This popular Mahāyāna practice was also carried over into Japanese Buddhism.

As Mahāyāna expanded to the north, it encountered the traditions of Tibet. Western scholars have frequently referred to the pre-Buddhist Tibetan religion as Bon, understanding Bon to refer to some form of primitive animism or shamanism.[37] Recent scholarship, however, is calling this understanding into question. David Snellgrove, on the basis of a thorough study of *bon-pos* texts, concludes that 'there are good reasons for believing the Buddhist yogis and hermits, and probably Hindu ascetics as well, had already familiarized the villagers of western Tibet with Indian teachings and practices before Buddhism was formally introduced by the Tibetan religious kings'.[38] Thus it may be that the followers of Bon (*bon-pos*) rose not from primitive animism or shamanism but from a form of Indian Buddhism – probably strongly influenced by some Tantric variety of Kashmir Hinduism. This Bon Buddhism seems to have been present in Tibet before the official introduction of orthodox (Chos) Buddhism to Tibet by the kings in the seventh and eighth centuries CE[39] and to have developed side by side with Chos as a parallel form of Buddhism. Thus the new influences that Bon introduced, including such things as 'methods of prediction', 'placating and repelling local divinities' and 'destroying enemies by fierce tantric rites', may have been influences from Hindu Tantrism.[40] Here again, as in the encounter with Chinese Taoism, the Buddhist ability to accommodate itself and merge with other forms is manifested.

In conclusion, then, it is the attitude of critical tolerance and the willingness to accommodate that have characterized Buddhism through the ages. From Gotama the Buddha's reaction to the various beliefs around him, to Chinese and Tibetan developments, it is this open and yet firm attitude that has dominated. Today in Europe and America this same critical openness is allowing Buddhist thought to interact with modern science and psychology in new and exciting ways. Buddhism is also dialoguing very creatively with Christianity, one of the most fruitful of the interreligious conversations going on today.[41]

Finally, it is of interest to note the attitude of a contemporary Mahāyāna Buddhist to other religions. The Dalai Lama has said on several occasions that it is not necessary for followers of other religions to convert to Buddhism – rather, they should become better Christians, Muslims, Jews, Hindus, etc. In an article published in 1981, the Dalai Lama states that the various religions have a common goal – the making of better human beings. The differences among religions should be recognized, but those differences also should be understood within the context of this common goal. Thus mutual respect should develop between all religions.

> Each system has its own value suited to persons of different disposition and mental outlook. At this time of easy communication we must increase our efforts to learn each other's systems. This does not mean that we should make all religions into one, but that we should recognize the common purpose of the many religions and value the different techniques that they have developed for internal improvement.[42]

7 RELIGIOUS PLURALISM AND THE FUTURE OF RELIGIONS

The time will soon be with us when a theologian who attempts to work out his position unaware that he does so as a member of a world society in which other theologians equally intelligent, equally devout, equally moral, are Hindus, Buddhists, Muslims, and unaware that his readers are likely to be Buddhists or to have Muslim husbands or Hindu colleagues – such a theologian is as out of date as is one who attempts to construct an intellectual position unaware that Aristotle has thought about the world or that existentialists have raised new orientations or unaware that the earth is a minor planet in a galaxy that is vast only by terrestrial standards. Philosophy and science have impinged so far on theological thought more effectively than has comparative religion, but this will not last.[1]

Religious pluralism is a special challenge facing the world religions today, yet in another sense religious pluralism has always been with us. As the preceding chapters have shown, each religion arose in a religiously plural environment and shaped itself in reaction to that pluralism. The creative tension pluralism generates has often been the catalyst for new insight and religious development. It was out of a welter of views – the Brāhmanical, Jaina, materialistic and agnostic – that Buddha's enlightenment arose. It was in the midst of the Meccan admixture of Jews, Christians, Zoroastrians, Manichaeans and others that the prophecy of Allah through Muhammad burst forth. It was in the midst of the worship of the numerous territorial gods of the ancient Near East that God covenanted with Abraham and Moses. It was the challenge of Gnosticism and Greek philosophy that helped early Christians to identify their separateness from Judaism. And plurality has been the strength of Hinduism up to the present day. Certainly there were times in the history of each of these religions when the pluralistic challenges receded to the background, often signalling a period of spiritual stagnation; Christianity through the Middle Ages and Islam just before the ṣūfī encounter with Hinduism are examples of this. And when the challenge of pluralism reasserted itself, it usually infused new life into the tradition that was confronted. Thus, although the challenge of religious pluralism is a crisis of our age, it is at the same time an opportunity for spiritual growth.

It is too early to detect the new contents and forms that will arise from the modern challenge of religious pluralism. But the analyses of the previous chapters indicate some preliminary outlines of the religions of the future – religions that will be able to live comfortably side by side in a global community. This chapter examines the major features of the current situation and then makes some observations as to the future of religions. The author's own view and guidelines for interreligious dialogue (based on the content of the previous chapters) are put forth in the second section of the chapter. The first section contains a summary of similarities of approach observed in chapters 1–6.

RELIGIOUS PLURALISM: THE CURRENT SITUATION

Our study of how each religion has responded and is responding to the challenge of religious pluralism has identified three general themes and common principles: 1) that religious pluralism can best be understood in terms of a logic that sees the One manifesting as the many – transcendent reality phenomenalizing as the various religions; 2) that there is a common recognition of the instrumental quality of particular religious experience; and 3) that spirituality is identified and validated by the superimposing of one's own criterion upon other religions. Also held in common are several difficulties posed by modern pluralism. Let us examine each of these points in detail.

A common logic: the One and the many

From the perspective of philosophy or theology, the logic that a source of reality is experienced in a plurality of ways seems to be the most satisfactory way of accounting for the fact of religious pluralism. The oldest formulation of this logic is encountered in the Vedic notion of the One that is called by many names. For Buddhism the causal law of *karma* is the one reality with which the religions are trying to cope. Judaism and Christianity share the biblical perception of all peoples and nations as under the one God; they also share Greek philosophy's notion of the Logos. In Islam there is the 'Mother Book' of which the earthly books of the various religions are copies. Contemporary scholars of religions such as Karl Jaspers,[2] John Hick[3] and Wilfred Cantwell Smith[4] also adopt this logic, as do current thinkers in each of these religions. The logic that the One is manifested in the many is both the oldest and the most contemporary explanation of religious pluralism.

The attempt to reduce all religions to one common universal – to reduce them all into one religion – has been unacceptable to these religions, and, as Charles Davis shows, it is philosophically unacceptable because it leads to a violation of the principle of freedom.[5] A universal religion would amount to religious coercion. Unity without diversity leads to a denial of freedom. Accordingly, plurality in matters of faith and morals should be accepted. With regard to the internal relationship between the One and the many, all religions would seem to agree that emphasis should be placed on the One as the creative source. Identifying the creative or spiritual source with the One rather than the many allows the many (the individual traditions) to change without destroying the One. It is a one-sided identity relationship. This is why the richness of plurality provides the dynamic to lead the many religions back to their creative source. Thus, the centre of gravity is kept in the One, without overthrowing the many. What is required is to use one's own particular religion in dialogue with the other traditions as the means of access to the deeper creative source.

Religion as instrumental

The diversity and plurality of religion underscore its instrumental function. The revelations, doctrines and spiritual disciples of the many religions are the means by which the One is reached. The sayings of the Buddha, the monastic rules, the philosophic schools and the Bodhisattvas all function as instruments of enlightenment in Buddhism. They are the 'boats' to help one across the river of *karma-saṁsāra* to enlightenment on the other side. But once the goal is reached, the boat that was employed is left behind. Buddhism is not Buddha's sayings or the monastic institution but the enlightenment experience itself – what Buddhadāsa called the *dhamma*. Similarly, in Hinduism the Vedas, though necessary, are left behind at the realization of *mokṣa* or release. The Vedas are the 'ladder' by which Brahman is reached. But when the soul has been released, when the instrumental function of the Vedic ladder has been accomplished, the Veda is no longer required. *Gurus*, ashrams, images and *yogis* are likewise instrumental in their function within Hinduism.

The scriptures, forms and practices of Western religions differ in that their instrumental function is never transcended in the experience of the devotee.[6] The Torah, New Testament and Qur'ān are never transcended and left behind in the way that Hindu or Buddhist scripture is transcended. But even though it cannot be totally transcended, scripture in the Western religions still functions as the instrument or means by which God is revealed. In a similar way, although the Western religions vary in their acceptance and use of theology, prayer, the singing of hymns and the partaking of sacraments, each religion employs these as the means by which the one God is responded to, gives grace and is known. Thus it becomes clear that much of what is commonly taken to be the core of the various religions is really a particular collection of instrumental means by which the One may be reached. Understood in this way, the various religions need not be treated as fixed, unchanging truths but rather as developing traditions of religious instrumentality.

Problems arise within religious pluralism when it is the forms of the various religions that are absolutized rather than the One. Both Karl Rahner, within Christianity, and Nāgārjuna, in Buddhism, agree on this point – although of course their understanding of the One is quite different. Both see religions as imperfect instrumental forms by which the One may be apprehended. To this the Jewish prophets, Muhammad and Śaṅkara would surely give assent. Much misunderstanding among religions can be avoided if the instrumental nature of the plurality of religious experience is grasped. In the past the lack of such awareness and the absolutizing of the instrumental forms of religion have often been the causes of religious conflict.

Wilfred Cantwell Smith has argued that the problem with much scholarly study of religion, especially in the modern West, is that it takes religions to be fixed, unchanging forms.[7] This reifying of religion has missed the cumulative and developing nature of religious traditions – a major plank in Troeltsch's analysis. Smith suggests that the various religions have never been distinct entities. In their instrumental forms, as the preceding chapters have demonstrated, the religions have constantly borrowed from and interacted with each other. Smith suggests that if scholars gave serious study to the Chinese concept of *san chiao* (the three traditions) and the Japanese concept of *Ryobu Shinto* (two-sided Shinto) a better understanding of this aspect of religious pluralism could be achieved.[8]

The superimposition of validating criteria

Another common feature observed in our study is the practice of responding to the challenge of pluralism by superimposing one's own criteria of validity upon the other religions. If, for the Christian, Christ is the validating criterion, then true spirituality within any other religion is to be identified by the superimposition of Christ upon that religion – thus Rahner's 'anonymous Christians' and Panikkar's 'unknown Christ of Hinduism'. For Buddhadāsa, the *dhamma* is the truth of all religions. For Islam, the Qur'ān is the validating revelation against which all others must be tested. Just as the Jews have been elected by God to fulfil a certain role in history, so other religions are to be understood in terms of their particular election by Yahweh. And because the one Brahman is, for the Hindu, the goal to which all paths must lead, Buddha, Christ, Muhammad and Moses may be validated as *avatāras* of Brahman. Fundamental to religious pluralism is the fact that one's commitment to truth within each tradition is experienced as absolute or decisive and is universalized by superimposing it upon the others. The reasons for this may well be found in the psychological and philosophical limits of human nature. This possibility will be explored later in this chapter. An important point to be emphasized here, however, is that the validating criteria adopted by each of the religions arose out of its contention with the challenge of pluralism. Each religion's validation of its traditions came after its contact with other religions. The criteria of Christianity, for example, were formulated after contact with Greek philosophy and Gnosticism. The same process can be observed in each of the religions.

Before moving on to discuss the future of religions, it is important to identify some dangers and difficulties in present-day religious pluralism. All the major world religions face these. An obvious area of difficulty is the missionary activity that occurs when the superimposition of one's own criteria upon the other is followed by efforts to convert the other. It is part of our nature as human beings to want to share our most treasured convictions with others. Often, as in the cases of Buddhism, Christianity and Islam, that tendency is reinforced by the teachings of the tradition. Difficulty ensues when this desire and direction to carry one's teaching to others are made militant or exclusivist. Our study indicates that militant or exclusivist approaches are today being severely questioned in terms of each tradition's own teaching. When accurate information about the other traditions is made available – as is the case in many places now – the resulting understanding usually produces a rethinking of the missionary philosophy and method. Examples can be seen in Islamic ṣūfism in India and in modern Christian theology. Pluralism will always demand that we share our particular understanding of religion with one another. If done in sympathy and respect for the integrity of the other, such sharing, as past and present examples demonstrate, can result in spiritual growth and enrichment for all. In the open experience of other traditions the possibility for conversion always exists. But, as the history of pluralism within each tradition shows, the result is more often one of the strengthening and enrichment of one's own religion. The alternative, attempting to attack or degrade other religions, has frequently produced both internal stagnation and often violent interreligious conflict of the sort that all religions would now see as a negation of spirituality.

Throughout the preceding chapters the problem of the divergence between the theistic religions and the non-theistic religions, such as Buddhism and Advaita Vedānta Hinduism (Taoism and Confucianism can probably be included here), continually reappeared. This problem has caused many significant difficulties for scholars of religion, often tempting them to solve the difficulty by uncritically imposing the concept of God on Advaita Vedānta and Buddhism – John Hick was noted as a scholar engaging in just such a 'solution.' Wilfred Smith attempts a more honest resolution of the problem.[9] Employing his corporate self-consciousness approach, he tries to demonstrate that as a general symbol for the transcendent, the term 'God' could be acceptable to Buddhist scholars. The Theravādin, imagines Smith, would agree that for purposes of general discussion the notion of *dharma* could be fruitfully compared with the concept of God in the Western religions. Buddhists have held *dharma* as a transcendent truth that is beyond the capabilities of words and is yet immediate and lived. In Mahāyāna Buddhism, the Bodhisattva as a symbol of the transcendent may be functionally parallel to the theistic term 'God'. For the Advaita Vedāntist, it may be Brahman symbolized as *sat* (pure being), *cit* (pure consciousness) and *ānanda* (pure bliss). The Buddhists and monistic Hindus might well be prepared to admit that conceptualizations differ across traditions, but because these people accord only secondary status to these conceptualizations, they do not become overly disturbed by such difficulties. Taken on that secondary level, the concept of 'God' might be accepted as a heuristic term in discussion across traditions. Smith does not suggest that we all simply agree to use the term 'God' and leave it at that. He strongly urges the necessity of learning each other's languages and thought forms. Only then will the vocabulary problem become soluble.[10] As a contribution to the inevitable process of learning each other's languages, he offers the following suggestion as a possible basis for discussion between theists and non-theists:

> that by the term 'God' one means a truth – reality that explicitly transcends conception, but insofar as conceivable is that to which man's religious history has at its best been a response, human and in some sense inadequate.[11]

Smith adds that his concept of religious history includes, in addition to Buddhism and Hinduism, the Western classical tradition and the metaphysical-humanist-idealist tradition in which transcendence appears as truth, beauty, justice and the good. In case someone were to assume that the provision of an encompassing description implies that all religions are true, or equally true, Smith responds as follows:

> That would be indeed silly. I, of course, hold that not even one 'religion' is equally true, abstractly in all its instances through history; rather, it becomes less or more true in the case of particular persons as it informs their lives and their groups and shapes and nurtures their faiths ... What I do urge is that the problem of religious truth is in principle not different but in practice much improved, if one take the whole of religion rather than a sector of it as the question's field.[12]

Although the findings of our current study would seem generally to support Smith's interpretation, there is one point on which we might find it necessary to differ. Smith strongly urges that 'our understanding of each other's concepts be anchored in history, even for history-transcending and self-transcending concepts such as "God".'[13] Although this assertion would be acceptable to Judaism and Christianity, it would seem unacceptable when applied to Islam, Hinduism and Buddhism. While Judaism and Christianity explicitly experience God's truth in and through history, it seems most unlikely that the Muslim, Hindu or Buddhist can share this perception. Though admitting that there is history in religion (i.e. traditions do change through time), they would not accept the idea that the truth is 'anchored' or revealed in that historical process; for them the truth is anchored and revealed in the reality that is behind or beyond history. As Smith urges, we must learn and respect each other's language and thought forms. In this instance his training as a modern Western historian has perhaps prevented him from following his own advice.

Yet another difficulty in contemporary religious pluralism is the conflict between constitutional statements of 'equality' (as found in the constitutions of the US and India) and religions that understand persons to be at different stages of spiritual realization and thus not equal (e.g. Hinduism's and Buddhism's law of *karma*). When such a conflict arises, as it now has in India, the requirement of equality may legally override the teachings and practices of a religion such as Hinduism and thereby violate religious freedom. Because constitutions calling for equality usually also enshrine the principle of religious freedom, a serious internal contradiction results. At this point the politicians, the lawmakers, usually throw up their hands and pass the problem on to the courts. Because the problem is not a legal one but a conflict of views or presuppositions (e.g. in the case of India, egalitarian humanism versus the *karma* theory of Hinduism), it is really a classic problem of pluralism. Here the experience and wisdom of religions could inform in a beneficial way the modern humanist or secularist. The problem and principles of religious pluralism are in many ways parallel to those of present-day cultural pluralism.[14]

The problem of equality is only one of many occasioned by modern cultural and religious pluralism. For instance, Islam perceives of itself as a state religion. Yet if it were to attempt to absorb or take over a nation such as the United States or Canada, which are constitutionally multicultural, it would be perceived as subversive. Again, religious and secular traditions and perceptions would clash, and this fact requires that Islam, as it increasingly finds itself a minority in pluralistic host cultures, reinterpret its perception of itself as a state religion. Many similar problems have arisen and will arise from the tensions generated by cultural and religious pluralism.

A threat to the creative contribution of pluralism to religion is that at times some members of religions react to the challenge of pluralism with militant exclusivism (e.g. Christian, Hindu or Islamic fundamentalism). Such a reaction is always to be regretted in that, as our study has suggested, it usually breeds spiritual stagnation and 'religious violence', as the history of modern Iran demonstrates. As in a family, the accepting of differences in the context of mutual respect and appreciation can be a powerful catalyst for good. Egocentric narrow-mindedness is always destructive and is the opposite of true religion in any tradition.

THE FUTURE OF RELIGIONS

We have noted that within modern Western thinking Schleiermacher inaugurated an approach to religion that was diametrically opposed to that of his predecessors. This shift in perspective had the effect of drawing attention to the universal nature of religious experience in its many different traditions – thus the relativizing approach of Ernst Troeltsch. In addition to turning attention away from metaphysics, rationalism or revelation, the focus on the humanity of religion has had the effect of highlighting some of the limitations in human nature that must be taken seriously in all future religion.

Future theology and the limits inherent in pluralism

For the purposes of this discussion, let us give the term 'theology' a broad, general meaning, namely, of knowledge or religious truth in all of its pluralistic forms. Although this may seem uncomfortable for a Buddhist or monistic Hindu, we ask acceptance of such a heuristic interpretation for purposes of our current discussion. The question to be examined is this: what are the limits to be respected in all future theologizing? Within the Christian religion Karl Rahner has discussed this issue at length. He demonstrates that pluralism requires a shift from the scholastic method of the past to a new approach that has not as yet been fully explored and articulated. But as a first step towards future theology, some important limitations can be stated – limitations that will apply to future thinkers in any religion.

Theology, says Rahner, can no longer follow the simplistic pattern of the past in which the problem of pluralism was overcome by application of the principle of non-contradiction – that is, when two theological positions were seen to be contradictory alternatives, then according to the principle of non-contradiction, by which both could not be correct at the same time, a decision would be made as to which of the positions was correct, and the pluralism or the contradiction would be overcome. This was the pattern that typified the scholastic theology of the past. It is a pattern that can no longer serve in the face of the challenge presented by the encounter of religions. As Rahner recognizes, theology finds itself in a new situation:

> The pluralism of which we are speaking here, rather, consists precisely in the fact that it is quite impossible to reduce the theologies and their representative thesis to a simple logical alternative in this manner, in the fact that they exist side by side with one another as disparate and mutually incommensurable.[15]

Rahner is speaking of the pluralism that he finds currently to be the case only within Christian theology. It is a pluralism that is insurmountable because no common basis can be found between the various theological schools upon which to arrive at a comparative understanding and logical judgement between alternatives. If Christians find this to be the case between the various theologies put forth within Christianity itself, then the difficulties certainly will be greater when the competing claims of the various religions are considered. The inescapable pluralism of all future theology has two limiting dimensions. First, there is the fact that rival viewpoints may adopt starting points so different that they will be able to establish little or no common intellectual ground. And without the basis of this common ground, individual propositions cannot be discussed in such a way as to arrive at a positive 'right' or 'wrong' judgement. Although the two partners in the dialogue may anticipate similarities and differences in their positions, the lack of a common ground, says Rahner, 'means that the representatives of the different schools cannot achieve, even indirectly, a position in which they can explain to one another consciously and unambiguously in what precisely the difference between their respective intellectual outlooks consist'.[16] Here Rahner is pointing to the experience that he has (and thinks others have) when one's partner in theological dialogue constantly proceeds from different starting points than one's own, uses terms differently and assumes points as established that are alien to one's own thinking. This results in no conclusion being reached and the discussion being broken off for lack of time or other reasons that make it impossible to continue. In any case, the lack of a common intellectual basis, which prevents the attainment of positive conclusions, is a limit that necessitates pluralism in theology.

A second limiting dimension that Rahner identifies as necessitating theological pluralism has to do with the finite nature of the human mind. All the various theological positions and full knowledge of the various world religions can no longer be mastered by any one mind. Even if a single world civilization or religion were to emerge, says Rahner, there would still be interior differences that would manifest in an increasing pluralism of theologies with respect to 'their methods, their structural developments, their outlooks, their terminologies, and the practical trends to which they give rise. These differences will be so great that as theologies it will be quite impossible for them to be covered by, or subsumed under any one single homogeneous theology.'[17] This means, then, that there cannot be any *one* theology, even when one's gaze is restricted to a particular religion. If, by reason of the limited capacity of the human mind, dogmatic judgements cannot be made within one religion, how much more must that be the case when theological reflection takes place within the larger context of the many religions. Within the context of the world religions, theological pluralism is the rule.

Both these limitations will have to be taken seriously by scholars functioning within a particular tradition or within the context of the world religions. Since the time of Nāgārjuna[18] in the East and Immanuel Kant[19] in the West, the intellectual limits of the human mind have been known – if not always respected. But perhaps more important for theologizing in a pluralistic context will be the first limitation – the lack of a common intellectual basis upon which dialogue or debate may be conducted. Theologians of one of the major Western religions – Judaism, Christianity or Islam – will quickly encounter this difficulty if in dialogue with Hindus they begin to think through their concept of creation or in dialogue with Buddhists they begin to scrutinize their notion of God. A common intellectual ground just does not seem to exist. Understanding, albeit partial and blurred, seems to come only when one group of theologians suspends its own viewpoint and attempts to adopt the assumptions of the other and see the universe through those alien concepts.

But here too certain psychological limits arise and must be taken seriously by the theologian. In any intellectual exercise in which theologians attempt to see with the concepts of another religion, the psychological dynamics of their minds will never allow them to be completely objective or neutral in their perceptions. A first impulse will be to identify similarities between their position and that of the others. Usually this signals an act of intellectual reductionism, or what Freud termed 'projection'.[20] Instead of a real similarity having been identified, the theologians have simply indulged in the self-protective mechanism of saying 'Oh yes, we see what you mean by that; it is exactly the same as we mean by this.' They project their viewpoint onto the persons of the other religion and then claim to discover that it is the same as their own. Of course this is very comforting in several ways. It suggests that there is only one truth after all, that they have it (probably in fuller or fullest measure, and thus implicitly or explicitly they claim superiority for their view) and that therefore no change is required. The true discovery, namely, that real difference does exist, naturally produces emotional insecurity and doubt that one's theological position is absolute.

This universal human characteristic of ego-attachment to one's own position has been given much attention by Nāgārjuna and other Mādhyamika Buddhists. They approached the problem as follows. Because human beings are by nature ego-attached to their own view or theological position, no amount of arguing from an opposed position will have any effect. The theologians in question will simply reinterpret an objection or counter position in such a way as to fit their system. In other words, by the mechanism of projection they will attempt to force their opponents off certain presuppositions and on to theirs. And because the opponents will be attempting to do the same (all are ego-attached to their positions and cognitively cannot let go), an endless and unhelpful debate will ensue. With this psychological insight in hand, the model developed by the Mādhyamika Buddhists for theological debate was simple and devastating. The Mādhyamika entered the debate with no theological position. The aim was to understand the position of an opponent so completely that the Mādhyamika would be able to find the internal inconsistencies inevitably present in every theological system and then by *reductio ad absurdum* argument bring the whole thing crashing down around the ears of the opponent. To be defeated by one's own system brings on a severe psychological shock – one that might even convince the theologian to give up theologizing permanently. And that, of course, was the very thing the Mādhyamika was hoping to accomplish. Once theologians put down their pens and let go of their favourite concepts, the way is cleared or emptied of intellectual obstacles so that they can finally see reality as a pure perception and live their lives appropriately.

The Mādhyamika and Freudian analyses both make clear that any attempt to conceptualize reality fully and objectively is inevitably tied to the finite limitation of one's cognitive processes and the self-centered, distorting emotions attached to those processes. The recent postmodern and feminist critiques offer further support to this conclusion.

When the above limitations are taken seriously and applied to current theological models, a helpful critique results. For the Christian, for instance, it means that there is no longer any ground upon which a theologian can make absolute claims for a particular theological position. For example, Hans Küng's argument that one should be a Christian because Jesus of Nazareth is 'ultimately decisive, definitive, and archetypal for man's relations with God, with his fellow man, with society'[21] is found to violate the limits of theologizing on at least two counts. The first problem, of course, is that Küng is making the very kind of absolute claim to knowledge that the finite limits of the human mind invalidate. Second, as Paul Knitter has pointed out in his careful assessment of Küng's argument, it is based on a badly blurred view of other religions.[22] In spite of Küng's warning to other theologians that they must not reach theological conclusions without a clear knowledge of the other world religions, his own understanding is shown to have been seriously distorted by the basic a priori of his thinking, namely, that Christ is the final norm for all religions.[23] Küng has engaged in Freudian projections (seeing Christ as the unknown fulfilment of all other religions) and intellectual reductionism (incorrect and simplistic understandings of other religions so as to fit them into his own categories).

Küng's approach can be classified with those of the Christocentric theologians reviewed in chapter 2. Whereas all religions are recognized (in varying degrees) to be particular manifestations of God, Christianity is seen as the only religion that fully (or that most fully) manifests God and therefore must serve as the criterion for all others. Theological approaches that presuppose a universal Logos as foundational for all religions and then identify the Logos as Christ are simply a variation on the same theme and suffer from the same failings of psychological projection and intellectual reductionism. If, for example, Jews were to be told that the basis of their religion was the Logos of which Jesus Christ was the criterion and manifestation, their response to such a theology would likely be that the theologian in question had never really understood the Jewish religion and indeed was taking a Christianized version of Judaism to be real Judaism. Christians frequently have the same sort of response when told by a Hindu that Christianity is fully encompassed within Hinduism as yet another particular manifestation of the one Brahman. It is not surprising that Christians find it difficult to recognize their own belief and practice in such a Hinduized version of Christianity. In all of these examples theological limitations have not been respected and the result proves unacceptable when seen in the context of religious pluralism.

Another approach, one that developed from the modern humanistic emphasis, resolves the problem by moving in the opposite direction. It attempts to overcome the difficulty by seeing Christianity, along with the other world religions, as simply various manifestations of one common humanity. This is the method frequently taken by theologians who have been seduced by the psychologists, sociologists and historians of religion. It is also a reductionism, but this time in the opposite direction. Instead of seeing the various religions as merely particular manifestations of the one divine, this solution reduces the transcendent experiences of the various religions to being no more than particular expressions of a common humanity. In the first instance, the human diversity of religious experience is reduced to a common transcendent reality; in the second, the plural experiences of the transcendent are reduced to a common human experience.

The implication of this discussion is that the Mādhyamika Buddhists are correct. When the limitations of theologizing are taken seriously, all future theologizing with the intent of establishing ultimate claims to knowledge must cease. Is the correct vision for the future one in which thousands of theologians of the various religions all around the world simultaneously put down their pens? What then, silence? Although the Mādhyamika Buddhists and modern sceptics and positivists might approve of this option, silence must be rejected as the correct vision for the future of theology and religions.

The future of religions in dialogue

The inherent desire to conceptualize and share religious experience is too deeply ingrained in human nature to render silence an acceptable answer. In fact the Mādhyamika themselves have been far from silent. Their prescription of silence was only intended to apply to claims of absolute knowledge. As long as that limitation is honoured, then discussion, including theological discussion, could take place. As a first step, then, let us attempt to indicate some of the presuppositions upon which the religious dialogue of the future should be grounded. These presuppositions will be drawn inductively from our prior analysis of the present situation in religious pluralism. The seven key presuppositions are these: 1) that in all religions there is experience of a reality that transcends human conception; 2) that that reality is conceived in a plurality of ways both within each religion and among all religions and that the recognition of plurality is necessary both to safeguard religious freedom and to respect human limitations; 3) that the pluralistic forms of religion are instrumental in function; 4) that what is absolute and decisive in any religion is one's commitment to truth, yet one's grasp of truth is and remains limited; 5) that the Buddha's teaching of critical tolerance and moral compassion always must be observed; 6) that through self-critical dialogue we must penetrate ever further into our own particular experience of transcendent reality (and possibly into the transcendent reality of others); and 7) that within the plurality of our interfaith encounter a focus on 'the suffering other' and 'the suffering earth' can provide a shared starting point for a dialogue towards mutual cooperation and understanding. Let us consider each of these in more detail.

Presupposition 1 simply states the recognition found in each religion surveyed, namely, that God, Brahman or *dhamma* is a transcendent reality which is over and above the mundane and which cannot be fully conceptualized. The presupposition does not judge whether transcendent reality is the same or different across religions. Such a judgement would be absolute, would exceed the limits of human knowledge and, therefore, is best left to God, Brahman, *dhamma* and so forth. The statement does, however, distinguish this experience and the resultant dialogue as religious (i.e. although acceptable to all religions it is not a statement the humanist or materialist could accept). This distinction would seem to be challenged by Wilfred Smith, who argues for the inclusion of the humanist – although he restricts inclusion to the rational humanist.[24] Certainly the merits of a dialogue involving all the possible pluralities within the global community is deserving of careful study. But, even if such a global dialogue were deemed advisable, there would still be a need for a separate caucus composed of those who could in some sense share an experience of transcendent reality.

Presupposition 2 arises from the existence and nature of religious pluralism and from the limitations on theologizing discussed above. It safeguards against claims of absolutism of a kind that would cause religious dialogue to self-destruct. It also safeguards religious freedom.

Presupposition 3, following from presupposition 2, gives importance to the instrumental function of religious forms through which religious experience takes place – that the revelations, doctrines and spiritual disciplines of the many religions are the means by which transcendent reality is reached. By implication the plurality of instrumental forms also points up the variety of spiritual dispositions among individuals – a fact that the religious absolutisms of the past have, to their detriment, often ignored.

Presupposition 4 is perhaps the most important and the most difficult. On the surface it might appear to conflict with presupposition 2, which safeguards the plurality of religions. It does not. The absolutism ruled out in presupposition 2 is the sort that would impose the experience of one's own commitment to truth upon all others – because one recognizes that one's grasp of that truth remains limited. This is the paradox that, as Langdon Gilkey puts it, has to be embraced and lived in the encounter of religions.[25] It is a recognition that deep religious commitment to truth is necessarily absolute and, as such, functions as the validating criteria for all of one's personal experience. This, however, does not impose it on others or rule out the recognition that other people have a similar absolute commitment to a particular truth claim, which, as stated in presupposition 2, will be different from one's own. As Jaspers correctly observes

> The language of transcendence, then, is spoken only in particular languages ... In such ... the truth which is heard is absolutely true, yet the speaking and hearing is such that it cannot be taken as universally or normatively true, but must admit the possibility of other, even of opposed, truths.[26]

Thus, one is able to honour one's own commitment to truth as absolute and at the same time respect the different absolute commitments to truth of others. In this way the limitations outlined above are respected, yet the necessity for absolute religious commitment to a particular religion is allowed. As Knitter points out, this distinction between one's commitment to truth and one's grasp of truth means 'that while there are no absolute expressions of truth, there are absolute commitments – there has to be if religion is going to play any kind of prophetic role in this threatened world'.[27] In an interreligious dialogue this would mean the preservation of our differences in dignity and mutual respect.

Presupposition 5 describes the character of mutual respect as one of critical tolerance and moral compassion. Standing secure in our difference we are encouraged to constructively criticize and so learn from one another. Our criticism is to be constructive, tolerant and undergirded by a moral compassion towards others. In such an atmosphere pluralism provides the opportunity for spiritual self-judgement and growth. It suggests that all theologizing activity should, as it were, be overheard by theologians of the other religions. The resultant theology would be more honest and humble than the theology we often have been accustomed to in the past.[28]

Presupposition 6 states that spiritual growth arises not from religious isolationism or exclusivism but rather in the context of religious pluralism. Our survey of each religion demonstrates that in all cases the creative periods were those marked by the challenge of pluralism. The presupposition is also substantiated by the experience of those now seriously engaged in dialogue, namely, that the result is an enriching and deepening of one's own religious experience. It remains for future dialogue to explore whether such spiritual deepening can reach a sense of a shared experience of transcendence (as Samartha reports) or, as Tillich puts it, a point where particularity breaks through to spiritual freedom – and to a vision of the spiritual presence in other expressions.

Presupposition 7 is an insight from Paul Knitter. Rather than searching for a theocentric, Christocentric or pluralist abstract concept upon which to ground the dialogue between religions, Knitter, as a result of his experience with liberation theology and religions other than his own, proposes a focus on the practice of religions towards the 'suffering other' and 'the suffering earth'.[29] Such a practical orientation, Knitter suggests, may provide powerful possibilities for the achievement of mutual understanding and cooperative ethical action on global problems. This insight of Knitter's has received empirical verification in my work over the past ten years as director of the Centre for Studies in Religion and Society at the University of Victoria in Victoria, British Columbia, Canada. A major part of the Centre's work has involved putting together teams of ethics theologians (from all the religions), scientists, social scientists and humanists to address major global problems. Different research teams have tackled: population, consumption and ecology; how to do health care ethics with cross-cultural sensitivity; religious conscience, the state and the law; and ethics and genetic engineering. Each of these has produced major books.[30] What is important for this discussion, however, is that, in the two- or three-year experience of each of these research teams the truth of Knitter's insight was borne out. While working on these major global challenges, those involved gained greater understanding of the participants from other religions and found cooperative ways for their traditions to respond. The problem that brought them together (e.g. the 'suffering earth' with its burden of overpopulation and excessive consumption) provided the common ground for dialogue far more successfully than if one had attempted to hammer out a theological concept as a basis or common ground for dialogue.

A basic prerequisite for future dialogue is that all participants have accurate information about each other's religion. Fulfilling this prerequisite is probably the single largest obstacle to the success of religious dialogue. The majority of people today are illiterate in their own religion as well as the religions of others. The academic discipline of religious studies has a major role to play in overcoming this problem. Intellectual knowledge of the facts of all religions is needed – but alone that will not be sufficient. We will not be able to empathize with the sense of transcendent reality that the forms of each religion seek to convey if only surface or intellectual knowledge is achieved. True empathy and understanding require that we learn each other's languages, for therein lie the important nuances of transcendent experience that are often lost in translation. The educational prerequisite for future dialogue is a stiff and serious one, requiring dedication and effort from all who would partake of this dialogue.

In the past many efforts at dialogue have failed because this prerequisite has not been fulfilled. Groups of well-meaning Jews, Christians, Muslims, Hindus and Buddhists have held polite and gracious gatherings and have returned home without having significantly entered into each other's thought forms. Although such meetings have produced a pious respect for others as fine religious people, they have not generated the deep self-criticism and spiritual renewal (presupposition 6) that future dialogue must achieve. If serious study, including thorough study of each other's languages, is to take place and develop, then religious studies departments will have an important and timely contribution to make. Universities in Canada, the United States, Australia and Europe offer sound, rigorous programmes of this kind. But elsewhere, in India for example, a serious weakness exists. Although the opportunity is provided for the serious study of Eastern religions – including the study of Sanskrit, Tibetan and Chinese languages – the same cannot be said for opportunities to study Western religions, Hebrew, Greek and Arabic. Until this fundamental deficiency is corrected, Indian participants in interreligious dialogue will be hampered by not having fulfilled the prerequisites for effective dialogue. The establishment of religious studies departments in which equal opportunity is provided for the study of all major religions and languages is an urgent need in Indian universities. Let us go one step further and hope that in the future seminaries throughout the world will understand and act upon the fact that this kind of study is a necessary prerequisite for meaningful theologizing.

In his book, *Towards a World Theology*, Wilfred Cantwell Smith gives careful attention to the importance of language in future religious dialogue. Although he agrees that knowledge of each other's languages is essential, he takes the further step of suggesting the need for some common operational or generic terms in which communication across religions can take place. He proposes the construction of conceptual categories to facilitate dialogue and attempts a beginning by redefining the terms 'faith', 'salvation', 'theology', and 'God'.[31] Although in this study we have made similar moves to facilitate discussion (e.g. our general use of theology), there is a very real danger in such an approach. Given the penchant of scholars to create their own cognitive universe through the construction of generic terms, the construction of such categories could lead to the formation of a meta-language, which would be yet one more thought form to add to those already existing. Of course this need not happen if scholars are careful not to give ontological status to their descriptive categories. The best safeguard against such a danger would be to let the various religions speak as much as possible in their own languages and thought forms. If in the course of dialogue useful and acceptable operational terms arise, then the process of communication will be improved. But for scholars to set out self-consciously to construct the generic terms for future dialogue (as Smith seems to propose) is dangerous and ill-advised. Knitter's proposal for praxis-based dialogue and study will help to avoid such problems.

The discussion of the above presuppositions and prerequisites is but an attempt at beginning to formulate the requirements for future religious dialogue. Accordingly, those presuppositions and prerequisites are necessarily sketchy, incomplete and in places probably misconceived. But they represent one attempt to reflect self-critically on the experience of the past and on that basis to formulate some guidelines for dialogue. For in such dialogue lies the future of religions.

NOTES

CHAPTER 1

1. Scholars differ in the way the term 'Judaism' is used. Some, notably Jewish scholars, see a continuity from ancient Israelite beginnings to the fully developed forms of Judaism, using this word to cover the entire history; for example, see Salo W. Baron, *A Social and Religious History of the Jews* (New York: Columbia University Press, 1952). Other scholars differentiate between classical Hebraism, ancient Israel from Abraham to the Babylonian exile, and Judaism as emerging after the Babylonian exile; for example, see W. F. Albright, *From the Stone Age to Christianity* (New York: Anchor, 1957). For the purposes of this book, the former interpretation is adopted.
2. Jacob Neusner, *The Way of the Torah: An Introduction to Judaism* (Belmont, CA: Dickenson, 1974), pp. 3–4.
3. Peter C. Craigie, *The Book of Deuteronomy* (Grand Rapids, MI: William B. Eerdmans, 1976), p. 28.
4. Ibid., pp. 377–8.
5. Ibid., p. 379.
6. R. J. Zwi Werblowsky, 'Judaism, or the Religion of Israel', in *The Concise Encyclopedia of Living Faiths*, ed. R. C. Zaehner (New York: Hawthorn Books, 1959), p. 31.
7. Ibid.
8. J. Kenneth Kuntz, *The People of Ancient Israel* (New York: Harper & Row, 1974), p. 356. See also Lam. 2:4; Ps. 137; Ezek. 1–24.
9. Ibid., p. 416.
10. Steven Fine, ed. *Sacred Realm: The Emergence of the Synagogue in the Ancient World* (New York: Oxford, 1996), p. 10.
11. E. R. Goodenough, *An Introduction to Philo Judaeus* (Oxford: Blackwell, 1962). See also 'Philo Judaeus', in *Encyclopedia Judaica* (Jerusalem: Keter, 1971).

12. See Raimundo Panikkar, *The Unknown Christ of Hinduism*, rev. edn. (Maryknoll, NY: Orbis, 1981); and John B. Cobb, Jr, *Christ in a Pluralistic Age* (Philadelphia: Westminister, 1975).
13. 'Philo Judaeus', in *Encyclopedia Judaica*.
14. 'Philosophy, Jewish', in *Encyclopedia Judaica*.
15. Cited in A. Cohen, *The Teachings of Maimonides* (New York: Ktav, 1968), pp. 116–17.
16. Cited in ibid., p. 120.
17. Moses Mendelssohn, *Jerusalem*, trans. Alfred Josepe (New York: Schocken, 1969).
18. Ibid., p. 66.
19. Ibid., p. 107.
20. Ibid., pp. 108–9.
21. Emil L. Fackenheim, *Encounters between Judaism and Modern Philosophy* (New York: Basic Books, 1973), p. 173.
22. Ibid.
23. Ibid., p. 174.
24. Ibid.
25. Ibid., p. 192.
26. Ibid., p. 197.
27. See Franz Rosenzweig, *The Star of Redemption*, trans. W. W. Hallo (New York: Holt, Rinehart & Winston, 1971); and *Judaism Despite Christianity: The 'Letters on Christianity and Judaism' between Eugen Rosenstock-Huessy and Franz Rosenzweig* (Tuscaloosa, AL: University of Alabama Press, 1969).
28. Nahum N. Glatzer, *Franz Rosenzweig: His Life and Thought* (New York: Schocken, 1953), p. xxiii.
29. Ibid., p. xxv.
30. Ibid., p. xxvi.
31. Rosenzweig, *Star of Redemption*, p. 416.
32. Glatzer, p. 203.
33. Rosenzweig, *Judaism Despite Christianity*, p. 68.
34. Ibid.
35. S. Daniel Breslauer, *The Ecumenical Perspective and the Modernization of Jewish Religion* (Missoula, MT: Scholars Press, 1978).
36. Ibid., p. 17.
37. Ibid., p. 18.
38. Ibid., p. 19.
39. Jacob B. Agus, *Dialogue and Tradition: The Challenges of Contemporary Judeo-Christian Thought* (New York: Abelard Schuman, 1971), p. 429.
40. Abraham J. Heschel, *The Insecurity of Freedom: Essays in Applied Religion* (New York: Farrar, Straus & Giroux, 1966), p. 182.
41. Breslauer, p. 20.
42. Breslauer, p. 21. Breslauer here identifies Agus, Gordis and Heschel.
43. Abraham J. Heschel, *Man Is Not Alone: A Philosophy of Religion* (New York: Harper & Row, 1951), p. 171.
44. Paul Tillich, *The Protestant Era* (Chicago: Phoenix, 1963), p. viii.

45. See Michael A. Meyer, *The Origins of the Modern Jew* (Detroit: Wayne State University Press, 1967).
46. Tillich, *Life and the Spirit*, vol. 3 of *Systematic Theology* (Chicago: University of Chicago Press, 1963), especially pp. 162–244. For a recent Jewish thinker who argues that Jews, in order to live in a pluralistic world, can and must surrender the conviction that their understanding of the Godhead is definitive and final, see Daniel Cohn-Sherbok, 'Jewish Religious Pluralism', *Cross-Currents*, 46, 1996, pp. 326–42.
47. Personal communication from Martin S. Jaffee, University of Washington, 15 October 1999.
48. Werblowsky, p. 49.
49. Ibid.
50. M. Amon (University of British Columbia, Vancouver) stated this in a letter to me in June 1983. See also Aviezen Ravitzky, *Messianism, Zionism and Jewish Religious Radicalism* (Chicago: University of Chicago Press, 1995).
51. Martin Buber and Hermann Cohen, 'A Debate on Zionism and Messianism', in *The Jew in the Modern World*, ed. P. R. Mendes-Flour and J. Reinharz (New York: Oxford University Press, 1980), pp. 448–53.
52. Israel, for example, includes in its Declaration of Independence the guarantee of 'freedom of religion'. It practises openness towards other religions, especially Christianity and Islam, on the basis of the biblical precept from Exod. 23:9, 'you know the heart of a stranger, for you were strangers in the land of Egypt'. The two major non-Jewish religions represented in Israel are Christianity and Islam. See Joseph Badi, *Religion in Israel Today* (New York: Bookman Associates, 1959), p. 55. For Orthodox Jewish comment see Mayer Schiller, 'We Are Not Alone in the World', *Tibbun*, 11, March 1996, pp. 59–60.

CHAPTER 2

1. For example, see Paul Tillich, *The Future of Religions* (New York: Harper & Row, 1966); J. M. Carmody, 'A Next Step for Catholic Theology', *Theology Today*, 32, 1976, pp. 371–81; Klaus Klostermaier, 'A Hindu Christian Dialogue on Truth', *Journal of Ecumenical Studies*, 12, 1975, pp. 157–73; R. H. Drummond, 'Christian Theology and the History of Religions', *Journal of Ecumenical Studies*, 12, 1975, pp. 389–405; John Hick, *God and the Universe of Faiths* (London: Macmillan, 1973); Hans Küng, *On Being a Christian* (New York: Doubleday, 1976); Karl Rahner, *Anonymous and Explicit Faith*, vol. 16 of *Theological Investigations* (New York: Seabury Press, 1979); Raimundo Panikkar, *The Trinity and the Religious Experience of Man* (London: Darton, Longman & Todd, 1973); J. A. T. Robinson, *Truth Is Two-Eyed* (London: SCM Press, 1979); W. C. Smith, *Towards a World Theology* (Philadelphia: Westminster Press, 1981); Alan Race, *Christians and Religious Pluralism* (Maryknoll, NY: Orbis, 1985); Paul Knitter, *No Other Name: A Critical Survey of Christian Attitudes Toward the World Religions* (Maryknoll, NY: Orbis, 1985); Gavin

D'Costa, *Theology and Religious Pluralism* (Oxford: Basil Blackwell, 1986); John Hick and Paul Knitter, eds, *The Myth of Christian Uniqueness: Toward a Pluralistic Theology of Religions* (Maryknoll, NY: Orbis, 1987); John Cobb, Jr and Christopher Ives, eds, *The Emptying God: A Buddhist–Jewish–Christian Conversation* (Maryknoll, NY: Orbis, 1990); Diana Eck, *Encountering God: A Spiritual Journey from Bozeman to Banaras* (Boston: Beacon, 1993); John Hick, *A Christian Theology of Religions: The Rainbow of Faiths* (Louisville, KY: John Knox, 1995); Jacques Dupuis, S.J., *Toward a Christian Theology of Religious Pluralism* (Maryknoll, NY: Orbis, 1997); Paul Knitter, *Jesus and the Other Names: Christian Mission and Global Responsibility* (Maryknoll, NY: Orbis, 1996). This list is by no means exhaustive. Of course it is also true that many fundamentalist or evangelical theologians are not prepared to entertain such fundamental changes of position.

2. Robley E. Whitson, *The Coming Convergence of World Religions* (New York: Newman, 1971).

3. John S. Dunne, *The Way of All the Earth* (New York: Macmillan, 1972). For an analysis of my personal experience in this regard see Harold Coward, 'Hinduism's Sensitizing of Christianity to Its Own Sources', *Dialogue & Alliance*, 7:2, 1993, pp. 77–85.

4. Lucien Richard, *What Are They Saying about Christ and World Religions?* (New York: Paulist Press, 1981), p. 3.

5. M. Wiles, 'Christianity Without Incarnation?', in *The Myth of God Incarnate*, ed. John Hick (Philadelphia: Westminster Press, 1977), p. 1.

6. E. D. Piryns, 'The Church and Interreligious Dialogue: Present and Future', *Japan Missionary Bulletin*, 4, 1978.

7. Ibid., p. 173.

8. Wilfred Cantwell Smith, *The Faith of Other Men* (New York: Harper & Row, 1972), pp. 9–23.

9. Piryns, p. 175.

10. K. S. Latourette, *A History of Christianity* (London: Eyre & Spottiswoode, 1955), p. 36.

11. Ibid., p. 79. Hugo Meynell has shown that it is just this identity relationship between Jesus and God that is crucial for Christian belief ('Myth in Christian Religion', *Theolinguistics*, 8, 1983, pp. 133–41).

12. J. Jeremias, *Jesus' Promise to the Nations* (London: SCM Press, 1967). Knitter has recently focused on this covenant relationship as a basis for reinterpreting the uniqueness of Christianity. Paul Knitter, *Jesus and the Other Names*, p. 174, note 6.

13. Jean Milet, *God or Christ: The Excesses of Christocentricity* (New York: Crossroad, 1981), p. 10. For a clear and balanced treatment of how much of this can be attributed to the historical Jesus and how much to the faith statements of the early Christian churches, see Marcus J. Borg, *Meeting Jesus Again for the First Time* (San Francisco: Harper, 1995).

14. Ibid., p. 20.

15. Richard, pp. 6–7.

16. Ibid., p. 7.

17. Milet, pp. 18–19.

18. Krister Stendahl, 'Notes for Three Bible Studies', in *Christ's Lordship and Religious Pluralism*, ed. G. H. Anderson and T. F. Stransky (Maryknoll, NY: Orbis, 1981), p. 10.
19. Ibid., pp. 15–17.
20. For a collection of Bible studies on key New Testament passages see Kenneth Cracknell, *Why Dialogue?: A First British Comment on the WCC Guidelines* (London: British Council of Churches, 1980).
21. Latourette, pp. 120–1.
22. Ibid., p. 122.
23. H. W. Robinson, *Inspiration and Revelation in the Old Testament* (Oxford: Oxford University Press, 1950).
24. Latourette, p. 123.
25. Ibid., p. 124.
26. Ibid.
27. Gerard Vallee, *A Study in Anti-Gnostic Polemics* (Waterloo, Canada: Wilfrid Laurier University Press, 1981), p. 99.
28. The following summary is taken from Latourette, p. 142ff.
29. Ibid., p. 143.
30. Jaroslav Pelikan, *The Growth of Medieval Theology (600–1300)*, vol. 3 of *The Christian Tradition* (Chicago: University of Chicago Press, 1977), p. 193.
31. Pelikan, *The Spirit of Eastern Christiandom (600–1700)*, vol. 2 of *The Christian Tradition*, p. 289.
32. Ibid., p. 240.
33. Ibid., p. 287.
34. See, for example, Jacob Needleman, *The New Religions* (Garden City, NY: Doubleday, 1970); and Harvey Cox, *Turning East* (New York: Simon & Schuster, 1977).
35. 'Declaration on the Relationship of the Church to Non-Christian Religions', in *The Documents of Vatican II*, ed. W. M. Abbott (New York: Guild Press, 1966).
36. At the World Council of Churches (WCC) central committee meeting in Addis Ababa in January 1971 a subunit on dialogue (DIF) was established in Geneva for the purpose of encouraging dialogue with other religions. In 1977 in the face of considerable opposition and charges of syncretism and the blunting of evangelism, the DIF was able to organize a worldwide consultation on the theme 'Dialogue in Community' in Chiang Mai, Thailand. Meetings and dialogue with other faiths have continued over the years. For example at the 1999 WCC meetings in Harare, scholars from various religions were invited to attend and a Hindu, Anatanand Rambachan, addressed the assembly. The WCC also publishes a journal dedicated to interfaith relations, titled *Current Dialogue*, now at volume 34.
37. See, for example, Cracknell.
38. At the annual meetings of the American Academy of Religion, religious pluralism has been the focus of an increasing number of panels and papers.
39. Immanuel Kant, *Religion within the Limits of Reason Alone* (New York: Harper Torchbooks, 1960).

40. Friedrich Schleiermacher, *On Religion* (New York: Harper & Row, 1958).
41. D. F. Strauss, *The Life of Jesus Critically Examined*, trans. M. Evans (New York: Calvin Blanchard, 1860).
42. Ernst Troeltsch, 'The Place of Christianity Among the World Religions', in *Christianity and Other Religions*, ed. John Hick and Brian Hebblethwaite (Glasgow: Fount, 1980), pp. 11–31.
43. Ibid., pp. 29–30.
44. Karl Barth, 'The Revelation of God as the Abolition of Religion', in *Christianity and Other Religions*, p. 32. The article is a reprint of chapter 17 of part 2 of *The Doctrine of the Word of God*, vol. 1 of *Church Dogmatics* (Edinburgh: Clark, 1961).
45. Ibid., p. 33.
46. Ibid., pp. 34–9.
47. Ibid., pp. 50–1.
48. See Richard, p. 12. For an excellent analysis of Barth in relation to other religions and Paul, see S. G. Wilson, 'Paul and Religion', in *Paul and Paulism*, ed. M. D. Hooker and S. G. Wilson (London: SPCK, 1982), pp. 339–54. Wilson conclusively shows that the positions of both Paul and Barth rest on a theological a priori, namely, that outside of the revelation of God in Christ all religion is by definition false.
49. See, for example, *Mekilta de Rabbi Ishmael*, trans. J. Lauterbach, vol. 2 (Philadelphia: Jewish Publication Society of America, 1976), p. 234.
50. The following summary is based on Demetrios J. Constantelos, 'An Orthodox Perspective', in *Christ's Lordship and Religious Pluralism*, pp. 181–90. The theocentric focus of Orthodox thought is also reflected in Kallistos Ware, 'The Spiritual Father in Orthodox Christianity', *Cross Currents*, 24, 1974, pp. 296–320.
51. Plato, *Crito* 47D–49B.
52. Constantelos, p. 186.
53. John Meyendorff, 'The Christian Gospel and Social Responsibility', in *Continuity and Discontinuity in Church History*, ed. E. G. Church and T. George (Leiden: E. J. Brill, 1979), p. 123.
54. Ibid., p. 126.
55. Ibid., p. 189.
56. Paul Tillich, *The Courage to Be* (London: Fontana, 1962), pp. 180–3. See also his *Systematic Theology* (Chicago: University of Chicago Press, 1951), vol. 1, p. 237; vol. 2, p. 150.
57. The following summary is based on Paul Tillich, *Christianity and the Encounter of the World Religions* (New York: Columbia University Press, 1963; reprinted in *Christianity and Other Religions*).
58. Ibid., p. 111 (in *Christianity and Other Religions*).
59. Ibid., p. 112.
60. Ibid., p. 121.
61. Tillich, *Systematic Theology*, vol. 1. A case can be made for including Tillich in the Christocentric category. Tillich does acknowledge that in the crucified Jesus are found the criteria under which Christianity must judge itself and also the other religions (*Christianity and the Encounter*

of the World Religions, p. 82). But the stress placed on the 'God above Gods' and 'the Holy Spirit', with comparatively light development of Christology in his *Systematic Theology*, led me to place Tillich in the theocentric group. He is clearly inclusivistic in his approach.

62. John Hick, 'Whatever Path Men Choose Is Mine', in *Christianity and Other Religions*, pp. 171–90.
63. Ibid., p. 180.
64. Ibid., p. 182.
65. Ibid., p. 183.
66. James D. G. Dunn, *Christology in the Making* (Philadelphia: Westminster Press, 1980), pp. 62–3. Contemporary New Testament scholarship is split between those who see Jesus as understanding himself to be a Jewish prophet revolutionary (e.g. Dominic Crossan) or spirit prophet (e.g. Marcus Borg) and those who see Jesus as proclaiming himself as a Jewish prophet, inaugurating the kingdom of God as Israel's Messiah, God's chosen one (e.g. N. T. Wright). See Marcus Borg and N. T. Wright, *The Meaning of Jesus: Two Visions* (San Francisco: Harper, 1999).
67. Hick, p. 185.
68. Ibid. Biblical scholars present them as faith statements of the early church.
69. Ibid., p. 186.
70. John Hick, *God Has Many Names* (London: Macmillan, 1980). Hick has continued to refine his position without any fundamental change. See his recent *A Christian Theology of Religions: The Rainbow of Faiths* (Louisville, KY: John Knox, 1995).
71. John Hick, 'The Theology of Religious Pluralism', *Theology*, 86, 1983, p. 336. For a comprehensive critique of Hick's theocentric pluralism see Gavin D'Costa, *Theology and Religious Pluralism: The Challenge of Other Religions* (Oxford: Basil Blackwell, 1986), pp. 22–51. Hick responds to criticism of his fundamental focus on God's universal salvific love (as unacceptable to Buddhists and some Hindus, for example) by substituting the term 'the Real' for God. D'Costa shows that this move does not help, but creates more problems in that unless God's universal love is the ultimate reality, 'the Real', Hick's pluralistic model falls apart. Thus, changing the name from 'God' to 'the Real' does not solve the problem for the non-theistic traditions such as Buddhism. D'Costa concludes that 'Hick's attempt to be genuinely accommodating to the religions of the world ends up by being accommodating to none including Christianity.' See Gavin D'Costa, 'The New Missionary: John Hick and Religious Plurality', *International Bulletin of Missionary Research*, 15, 1991, p. 66. Other critiques of Hick include John Lyden, 'Why Only "One" Divine Reality? A Critique of Religious "Pluralism",' *Dialogue & Alliance*, 8, 1994, pp. 60–74; and Paul Eddy, 'Religious Pluralism and the Divine: Another Look at John Hick's Neo-Kantian Proposal', *Religious Studies*, 30, 1994, pp. 467–78. Eddy concludes that D'Costa's characterization of Hick's position as a 'transcendental agnosticism' is correct.
72. Wilfred Cantwell Smith, *The Faith of Other Men*, p. 98.

73. Ibid., p. 123.
74. Ibid., p. 129.
75. Ibid., pp. 130–1.
76. Ibid., p. 132.
77. Ibid., p. 133.
78. Ibid., p. 139.
79. Ibid.
80. Wilfred Cantwell Smith, *The Meaning and End of Religion* (New York: Harper & Row, 1978), p. 140.
81. Ibid., p. 201.
82. Ibid.
83. Wilfred Cantwell Smith, 'Participation: The Changing Christian Role in Other Cultures', in *Religious Diversity*, ed. W. G. Oxtoby (New York: Harper & Row, 1976), pp. 131–2.
84. Smith, 'Objectivity and the Humane Sciences: A New Proposal', in *Religious Diversity*, p. 178.
85. Wilfred Cantwell Smith, *Towards a World Theology* (Philadelphia: Westminster Press, 1981), p. 89. For a critique of this book see John Berthrong, 'The Theological Necessity of Pluralism', *Toronto Journal of Theology* 5, 1989, pp. 188–205.
86. Ibid., p. 103.
87. Ibid.
88. Paul Knitter, *No Other Name?* p. 32.
89. Ibid., p. 219.
90. Paul Knitter, 'Toward a Liberation Theology of Religions', in *The Myth of Christian Uniqueness*, ed. John Hick and Paul Knitter (Maryknoll, NY: Orbis, 1987), p. 181ff.
91. Stendahl, pp. 7–18.
92. See Hick, 'Whatever Path Men Choose Is Mine', p. 179.
93. John Cobb, *Christ in a Pluralistic Age* (Philadelphia: Westminster Press, 1975).
94. Wolfhart Pannenberg, *Jesus – God and Man* (Philadelphia: Westminster Press, 1968), p. 37. For a recent assessment see Steffen Losel, 'Wolfhart Pannenberg's Response to the Challenge of Religious Pluralism: The Anticipation of Divine Absoluteness', *Journal of Ecumenical Studies*, 34, 1997, pp. 499–519.
95. Pannenberg, 'The Revelation of God in Jesus of Nazareth', in *Theology as History*, ed. J. M. Robinson (New York: Macmillan, 1967), p. 133.
96. Cited in Waldron Scott, '"No Other Name" – An Evangelical Conviction', in *Christ's Lordship and Religious Pluralism*, pp. 59–60.
97. Cited in ibid., p. 65.
98. Ibid.
99. Ibid., p. 68.
100. Clark Pinnock, 'An Inclusivist View', in *Four Views on Salvation in a Pluralist World*, ed. D. L. Akholm and T. R. Phillips (Grand Rapids, MI: Zondervan, 1996), p. 95.
101. Ibid., p. 106.
102. Ibid., p. 114.

103. Karl Rahner, 'Christianity and the Non-Christian Religions', in *Christianity and Other Religions*, pp. 52–79.
104. Ibid., p. 63.
105. Ibid., pp. 76–7.
106. Ibid., p. 78.
107. Richard, p. 35.
108. Gavin D'Costa, *Theology and Religious Pluralism*. See also his *John Hick's Theology of Religions: A Critical Evaluation* (Lanham, MD: University Press of America, 1987), and 'The New Missionary: John Hick and Religious Plurality'.
109. D'Costa, *Theology and Religious Pluralism*, pp. 117–36. D'Costa has a new book due out from Orbis in spring 2000, which may well develop these themes.
110. Jacques Dupuis, S.J., *Toward a Christian Theology of Religious Pluralism*.
111. Ibid., p. 10.
112. Ibid., p. 23.
113. John V. Taylor, 'The Theological Basis of Interfaith Dialogue', in *Christianity and Other Religions*, pp. 226–7.
114. Ibid., p. 218.
115. Ibid., p. 226.
116. Stanley J. Samartha, *Courage for Dialogue* (Maryknoll, NY: Orbis, 1981).
117. Ibid., p. 96.
118. Ibid., p. 97.
119. Ibid., p. 98.
120. Ibid., p. 99.
121. Ibid., p. 12.
122. Ibid., p. 98.
123. Raimundo Panikkar, *The Unknown Christ of Hinduism*, rev. edn. (Maryknoll, NY: Orbis, 1981), p. 7. For an assessment of the significance of Panikkar's thought for the discussion of 'theoretical pluralism' see Gerald Larson, 'Contra Pluralism', *Soundings*, 73, 1990, pp. 303–26.
124. Ibid.
125. Harold Coward, 'A Critical Analysis of Raimundo Panikkar's Approach to Inter-Religious Dialogue', *Cross-Currents*, 29, 1979, pp. 183–90.
126. Panikkar, p. 7.
127. Ibid., p. 12.
128. Ibid., p. 25.
129. Ibid., p. 26.
130. Ibid., p. 27.
131. Ibid., p. 29.
132. Ibid., p. 30.
133. Ibid., p. 14ff.
134. Ibid., p. 21.
135. Ibid., p. 22.

136. Ibid.
137. Ibid.
138. Panikkar, *The Trinity and the Religious Experience of Man* (Maryknoll, NY: Orbis, 1973), p. 42.
139. Ibid., p. 43.
140. Ibid., p. 52.
141. Ibid., p. 54.
142. Ibid., p. 58. See also Raimundo Panikkar, 'The Jordan, the Tiber and the Ganges', in *The Myth of Christian Uniqueness*, ed. John Hick and Paul Knitter (Maryknoll, NY: Orbis, 1987), pp. 89–116.
143. Paul Knitter, *Jesus and the Other Names*.
144. Ibid., p. 1.
145. Ibid., p. 16.
146. Ibid., p. 17.
147. Ibid., p. 19.

CHAPTER 3

1. J. A. Hutchinson, *Paths of Faith*, 3rd edn (New York: McGraw-Hill, 1981), p. 399.
2. Ibid., p. 400.
3. P. C. Craigie, *The Problem of War in the Old Testament* (Grand Rapids, MI: William B. Eerdmans, 1978), p. 22.
4. Muslims did form minority groups, for example in the Ottoman empire before 1516, in the Moghul empire, and under Umayyad rule in Spain.
5. Jacques Waardenburg, 'World Religions as Seen in the Light of Islam', in *Islam: Past Influence and Present Challenge*, ed. A. Welch and P. Cachia (Edinburgh: Edinburgh University Press, 1979), pp. 248–9.
6. Yvonne Haddad, 'The Islamic Alternative', *The Link*, 15, 1982, p. 2.
7. 'Abd al-Tafāhum, 'Doctrine', in *Islam*, vol. 2 of *Religions in the Middle East: Three Religions in Concord and Conflict*, ed. A. J. Arberry (Cambridge: Cambridge University Press, 1969), p. 393.
8. Ibid.
9. Fazlur Rahman, *Major Themes of the Qur'ān* (Chicago: Bibliotheca Islamica, 1980), p. 163.
10. Ibid., p. 164.
11. Ibid.
12. Cited in ibid., p. 165.
13. Cited in ibid., p. 167.
14. Cited in Rahman, *Islam* (New York: Anchor, 1966), pp. 15–16.
15. Ibid., p. 23.
16. See, for example, M. Perlmann, 'The Medieval Polemics between Islam and Judaism', in *Religion in a Religious Age*, ed. S. D. Goitein (Cambridge, MA: Association for Jewish Studies, 1974), pp. 103–38.
17. Waardenburg, p. 255.
18. Ibid. Waardenburg supplies an itemized list of authors and works.
19. Ibid., p. 256.
20. Ibid.

21. Ibid., p. 257. This argument turned into a two-edged sword because Muslim scholars then read the Torah and found mention of the coming of Muhammad and Islam.
22. Ibid., p. 258.
23. W. Montgomery Watt, 'The Christian Criticized in the Qur'ān', *Muslim World*, 57:3, 1967, pp. 197–201.
24. Waardenburg, p. 259.
25. Detailed evidence for these statements is given in Waardenburg, pp. 260–1.
26. Ibid.
27. See H. G. Dorman, Jr, *Toward Understanding Islam: Contemporary Apologetic of Islam and Missionary Policy* (New York: Columbia University Press, 1948). See also Tarek Mitri, 'Minority Rights in a Christian–Muslim Perspective', *Current Dialogue*, 33, 1999, p. 47.
28. William Shepard, 'A Modernist View of Islam and Other Religions', *Muslim World*, 65:2, 1975, pp. 79–92.
29. Ibid.
30. Ibid., p. 91.
31. Ibid., p. 88.
32. M. Freedman, *Journal of the American Oriental Society*, 95, 1975, p. 219.
33. Rahman, *Islam*, p. xxii.
34. Ibid.
35. The above summary of Buddhism in medieval Islam is based on Waardenburg, pp. 251–2.
36. Rahman, *Islam*, p. 159.
37. Aziz Ahmad, *Studies in Islamic Culture in the Indian Environment* (Oxford: Clarendon Press, 1964), pp. 125–6.
38. R. A. Nicholson, *The Mystics of Islam* (1914; reprint, Chester Springs, PA: Routledge, 1962), pp. 16–17.
39. Waardenburg, p. 253.
40. Ibid.
41. Ibid., p. 254. Friedmann's articles are: 'The Temple of Multān: A Note on Early Muslim Attitudes to Idolatry', *Israel Oriental Studies*, 2, 1972, pp. 176–82; and 'Medieval Muslim Views of Indian Religions', *Journal of American Oriental Society*, 95:2, 1975, pp. 214–21.
42. Ibid.
43. Ibid., p. 255.
44. Cited in Seyyed Hossein Nasr, *Ṣūfī Essays* (New York: Schocken, 1977), p. 139.
45. Cited in ibid., p. 140.
46. Ibid., p. 139.
47. Annemarie Schimmel, *Mystical Dimensions of Islam* (Chapel Hill, NC: University of North Carolina Press, 1975), p. 361.
48. Nasr, p. 141.
49. Ahmad, p. 167.
50. He would appear in council with the Hindu *tilak* mark on his forehead and celebrate Dewali with the ardency of a devout Brahmin. He would also wear a Parsee girdle and prostrate himself before the sun in typical

Parsee fashion. Jain devotees convinced him of the validity of *ahimsā*, and spokesmen of Sikhism found Akbar an attentive listener. Taoist and Confucian scholars arrived from China and Buddhist monks from Sri Lanka. In 1578 he sent to Portuguese Goa for representatives of Christianity. See David Carroll, *The Taj Mahal* (New York: Newsweek Books, 1972), p. 40.

51. Ahmad, p. 167.
52. Carroll, p. 41.
53. Ahmad, p. 169.
54. Ibid., p. 176.
55. Ibid., 180. Zoroastrianism not only influenced Akbar but continues to inform Iranian Shia, particularly in doctrines of dualism (e.g. good versus evil). See articles on 'Islam' and 'Zoroastrianism' in *A New Handbook of Living Religions*, ed. John R. Hinnells (Oxford: Basil Blackwell, 1997).
56. Ibid., p. 175.
57. M. G. S. Hodgson, *The Gunpowder Empires and Modern Times*, vol. 3 of *The Venture of Islam* (Chicago: University of Chicago Press, 1974), p. 80.
58. Yvonne Haddad, 'The Qur'ānic Justification for an Islamic Revolution: The View of Sayyid Qutb', *Middle East Journal*, 37, 1983, p. 15.
59. Ibid., p. 18.
60. Ibid., p. 26.
61. Ibid., p. 28.
62. This discussion is based on Sheila McDonough, *Muslim Ethics and Modernity: A Comparative Study of the Ethical Thought of Sayyid Ahmad Khan and Mawlana Mawdudi* (Waterloo, Canada: Wilfrid Laurier University Press, 1984).
63. Ibid., p. 44.
64. Grant Mclure, 'Sayyid Ahmad Khan's Muslim Revival', unpublished MA thesis, University of Victoria, Victoria, BC, Canada, 1998.
65. McDonough, p. 56.
66. Ibid., p. 57.
67. Ibid., p. 76.
68. Ibid., p. 113.
69. Ibid., p. 115.
70. Waardenburg, p. 266.
71. Nasr, p. 139.
72. Yvonne Haddad, 'Muslims in Canada', in *Religion and Ethnicity*, ed. Harold Coward and Leslie Kawamura (Waterloo, Canada: Wilfrid Laurier University Press, 1978), p. 85.
73. Ibid.
74. Nasr, p. 148.
75. Cited in ibid., p. 149. Westerners often embrace ṣūfism in its attractive aspects (love, song, poetry, dance) but not as an integral part of *sharī'ah*-centred Islam. This is disturbing to devout Muslims, who view it as an inauthentic appropriation.
76. Waardenburg, pp. 268–9.

CHAPTER 4

1. 'World Religion Statistics', in *Brittanica Book of the Year* (Chicago: Encyclopædia Brittanica, 1997). See also Denis Maceoin, 'Baha'ism', in *A New Handbook of Living Religions*, ed. John R. Hinnells (Oxford: Basil Blackwell, 1997), p. 619.
2. Seena Fazel, 'Religious Pluralism', in *Baha'i Encyclopedia*, in preparation, but posted on http://bahai-library.org/encyclopedia/pluralism.html
3. Ibid. See also Juan R. I. Cole, '"I am all the Prophets": The Poetics of Pluralism in Baha'i Texts', *Poetics Today*, 14:3, 1993, pp. 447–76.
4. William S. Hatcher and J. Douglas Martin, *The Bahá'í Faith: The Emerging Global Religion* (San Francisco: Harper & Row, 1984), pp. 25–6.
5. Juan R. I. Cole, 'Baha' Allah', in *Encyclopedia Iranica* (Boston: Routledge & Kegan Paul, 1988), vol. 3, pp. 422–9.
6. 'The Writings of Bahá'u'lláh', quoted in Hatcher and Martin, p. 3.
7. Ibid.
8. Hatcher and Martin, p. 5.
9. Ibid., p. 40.
10. Ibid., p. 56.
11. Ibid., pp. 64–5.
12. Seena Fazel, 'Religious Pluralism', in *Baha'i Encyclopedia*. The author cites Shoghi Effendi, letter, 19.11.45.
13. Ibid.
14. Ibid.
15. Ibid.
16. Ibid.
17. Ibid.
18. Ibid.
19. As quoted in ibid.
20. Cole.
21. Ibid., p. 448.
22. Ibid., p. 449.
23. Ibid., p. 450. There is also an acceptance of aboriginal messengers in Baha'i thinking, although the names of individual aboriginal manifestations are not known. See Christopher Buck, 'Native Messengers of God in Canada? A Test Case for Baha'i Universalism', *Baha'i Studies Review*, 6, 1996, pp. 97–134.
24. Moojan Momen, 'Relativism: A Basis for Baha'i Metaphysics', in *Studies in Honor of the Late Hasan M. Balyuzi*, ed. Moojan Momen (Los Angeles: Kalimat Press, 1988), pp. 185–217.
25. Ibid., p. 195.
26. Ibid., p. 202.
27. For modern Western and Eastern approaches to negative theology see *Derrida and Negative Theology*, ed. Harold Coward and Toby Foshay (Albany, NY: State University of New York Press, 1992).
28. Momen, p. 203.
29. As quoted in ibid., p. 204.

30. Ibid., p. 211.
31. Ibid.
32. Seena Fazel, 'Interreligious Dialogue and the Bahā'ī Faith', in *Revisioning the Sacred: New Perspectives on a Baha'i Theology*, ed. Jack McLean (Los Angeles: Kalimat Press, 1997), pp. 137–52.
33. Ibid., p. 139.
34. As quoted in ibid., p. 140.
35. William Garlington, 'Baha'i Bhajans: An Example of the Baha'i Use of Hindu Symbols', *Occasional Papers in Shaykhi, Babi and Baha'i Studies*, 2:1, 1998, pp. 1–12.
36. Ibid., p. 1.
37. Ibid., p. 3.
38. Ibid.
39. Ibid.
40. Ibid.
41. The *bhajan* 'The Call of Baha'i', quoted in ibid., p. 5.
42. Ibid., p. 6.
43. Ibid.
44. Ibid., p. 9.

CHAPTER 5

1. W. D. O'Flaherty, ed., *Karma and Rebirth in Classical Indian Traditions* (Berkeley, CA: University of California Press, 1980), p. 139.
2. T. R. V. Murti, *The Central Philosophy of Buddhism* (London: Allen & Unwin, 1960), pp. 11–12.
3. Ibid., p. 12.
4. P. T. Raju, 'The Development of Indian Thought', *Journal of the History of Ideas*, 13, pp. 528–50.
5. See *Chāndogya Upaniṣad*, chapter 6.
6. Alain Danielou, *Hindu Polytheism* (New York: Pantheon, 1962), pp. 3–4.
7. Ibid., p. 5.
8. Ibid., p. 9.
9. Raju, p. 533.
10. *The Māṇḍūkyopaniṣad with Gauḍapāda's Kārīkā*, trans. Swami Nikhilananda (Mysore, India: Sri Ramakrishna Ashrama, 1968).
11. A. L. Basham, *The Wonder that Was India* (New York: Grove, 1959), p. 265.
12. David M. Miller and Dorothy C. Wertz, *Hindu Monastic Life and the Monks and Monasteries of Bhubaneswar* (Montreal: McGill-Queen's University Press, 1976), p. 4.
13. David Miller, 'The Guru as the Centre of Sacredness', *Studies in Religion*, 6:5, 1976–7) pp. 527–33.
14. *The Vishṇu Purāṇa*, trans. H. H. Wilson (Calcutta: Punth Pustak, 1972), pp. 269–70.
15. Ibid., p. 272. Some commentators even suggest that the destruction of the Daityas refers to the actual destruction of the Buddhists by the invading Moghuls (see p. 272, note 8).

16. Vettam Mani, *Purāṇic Encyclopedia* (Delhi: Motilal Banarsidass, 1975), p. 165.
17. Basham, p. 265.
18. Jan Gonda, *Change and Continuity in Indian Religion* (London: Routledge, 1965), pp. 7–8.
19. Ibid., p. 10.
20. Wendy Doniger O'Flaherty, *The Origins of Evil in Hindu Mythology* (Delhi: Motilal Banarsidass, n.d.), p. 375.
21. Ibid., p. 377.
22. Ibid. See, for example, the *Bhagavad-Gītā's* prescription against the mixing of castes.
23. Ibid., p. 378.
24. Ibid., p. 379.
25. Cited in ibid., p. 378. The quote is from the *Mahimnastotra*.
26. Basham, p. 344.
27. S. A. A. Rizvi, 'The Muslim Ruling Dynasties', in *A Cultural History of India*, ed. A. L. Basham (Oxford: Clarendon Press, 1975), p. 245.
28. J. Estlin Carpenter, *Theism in Medieval India* (Delhi: Oriental Books Reprint, 1977), p. 451.
29. Ibid., p. 452.
30. Cited in ibid., p. 455.
31. Kshitimohan Sen, *Medieval Mysticism of India* (Delhi: Oriental Books Reprint, 1974), p. 88. The author goes on to say that Kabir's forefathers were among the early converts from Hinduism to Islam.
32. Carpenter, p. 457.
33. Kshitimohan Sen, p. 91.
34. Ibid., p. 100.
35. Ibid.
36. Carpenter, p. 463.
37. See H. G. Coward, *The Sphoṭa Theory of Language* (Delhi: Motilal Banarsidass, 1980).
38. Carpenter, p. 467.
39. Cited in Kshitimohan Sen, p. 98.
40. Carpenter, p. 504.
41. Raju, p. 540.
42. Kshitimohan Sen, pp. 102–3.
43. W. H. McLeod, *Guru Nānak and the Sikh Religion* (Oxford: Clarendon Press, 1968).
44. N. G. Barrier, *The Sikhs and Their Literature* (Delhi: Manohar, 1970), p. xix.
45. Ibid., p. xx.
46. Ibid., p. xxxiv.
47. Ibid., p. xxxviii ff.
48. Carpenter, p. 485.
49. Ibid.
50. Ibid., p. 521ff. The summary that follows is based upon the section entitled 'Note on Christianity in India'.

51. W. T. De Bary, ed., *Sources of Indian Tradition*, vol. 2 (New York: Columbia University Press, 1969), pp. 1–2. See also Antony Copley, *Religions in Conflict: Ideology, Cultural Contact and Conversion in Late Colonial India* (Delhi: Oxford University Press, 1997) for an examination of the impact of Christian missionary endeavours on Hinduism. The author argues that India's traditional Hindu institutions successfully warded off this Christian missionary challenge.
52. Raju, p. 540.
53. De Bary, pp. 23–5.
54. Ibid., p. 26.
55. Rāmmohun Roy, 'Letter to the Editor of the *Bengal Hurkanu*' (23 May 1823), in De Bary, p. 28.
56. Rāmmohun Roy, 'In Defence of Hindu Women', in De Bary, pp. 29–32.
57. De Bary, p. 50.
58. Ibid., p. 51.
59. Rāmmohun Roy, 'Letter on Education', in De Bary, pp. 40–3.
60. De Bary, p. 64.
61. Keshub Chunder Sen, 'Jesus Christ: Europe and Asia', in De Bary, pp. 68–9.
62. Keshub Chunder Sen, 'We Apostles of the New Dispensation', in De Bary, p. 75.
63. Ibid., p. 76.
64. Ibid., pp. 76–77.
65. See 'A Debate with a Christian and a Muslim', in De Bary, pp. 79–81.
66. G. R. Thursby, *Hindu–Muslim Relations in British India* (Leiden: E. J. Brill, 1975), p. 13.
67. Swami Dayānanda Sarasvatī, 'Light of Truth', cited in ibid., p. 13.
68. Thursby, p. 14.
69. De Bary, p. 77.
70. Thursby, pp. 34–73.
71. Raju, p. 546.
72. S. Radhakrishnan, *Eastern Religions and Western Thought* (Oxford: Clarendon Press, 1939).
73. Ibid., p. 18.
74. Ibid., pp. 20–21.
75. Ibid., p. 21.
76. Ibid., p. 306.
77. *Ṛg Veda* 1:164:46.
78. Radhakrishnan, p. 308.
79. Ibid., p. 310.
80. Ibid., p. 312.
81. Ibid., p. 313.
82. Ibid., pp. 316–17.
83. Ibid., p. 324.
84. Ibid., p. 327.
85. Ibid., 328. This view is consistent with C. G. Jung's notion of archetypes as racial memories.
86. *Bhagavad-Gītā* 3:26.

87. Radhakrishnan, p. 329.
88. Ibid., p. 335.
89. Ibid., p. 337.
90. Ibid., p. 338.
91. Anantanand Rambachan, 'May God, Your God, Our God, No God?', in *Current Dialogue*, 33, 1999, p. 38.
92. Ibid., p. 39.
93. Ibid., p. 40.
94. Ibid.
95. Ibid.
96. Robert D. Baird, 'Religion and the Secular: Categories for Religious Conflict and Change in Independent India', in *Religion and Social Conflict in South Asia*, ed. Bardwell Smith (Leiden: E. J. Brill, 1976), p. 47.
97. Ibid., p. 48.
98. Ibid., p. 50.
99. Ibid., p. 52.
100. Baldrishna Govind Gokhale, 'Dr. Bhimrao Ramji Ambedkar: Rebel against the Hindu Tradition', in *Religion and Social Conflict in South Asia*, p. 21.
101. Ibid., p. 22.
102. For an extended examination of this problem see Harold Coward, 'India's Constitution and Traditional Presuppositions Regarding Human Nature', in *Religion and Law in Independent India*, ed. Robert D. Baird (Delhi: Manohar, 1993), pp. 23–39.
103. See Ainslie T. Embree, *Utopias in Conflict* (Delhi: Oxford University Press, 1992); and Lise McKean, *Divine Enterprise: Gurus and the Hindu Nationalist Movement* (Chicago: University of Chicago Press, 1996).
104. The following is based on Lise McKean's analysis of Savarkar in *Divine Enterprise*, p. 71ff.
105. See, for example, the chapter on 'Gandhi and Religious Pluralism', J. F. T. Jordens, in Harold Coward, ed., *Modern Indian Responses to Religious Pluralism* (Albany, NY: State University of New York Press, 1987), pp. 3–18.
106. Cynthia Keppley Mahmood, 'Ayodhya and the Hindu Resurgence', *Religion*, 24, 1994, pp. 73–80.
107. Ibid., p. 75.
108. Ibid.
109. Ainslie T. Embree, *Utopias in Conflict: Religion and Nationalism in Modern India* (Delhi: Oxford University Press, 1992).
110. Robert N. Minor, 'Sarvepalli Radhakrishnan on the Nature of "Hindu" Tolerance', *Journal of the American Academy of Religion*, 50, 1982, p. 276. See also J. Duncan and M. Derrett, 'Unity in Diversity: The Hindu Experience', *Baharata Manisha Quarterly*, 5, 1979, pp. 21–6; and Robert N. Minor, *Radhakrishnan: A Religious Biography* (Albany, NY: State University of New York Press, 1987).

CHAPTER 6

1. Although there is considerable debate in recent literature as to the use of the term 'religion' for anything other than the theistic traditions, I have not entered into that debate here. I simply assume the use of the term current in contemporary scholarship, in which the earlier, narrow definition of religion has been broadened so as to include both Hinduism and Buddhism. Many contemporary Buddhists seem also to accept this view. See, for example, Buddhadāsa Bhikkhu's view that Buddhism can be called a religion, in *Dharma – The World Saviour* (Bangkok: Friends Muslim Mission, n.d.), p. 10. See also Seyfort Ruegg, 'On the Supramundane and the Divine in Buddhism', *Tibet Journal*, 1, 1976, p. 25.
2. K. N. Jayatilleke, *The Buddhist Attitude to Other Religions* (Kandy, Sri Lanka: Buddhist Publication Society, 1975).
3. Arnold Toynbee, *A Historian's Approach to Religion* (London: Oxford University Press, 1956), p. 272.
4. Arnold Toynbee, *America and the World Revolution* (New York: Oxford University Press, 1962), p. 49.
5. Edward Conze, *Buddhism: Its Essence and Development* (New York: Harper, 1959).
6. Edward J. Thomas, *The History of Buddhist Thought* (London: Routledge & Kegan Paul, 1967), p. 91.
7. Thomas, p. 11ff.
8. Jayatilleke, p. 3.
9. Ibid., p. 14.
10. Cited in ibid., p. 17.
11. Ibid., p. 17.
12. Ibid., p. 19.
13. Ibid., p. 20.
14. Ibid., p. 22.
15. Ibid.
16. *Majjhima Nikāya* 1:515–18.
17. Jayatilleke, p. 23.
18. Cited in ibid., p. 24.
19. Ibid., p. 28.
20. Ibid., p. 29.
21. Personal communication from David Loy, 25 October 1999.
22. Buddhadāsa, *No Religion* (Bangkok: Sublime Life Mission, n.d.).
23. Buddhadāsa, *Dharma – The World Saviour*, p. 16.
24. Buddhadāsa, *No Religion*, p. 16ff.
25. This point is clearly made by T. R. V. Murti when he states, 'Śūnyatā is not positivism: it has a spiritual goal' (*The Central Philosophy of Buddhism* (London: Allen & Unwin, 1960), p. 331).
26. See ibid., chapter 5, pp. 121–43.
27. See ibid., p. 337.
28. Cited in ibid.

29. Y. Krishnan, 'Buddhist Challenge and Hindu Response', *Studies in Pali and Buddhism* (Delhi: Motilal Banarsidass 1979), pp. 217–27.
30. Ibid., p. 225.
31. Ibid.
32. *Chao Lun: The Treatises of Seng-chao*, trans. W. Liebenthal (Hong Kong: Hong Kong University Press, 1968), p. 21.
33. Ibid.
34. Ibid., p. 22.
35. Ibid.
36. Heinrich Dumoulin, ed., *Buddhism in the Modern World* (New York: Collier Books, 1976), p. 160.
37. David S. Snellgrove, *The Nine Ways of Bon* (Boulder, CO: Prajnā Press, 1980), p. 20.
38. Ibid., p. 15.
39. Per Kvaerne, 'Aspects of the Origin of the Buddhist Tradition in Tibet', *Numen*, 19, 1972, p. 32.
40. Snellgrove, p. 12.
41. See, for example, the journal *Buddhist–Christian Studies*, University of Hawaii Press. See also David Loy, ed., *Healing and Deconstruction: Postmodern Thought in Buddhism and Christianity* (Atlanta, GA: Scholars Press, 1996) for an example of the creative nature of this dialogue in academia.
42. Dalai Lama, 'Spiritual Contributions to Social Progress', *Tibetan Review*, 16, November 1981, p. 18.

CHAPTER 7

1. Wilfred Cantwell Smith, 'The Christian in a Religiously Plural World', in *Religious Diversity*, ed. W. Oxtoby (New York: Harper & Row, 1976), p. 9.
2. See John F. Kane, *Pluralism and Truth in Religion* (Chico, CA: Scholar Press, 1981).
3. John Hick, *Philosophy of Religion* (Englewood Cliffs, NJ: Prentice Hall, 1973).
4. Wilfred Cantwell Smith, *Towards a World Theology* (Philadelphia: Westminster Press, 1981).
5. Charles Davis, 'Religious Pluralism' lecture read at the annual meeting of the Canadian Society for the Study of Religion, Montreal, May 1980.
6. Schleiermacher does say that scriptures are mainly for beginners in religion (*On Religion* (New York: Harper & Row, 1958), p. 34), and Paul Tillich does stress the self-transcending quality of scripture (it participates in that to which it points) (*Dynamics of Faith* (New York: Harper & Row, 1957)). But neither would allow the total transcendence of scripture found in Advaita Vedānta and Buddhism. It is also true that within Hinduism (e.g. Pūrva Mīmāmsā, Vsistādvaita Vedānta, *bhakti*) and in certain forms of Jodo Shinshu Buddhism total transcendence of instrumental forms is not accepted.

7. Wilfred Cantwell Smith, 'Traditions in Contact and Change: Towards a History of Religion in the Singular', in *Traditions in Contact and Change*, ed. P. Slater et al. (Waterloo, Canada: Wilfrid Laurier University Press, 1983), pp. 1–23.

8. Ibid.

9. Smith, *Towards a World Theology*, pp. 137–39, 151–3, 183ff.

10. Ibid., p. 184.

11. Ibid., p. 185. John Hick has begun using the term 'The Real' to deal with this problem. See John Hick, *A Christian Theology of Religions* (Louisville, KY: Westminster John Knox Press, 1995), pp. 57–82.

12. Ibid., p. 187.

13. Ibid., p. 186.

14. See, for example, Richard E. Wentz, *The Culture of Religious Pluralism* (Boulder, CO: Westview, 1998).

15. Karl Rahner, *Confrontations 1*, vol. 11 of *Theological Investigations*, trans. David Bourke (London: Darton, Longman & Todd, 1974), p. 7.

16. Ibid. Knitter's suggestion that one shift from theological theory to each religious practice in responding 'to suffering persons and suffering earth' in today's global crisis may succeed in providing a common ground upon which to conduct dialogue. Paul Knitter, *Jesus and Other Names* (Maryknoll, NY: Orbis, 1996).

17. Ibid., p. 139. Dupuis' attempted study of God's grand plan for the pluralism of religions does not take this limitation seriously (see chapter 2 of this book). Jacques Dupuis, S.J., *Toward a Christian Theology of Religious Pluralism* (Maryknoll, NY: Orbis, 1997).

18. Nāgārjuna, *Mūlamādhyamikakārikā*, trans. K. K. Inada (Tokyo: Hokuseido Press, 1970). Nāgārjuna's dates are given as *c.* 150–250 CE.

19. Immanuel Kant, *Religion within the Limits of Reason Alone* (New York: Harper, 1960).

20. Calvin S. Hall, *A Primer of Freudian Psychology* (New York: Mentor, 1958), pp. 89–91.

21. Hans Küng, *On Being a Christian* (New York: Doubleday, 1976), p. 123. Küng now has better knowledge of other religions and has shifted his approach to focus on finding a common ethic but remains tied to the 'finality of the Christ event'. See Knitter, *Jesus and Other Names*, p. 9.

22. See Paul Knitter, 'World Religions and the Finality of Christ: A Critique of Hans Küng's *On Being a Christian*', *Horizons*, 5, 1978, pp. 151–64.

23. Ibid., p. 156.

24. Smith, *World Theology*, pp. 123, 145ff.

25. As quoted by Knitter in, 'Making Sense of the Many', *Religious Studies Review*, 15, 1989, p. 207. I am indebted to Knitter for his formulation of this presupposition.

26. Jasper's position is paraphrased by Kane, p. 113.

27. Knitter, 'Making Sense of the Many', *Religious Studies Review*, 15, 1989, p. 207.

28. In a recent article Heinrich Ott stresses the 'openness' required for dialogue: 'Dialogue between the religions has to be so open that it requires no common doctrinal presuppositions and expects no doctrinal

results. Rather, this dialogue leads simply to a mutual respect in which the experience of one religion enlightens the other and allows itself to be enlightened by the other' ('Does the Notion of "Mystery" – as Another Name for God – Provide a Basis for a Dialogical Encounter between the Religions?', in *God: The Contemporary Discussion*, ed. F. Sontag and M. D. Bryant (New York: Rose of Sharon Press, 1982), p. 15).

29. Knitter, *Jesus and the Other Names*, p. 10ff.
30. For examples of the resulting books see: Harold Coward and Dan Maguire, eds, *Visions of a New Earth: Religious Perspectives on Population, Consumption and Ecology* (Albany, NY: State University of New York Press, 2000); Harold Coward and Pinit Ratanakul, eds, *A Cross-Cultural Dialogue on Health Care Ethics* (Waterloo, Canada: Wilfrid Laurier University Press, 1999); and John McLaren and Harold Coward, eds, *Religious Conscience, The State and the Law* (Albany, NY: State University of New York Press, 1999).
31. Smith, *World Theology*, pp. 180–91.

INDEX